PRAISE FOR MICHAEL SMITH'S BEST-SELLING BIOGRAPHY,
AN UNSUNG HERO: TOM CREAN, ANTARCTIC SURVIVOR

This book is a remarkable tribute to one of Ireland's great polar explorers. Michael Smith's excellent biography finally puts Tom Crean where he has long deserved to be – in the limelight amongst the other great figures of the Heroic Age of Exploration.
— Jonathan Shackleton

Well-written and beautifully produced. — The Times, London

This is a moving account of a genuine hero – modest, honest and powerful . . . timely in an age when we put down our heroes. Frank Delaney

. . . compulsive reading. An inspiring and quite remarkable story . . .
— The Irish Times

This is a remarkable book about a remarkable man. — Sunday Tribune

Michael Smith has made a great and welcomed addition to the history of Antarctic exploration. A man like Tom Crean who survives three Antarctic expeditions and returns to his Irish village to open a pub called 'The South Pole Inn' is a man worth knowing about and Smith tells the story well.
— Robert B. Stephenson, Coordinator, The Antarctic Circle

It's a wonderful Kiplingesque yarn about a great Irishman who didn't have to die to become a hero. — Irish Independent

I've read all the books, repeated most of Shackleton's boat routes as well as that of the Worst Journey, plus written a book of my own on polar exploration – but this old, bold tale, told well, is one I couldn't put down.
—Galen Rowell, author of *Poles Apart: Parallel Visions of the Arctic and the Antarctic*

Michael Smith has written a splendid biography of Crean.
— The Nautical Magazine

. . . Creates a fascinating word picture of this astonishing man.
— Irish Examiner

I Am Just Going Outside

Captain Oates – Antarctic Tragedy

Dedication

To Barbara, Daniel and Nathan

I Am Just Going Outside
Captain Oates – Antarctic Tragedy

Michael Smith

British Library Cataloguing in Publication Data:
A catalogue record for this book is available
from the British Library

Copyright © Michael Smith 2002, 2003, 2006

ISBN 978-1-86227-355-9

First published in the UK in 2006 by
Spellmount, an imprint of The History Press
The Mill, Brimscombe Port
Stroud, Gloucestershire. GL5 2QG
www.thehistorypress.co.uk

Reprinted 2012

Printed and bound in England.

Contents

Notes

Temperatures are generally given in the form used at the time, Fahrenheit. But conversions into the modern usage of Centigrade are provided. For example, water freezes at 32°F which is equal to –0°C, –20°F is –29°C and –40°F is –40°C. The body temperature of 98.4°F is 37°C.

Many of the distances of the age were measured in geographical or nautical miles, which is 1/60th of a degree of latitude or 6,080 feet (1.85 kilometres), the equivalent of 1.15 statute miles (1.60 km). Where appropriate, conversions are given.

Weights are listed in the Imperial form, the measure used at the time. For example, there are 2,240 lbs (1,016 kilograms) in a ton. Conversions into metric are given where considered helpful.

Money is written into contemporary units of pounds, shillings and pence (£ s d), but has been converted into current day purchasing power to provide a clearer indication of the relative sums involved. The conversion formula is provided by the Bank of England and illustrates the amount of money required at March 1999 to purchase £1 of goods on the chosen date in history. For example, it would require £52.94 today to purchase the equivalent £1 of goods in 1900.

During the Heroic Age of Polar exploration, the Ross Ice Shelf in Antarctica was known as the Ross Barrier, the Great Ice Barrier or simply the Barrier and the contemporary name is used in this book.

The punctuation and spelling used in original correspondence and diaries, however erratic, have been faithfully repeated.

Acknowledgements

This book could not have been written without the valuable assistance of many considerate people, who willingly provided generous access to relevant information, gave valuable advice and offered friendly encouragement.

I am especially grateful to Jenny Streeter, Curator of the Gilbert White Museum-Oates Memorial Museum at Selborne, Hampshire, who was endlessly patient and helpful over a very long period. Her independent guidance and encouragement were invaluable and freely given in the very best traditions of literary research.

Robert Headland at the Scott Polar Research Institute, Cambridge was a generous source of information and gave me access to the Institute's exceptional archive material, for which I am especially grateful. William Mills and Shirley Sawtell, also at SPRI, were especially helpful with information held in the library and always patient with my enquiries.

Captain (Retd) W. Alan Henshall, Assistant Regimental Secretary of the Royal Dragoon Guards, was generous with his access to the Regiment's archive material and has allowed me to quote freely.

I am particularly grateful to the following people and general staff at the other libraries, museums, research institutes and universities who gladly allowed me access to their archive material and were always considerate and helpful. Meredith Davies at Battersea District Library, London (BDL); British Colombia Archives, Victoria, Canada (BCA); Cambridge University Library, Cambridge (CUL); Dr Steven Blake at Cheltenham Art Gallery & Museums, Cheltenham (CAG); Essex County Archives, Essex Record Office, Chelmsford (ECA); Penny Hatfield at Eton College Archives, Eton (EC); the General Medical Council (GMC); Public Record Office, London (PRO): Dr Andrew Tatham and Huw Thomas at the Royal Geographical Society, London (RGS); Sharon McIntyre at The Shaftesbury Society, London (SS); Suffolk County Libraries & Heritage, Bury St Edmunds, Suffolk, (SCL); West Yorkshire Archives, Leeds (WYA).

Sue Limb and Major General Patrick Cordingley, earlier biographers of Lawrence Oates, were supportive and offered great encouragement and useful advice. Sue Limb also readily shared her personal memories of Violet Oates and was always endlessly patient with my questions. She also gave her generous approval for me to quote from her book, *Captain Oates: Soldier and Explorer.* Janet Crawford, the granddaughter of Louis Bernacchi, kindly gave me permission to quote from her grandfather's book, the first biography of Oates, *A Very Gallant Gentleman.*

I am just
going outside

I must place on record my thanks to Lord Kennet who allowed me access to the Kennet family papers, particularly the diaries and correspondence of Lady Kennet (Kathleen Scott). The Hon Broke Evans, son of Edward R.G.R. 'Teddy' Evans (Lord Mountevans), offered encouragement and gladly shared his valuable understanding of Polar affairs. The Society of Authors, on behalf of the Bernard Shaw Estate, allowed me to quote from the letters of G.B. Shaw.

Angela Mathias kindly allowed me to quote from her husband's book, *The Worst Journey in the World*. I am also grateful that Hermann Gran generously permitted me to extract references from *The Norwegian With Scott: Tryggve Gran's Antarctic Diaries 1910–13*.

David Wilson, allowed me to inspect documents relating to his great-uncle, Edward Wilson, at Cheltenham Art Gallery & Museum and to quote from his book, *Cheltenham in Antarctica*. A.G.E. Jones also offered useful wisdom on the affairs of Cecil Meares.

Klaus Marx, a former headmaster of Willington School and authority on Lawrence Oates' period in Putney, kindly shared his knowledge and willingly gave me free access to much useful material about his early life. I am especially grateful for being allowed to listen to his original recording of Tryggve Gran's speech on Oates delivered in 1972.

I want to record my grateful thanks to Tony Dagnall, Churchwarden at St Mary the Virgin, Gestingthorpe, who was enormously obliging and constructive with his advice and knowledge on the village so closely associated with the Oates family. Local people, Ashley Cooper, Cecil Pannell and Frances Teverson were also very helpful in providing me with their anecdotes and personal recollections of the Oates family at Gestingthorpe. Corinna Brown, a resident for many years, generously provided me with a guided tour of Gestingthorpe Hall, which added to my understanding of the subject. Vera Hodsoll of the Eastbourne Local History Society willingly shared her local knowledge.

Dr Charles R. Bentley, Professor Emeritus of Geophysics, Geophysical and Polar Research at the University of Wisconsin, US, graciously showed me the results of his research into glaciology and the probable locations of the bodies of Lawrence Oates and his four companions on the Southern Journey.

I also owe considerable thanks to Dr Evan Lloyd of The Western General Hospital, Edinburgh who provided me with invaluable professional guidance and insight into the effects of frostbite. Staff at the British Dyslexia Association were particularly helpful with advice and guidance into the mysteries of this particular affliction. I am very grateful.

Alison Delanty was a welcome source of knowledge and understanding about horses.

I should like also to record my thanks to Sara Wheeler for her thoughtful contributions.

I owe a special debt to Gillian Ward, who was courteous and patient with my inquiries about her mother and the relationship with Lawrence Oates. The investigation into Oates' child was undertaken entirely at my instigation and she never sought any personal gain from her knowledge. But her generous assistance was invaluable in shedding light on this episode and I am very grateful. Angela Wilson was immensely helpful in providing considerable information, correspondence and memories of her friend, Kathleen Gray.

Joan Keen of the Glasgow & West of Scotland Family History Society, Ian McKendrick and Margaret McKendrick were particularly thoughtful in supplying useful support and genealogical details about Henrietta Learmont McKendrick.

My agent, Anne Dewe, also deserves my gratitude for her support.

It should be recorded that most of the present day Oates family was evidently opposed to publication of this book about their most famous ancestor and was deliberately obstructive and unhelpful towards my research. An honourable character like Oates would not be impressed.

The one exception was Laurie G. Oates, the great-nephew of Lawrence Oates, who was very considerate and offered some useful guidance on the family. I am grateful to him.

I have made every reasonable effort to trace copyright holders of documents and photographs in the course of my researches, which has proven difficult in some cases after such a long passage of time. Accreditation has been given where it can be properly established. I hope I will be forgiven if there are any unintentional omissions.

On a personal note, I must thank my wife, Barbara, who has been considerate, thoroughly supportive and ceaselessly patient. My sons, Daniel and Nathan, were also important during the writing of this book and lent their own enthusiastic support.

Michael Smith
August 2002

Preface

'I am just going outside and may be some time.'

Most people will know that these simple words, so famous and so often repeated over the past decades, were uttered by Captain Lawrence Oates who, according to legend, gallantly gave his life to help save his comrades in an Antarctica blizzard during Captain Scott's tragic last expedition. There are few phrases in the English language that are so instantly recognisable or so enduring, or that capture the imagination to such an extent. From the moment that his tragic words and the circumstances of his death arrived in the public domain in 1913, Oates became a symbol of gallantry and heroism and a national icon.

Oates was at centre stage of the Scott disaster and the expedition's most unfortunate victim. It was a tragedy which left such an impression on the national psyche that 100,000 British soldiers, who themselves were staring death in the face from the trenches of the First World War, were shown pictures of Oates and his comrades as an example of how to die nobly. One senior military chaplain wrote from the Front that the tragedy was '. . . just the thing to cheer and encourage us out here . . .' Oates was the finest example of how, if nothing else, Britons knew how to die.

With hindsight, it is easy to understand how the country sought to draw strength from Oates. The Old Order was changing and war had accelerated the change. The reforms of the Edwardian age had left many Britons bewildered and uncertain, the Empire was under intense strain in places like Ireland and India, and the map of Europe was being re-drawn by the war.

Oates was a symbol of Britishness at a time when the country was under most pressure and people drew strength from his heroism. It was a time for heroes, unlike the modern day preoccupation with villains.

However, the man behind the memorable words, Lawrence Edward Grace Oates, remains something of an enigma. He is a mysterious, largely unknown character, whose fame arises chiefly from his short valedictory remark and miserable death in the most inhospitable and remote place on earth.

However, there was far more to Lawrence Oates than a distinguished death.

Oates was undoubtedly a hero, a cool-headed man of tremendous courage. He might have won the Victoria Cross during a distinguished army career.

But he was a reluctant hero, a quiet man who was uncomfortable in the limelight and hated convention and what he called 'fuss'. He would have been utterly repelled by the attention and hero worship which has followed him since his death in 1912.

On the surface, Oates was just another member of the Landed Gentry, who emerged from one of England's oldest families at the end of the Victorian age to an enviable position of inherited wealth and social position. The trappings of privilege took him from the family's country estate to Eton and onto a commission in an élite cavalry regiment. It also gave him a lazy, self-indulgent life hunting, playing polo and attending an endless merry-go-round of parties and social functions for the idle rich.

Beneath the surface the Oates story is different. He was always something of an outsider, a man who disliked the strict conventions of the Victorian era into which he was born and yet struggled to come to terms with the reforms of Edwardian Britain. He was a contradiction, a person who epitomised the English country squire but was no dandy. He rejected the rigid social customs, ignored class distinction and deliberately wore shabby clothes to emphasise his abhorrence of social status. He was informal in an age of formality.

The other side of Oates was that he was dominated by his austere and over-powering mother, a formidable woman who exercised a powerful control over his life from the stuffy drawing room of the grand manorial home and who could never come to terms with his death. It was a control she continued to exercise long afterwards. Her obsessive love for her son also meant that she was among the first to raise uncomfortable questions about the official version of Scott's ill-fated expedition, which killed her son.

Oates played a prominent role in the key events which shaped the Scott tragedy and was the only one of the five men who perished on the terrible Polar journey to offer an alternative perspective on the unfolding catastrophe. Contemporary scraps of diaries and letters reveal a different picture from the conventional story of gallant failure by the harmonious and unlucky British explorers. Oates did not suffer fools gladly and his writings are typical pieces of iconoclasm offering a sardonic and alternative outlook on the disaster.

Scott's doomed expedition has been the subject of wholesale revision in the past few years, with many seeing it as the symbolic passing of an age. It is equally fitting to reassess the enterprise's most unfortunate figure, Lawrence Oates.

A new biography is long overdue. The first, written in the 1930s, was severely hampered by Oates' mother and the author was unable to penetrate too deeply into his life. The second was effectively compiled 35 years ago in a different historical climate and eventually published twenty years ago.

Since then considerable new material has emerged, including significant family documents and public files, which were kept secret for 75 years and have since been opened. There are also important new details about his private life.

This new information, coupled with the fresher perspective on Polar history provided by the newer generation of writing and the unrelenting interest in the Heroic Age of exploration, makes a compelling case for a fresh look at Lawrence Oates.

1

Deep roots

Lawrence Oates sprang from deeply rooted English stock. The Oates family can proudly claim to be among the oldest in the country and, thanks to an ancient preoccupation with its own lineage, can trace the line back with considerable accuracy for almost 1,000 years.

The name Oates is thought to derive from the Christian name, Odo, which became Ode. Later it developed to Ode-son, or Ote-son and eventually Otes, before the present form of Oates. The earliest traces of the family can be found in Essex, although during the seventeenth, eighteenth and nineteenth centuries the name was more generally associated with Yorkshire.

An Otes or Oates was on the battle roll at Hastings in 1066 and an Otes owned the Manor of Gestingthorpe, Essex, at the time of the Domesday Book shortly afterwards. William Fitz Otto had been Sheriff of Essex and Hartford from 1181 to 1191 and John Otes held the manor of Little Laver, Essex, during the fourteenth century.

The Yorkshire connection first emerges in the fifteenth century when William Otes of Southowram built a large house, Shibden Hall, near Halifax. Successive generations of the Otes family were members of the area's rising merchant classes in Tudor and Elizabethan England, mainly woollen cloth traders and prominent landowners who built up considerable wealth. They included Thomas Otes of Thornhill Lees, near Dewsbury, born in 1554 and educated at Oxford, and a little later, Lawrence Otes, who owned a large amount of land at Woolley, near Barnsley, during the seventeenth century.

The military connection also stretches back through the centuries. George Oates of Low Hall, near Leeds, commanded a company of the Trained Bands militia pitched against Bonnie Prince Charlie during the Stuart Rebellion of 1745.

As a member of the flourishing mercantile classes, he turned his commercial wealth into property and became a sizeable landowner in the area.

George Oates was born in 1717 and put down further Yorkshire roots in 1765 when he bought Carr House with about 50 acres and a share of the manor and lordship of Chapel Allerton, Leeds. The site formed part of the old-established Meanwood estate to the north-west of Leeds. The transaction began an association between the Oates family and Meanwood which lasted for almost 150 years and provided a direct link to Lawrence Oates in the early twentieth century.

Meanwood passed to George Oates' son, Joseph, who further extended the family's interest in the area by purchasing another portion of the estate and establishing Westwood Hall. Joseph raised six children, including the youngest son, Edward, who was born in 1792. Edward Oates enjoyed a good deal of his earlier life living on the Mediterranean island of Malta before returning to Yorkshire in middle age. He finally came home in 1836 to marry Susan Grace, the only surviving child of Edward Grace, another established cloth merchant and magistrate from nearby Burley, in Leeds. He needed a home for his family and turned to another slice of the Meanwood estate, which had fallen into appalling disrepair. Edward Oates knocked down some farm buildings on the estate in 1838 and built a new family home, which he called Meanwoodside. Susan Oates further extended the property by demolishing the remaining farmhouses after Edward's death. The handsome manorial home, with an unusual green slate roof, would eventually pass into the hands of Lawrence Oates.[1]

Edward was 44 years old when he married Susan. The union produced five children in the following eight years. Edward Grace and Emily died in childhood and the youngest, Charles, went to Cambridge and built a successful career as a barrister in London's Inner Temple.

But to his two other sons, Edward Oates had passed the fondness of travel and adventure. Francis Grace, widely known as Frank, was born in 1840 and William Edward a year later. William's arrival into the world was recorded in Edward Oates' diary with a casual entry: 'Little boy born about 4 am.'

Both young men, who were born at Meanwoodside, grew to become inveterate travellers, naturalists and sportsmen, establishing their reputations as classic gentlemen explorers and big-game hunters of the mid-Victorian age. They were both tall and handsome, William's strong good looks topped off by a fashionable flowing moustache. However, Frank had to combat poor health in his early adult life, suffering long periods of illness as a young man before setting off on his travels. He went to Christ Church, Oxford, in 1861 but did not take a degree because of illness.

Frank Oates. Laurie's Uncle Frank was the archetypal Victorian gentleman-explorer, whose travels took him into the vast unexplored regions of Africa. He died of malaria in 1875 on a long trek to the Victoria Falls. (White Oates Museum)

Both were Fellows of the Royal Geographical Society and Frank and William Oates occasionally followed in the pioneering footsteps of Doctor David Livingstone on their trips to Africa. When their father died in 1865, he left the two adventurous brothers a sizeable inheritance and private income, which gave them greater freedom further to indulge their passions.

The Oates brothers were renowned hunters but not merely trophy hunters. In later life William was an energetic member of a special committee established by the Royal Geographical Society to conserve rare species of African wildlife. The RGS remembered William as an 'active and useful member' of the conservation committee which, among other things, was ahead of its time in demanding government grants to establish special hunting-free areas to protect and preserve animals threatened with extinction.[2]

Frank and William Oates set off from Southampton in March 1873 at the start of a prolonged trip of exploration and research to the largely unknown Zambesi. The brothers started from Durban and plunged deep into northern Transvaal, where hostile local tribes frequently halted their progress. After a lengthy journey together, Frank Oates decided to press on alone into more remote areas of Matabeleland, in the west of what is today Zimbabwe. He reached the Zambesi River and on New Year's Day 1875 Frank Oates became only the fifth Westerner to see the magnificent Victoria Falls, discovered twenty years earlier by Livingstone.

But disaster struck on the return journey when the gentleman-explorer was attacked by malaria near the village of Makalaka, about 80 miles north of the Tati River. After a twelve-day struggle, he died on 5 February 1875 surrounded by his prized assortment of rare animal skins, birds and reptiles. Dr Bradshaw, a local English surgeon in the area, pronounced that Frank Oates, at only 35, had died of 'Zambesi fever'.

The results of Frank's findings were edited by his younger brother, Charles, and published posthumously in a weighty tome entitled *Matabele Land and the Victoria Falls*, which received solid critical acclaim.

William Oates continued to make further trips into the African hinterland, frequently using his gun to increase his sizeable collection of valuable wildlife specimens and employing his natural artistic skills to record the sights with a series of attractive watercolours. Contemporary reports record that he 'bagged' a large number of waterbuck, blue wildebeest, zebra and white rhinoceros, plus many species of birds. It was described as 'a private collection of almost unique interest' and some of the rare trophies adorned his home, while others were eventually presented to the British Museum.

William's appetite for travel and adventure was not dulled by Frank's untimely death. He went as far as India and America and on one summer yachting trip William ventured as far north as Spitzbergen above the Arctic Circle.

William's voyaging – like that of his father – came to a temporary halt in September 1877 when he married Caroline Annie Buckton, the 23-year-old second daughter of Joshua Buckton, also from the Meanwood area of Leeds. Indeed, the families had closer ties since Caroline was William's second cousin.

Four children were born during the first six years of their marriage. The first child, Lillian Mary, was born in June 1878, precisely nine months after their wedding. Another daughter, Violet Emily, arrived in 1881 and the youngest son,

Bryan William Grace was born in 1883. The eldest son was born at 6.20 am on 17 March 1880 and named Lawrence Edward Grace Oates. The middle names were chosen out of respect for William's parents. But to almost everyone, he was known as Laurie, despite the 'w' in his full name.

It was a happy, comfortable marriage for the well-off couple, whose inherited wealth provided a substantial income and ensured there was no need for William to work. Apart from odd trips, William's main activity was painting and he would regularly take his colours out to the local common and other beauty spots where he found real peace. His financial independence was further emphasised on Laurie's birth certificate, where William simply described his job as 'gentleman'.

William Oates was a millionaire by today's standards, who made his money as an absentee landlord and private shareholder. He generated a substantial income from rents on numerous properties, including well-appointed office premises at South Parade in the centre of Leeds and cottages and workshops elsewhere in the city. He also owned a sizeable portfolio of shares and was particularly fond of fashionable Victorian railway stocks.

However, the demands of family life presented William Oates with a problem. By the age of 42, he was the father of four children under the age of six and the newly-acquired responsibilities necessitated that the Oates family find a permanent home. It was time for the traveller to lay down some foundations.

This was a radical departure, since during the early years of marriage, William and Caroline were constantly on the move, both in England and abroad. The itinerant family lived in a variety of temporary homes, in places like Leeds, London and assorted English seaside resorts such as Whitby and Hastings. Interspersed were occasional visits overseas as William continued to travel as parental circumstances allowed.

The transitory nature of their existence was reflected by each of the four children having a different birthplace over the six-year period. Only the youngest, Bryan, was born in the Oates family home at Meanwood. The eldest, Lillian, was born in the German city of Dusseldorf and Violet at Ewe Cote, a small hamlet outside Whitby which became a regular retreat in the 1880s.

Laurie Oates was born at 3 Acacia Villas, Putney, south-west London, in a comfortable, unpretentious boarding house specially rented for the purpose of Caroline Oates' confinement in the spring of 1880. Less than a year later, the boarding house and street were reclassified by the local council as 93 Upper Richmond Road, Putney. In 1904 the house was again renumbered to 111 Upper Richmond Road on what is today the busy, congested London thoroughfare called the South Circular Road.[3]

*The first photograph of Lawrence
Oates, cradled by his doting
mother Caroline. She called him
'Baby Boy' long into childhood. To
everyone else he was known as
Laurie.*

The obvious choice of a permanent family home was the Meanwood estate in Leeds, William's birthplace. But the property was still occupied by his mother, Susan, and after her death in 1889 it would pass to his younger brother Charles. It was not the ideal home for which the Oates family longed and they continued to look away from Yorkshire for their new home. William, the eldest in the Oates family, was lord of the manor without a manorial home.

The search was further complicated by the fact that Caroline Oates had taken to the London area and she had become the driving influence in the family. To emphasise the fondness for London, the family took lodgings in Chepstow Village, Notting Hill, and Caroline personally set about the task of finding a home in the capital, inspecting numerous properties in smart places like Hampstead, Swiss Cottage and Kensington. After a lengthy search, they finally found something suitable in April 1885.

Their choice was a solid three-storey detached property at 263 Upper Richmond Road, Putney, only a short distance from where Laurie was born.[4] A cousin, Dr Robert Oates, lived nearby. For the first time the family was able to begin building a permanent home among the quiet open spaces of a leafy London suburb. The detached red-brick home, which had a small crescent-shaped driveway and a large walled garden at the rear, suited their purpose.

Putney at the time was a prosperous, growing area with busy market gardens and a scattering of large family houses, including the London mansion of the American millionaire financier and industrialist, John Pierpont Morgan. Open fields surrounded the ribbon development of substantial Victorian villas which were springing up along the main arteries like Upper Richmond Road and Putney High Street. Arnold Bennett once observed that the existence of Putney 'seemed to approach the Utopian, it breathed the romance of common sense, kindliness and simplicity'.

William Oates, the wealthy, carefree wanderer, was easily dominated by Caroline, a strong-minded matriarch who epitomised the strict Victorian mother figure. She was a stern, severe-looking woman who was entirely comfortable with the strict disciplines and rigid social conventions of the age, a natural Victorian.

Her one indulgence was the church, which she embraced with a suitably restrained passion. She was fully at home in solemn surroundings and, wherever the Oates family travelled, Caroline would always seek out the nearest place of

'Baby Boy'. Laurie Oates aged about one year, complete with fashionable curls. (White Oates Museum)

*Caroline Oates. The buttoned-up
personification of Victorian motherhood
became obsessively devoted to her eldest
son, Laurie.*

worship. From good Anglican stock, she devoted a considerable amount of time
and money to supporting the church and found true contentment in her strong
religious beliefs.

As the rock of the family she represented permanence and stability for the four
children. Her potent mixture of traditional Yorkshire bluntness and the English
landed gentry's unshakeable belief in their own superiority gave Caroline Oates a
powerful, almost regal presence. She called her husband Willie and those closest
called her Carrie, but she was not someone who encouraged familiarity. She was
a devoted, generous mother, though with assistance of willing nannies,
governesses and maids this was not as demanding as for the vast majority of
Victorian women with four young children. Nonetheless, Caroline Oates was a
caring, considerate woman who undoubtedly loved her children.

But from a very early age, her four youngsters were split into two distinct
cliques. In one group was Lillian, Violet and Bryan, in the other, Laurie.

2

Mother's boy

Laurie Oates was mother's boy. She indulged him and lavished affection on him, frequently at the expense of the other three children. His younger sister, Violet, said that her strict mother would often get irate with the others for some minor misdemeanour, but she never got angry with Laurie. Laurie was always 'Baby Boy' to Caroline Oates, a term of affection which lingered long after her youngest, Bryan, was born. In fact, he remained 'Baby Boy' for an unhealthily long period of his life. Very little of his activities and habits escaped her attention as Caroline fussed and fretted over the child. Her simple motherly love grew into deep devotion and before long was bordering on obsession.

Aside from obsessive love, Caroline also extended her devotion to Laurie in more tangible ways. She always ensured that Laurie was given far more money and other gifts than his brother and sisters. The differences were so pronounced that, even as a child, Laurie regularly received more than the combined allowances of Lillian, Bryan and Violet.[1] It was a fiscal favouritism which would last deep into adulthood.

Caroline Oates, despite her frosty exterior, was a woman of considerable generosity, who always supported charities and causes, particularly those linked to the church. Her allowances to the children were equally generous and frequently topped up with additional gifts and presents. In later life, she supplemented their annual allowances with more substantial gifts of stocks and shares and later gave Bryan the money to buy a farm. But whatever she gave, Laurie always received more than Lillian, Violet and Bryan. She made no attempt to disguise her favouritism.

She was a meticulous person who kept detailed household accounts recording every penny spent, right down to trivial items like the cost of postage stamps or

Quartet. The four children of William and Caroline Oates, pictured in the late 1880s at their home in Putney, London. They are (left to right) the eldest Lillian, Laurie, Violet and the youngest, Bryan.

the precise sum dropped into the weekly church collection. Or in the case of her children, how the scales were weighted heavily in favour of 'Baby Boy'.

It is not entirely clear why Caroline Oates singled out Laurie for the special attention. The first-born son often holds a particular place in a mother's affections and there is little doubt that Caroline was overjoyed at the birth of Laurie. But her diary gives few clues as to why she would later develop her excessive devotion to the youngster. 'Baby is so bonny, dear little thing,' she wrote.

One plausible explanation is that the boy's uncertain health gave her grounds for concern and it may be that she was simply being over-protective of the child. He caught measles at the vulnerable age of fifteen weeks and from the outset, Laurie was more susceptible than most to everyday minor chills and coughs. She described him as a 'pathetic little boy'. The slightest cold went to his chest, he was occasionally short of breath and his little hands often turned blue. She responded by devoting even more attention, frequently sitting up through the night keeping a watchful eye on the weak child. Caroline conceded that Laurie had been 'extremely delicate' as a child and only recovered through 'much loving care and attention'.[2]

A visit to the Wimpole Street surgery of Dr Gunn in London showed that Laurie's illness was inflammation of the left lung, which was probably a touch of tuberculosis. Caroline Oates sought a second opinion and was advised to give the youngster some fresh sea air and even a warmer climate overseas. Initially, she took the familiar Victorian remedy of regular trips to the seaside. There were frequent outings to Sidmouth, Devon and back to Whitby where, for the first time, Laurie was given his own donkey to ride. It was the start of his love affair with horses.

As winter approached Caroline finally decided to take him abroad. This left the problem of what to do with the other three children. Christmas was near and all the children were under eight years of age. For Caroline there was little to consider. She left them behind.

A week before Christmas 1885, Mr and Mrs Oates waved goodbye to seven-year-old Lillian, Violet, aged four, and Bryan, who had just reached his second birthday, and set off for the sunshine of South Africa with Laurie. Caroline was a bad sailor and dreaded the long sea trip. But Laurie always came first.

By early January 1886 the damp chill of a London winter had been gratefully swapped for the warm summer breeze at a friend's house outside Cape Town. Later they moved 80 miles inland to stay with cousins at Caledon, south-east of Cape Town. It was a largely enjoyable spell, particularly for the young Laurie, who had the undivided attention of his parents and basked in the balmy climate and his mother's love.

Although Caroline inevitably felt some guilt about leaving her other three children 6,000 miles away, her priorities were clear and it was a good opportunity for William to introduce the pleasures of travel to his son. It had been little more than a decade since the adventurer had travelled on the same African Continent with his brother. Together they fished, walked the hills and enjoyed the pleasant fresh air. All the while Caroline stood guard over her son, watching and fretting. 'Baby Boy' was never far from her side.

After three months the Oates family felt it was safe to return to England, where they were reunited with the three children for a family holiday at Sidmouth. However, the long break from the English winter had not cured the young boy's ills and a year later, William Oates again took Laurie to South Africa for the winter. This time, Caroline remained in London with her other three children, though not without some anxiety. The parting from Laurie was purgatory and she set aside her own worries with seasickness to sail to Madeira alone to meet him on the return journey in March 1887. Once again, the other three children were left behind with assorted relatives and nannies.

*Father and son.
Laurie, aged six, en
route to South
Africa in 1886 with
his father, William.
Laurie was taken to
the warmth of South
Africa on several
occasions to help his
constant battle
against ill health.*

Despite his occasional bursts of illness, Laurie was a typically energetic lad, happiest with outdoor games and the adventurous pursuits of little boys. His health did not prevent him developing a passion for sports of all kinds and a particular keenness for horses.

Not long after coming back to England in 1886, Caroline Oates turned her attention to Laurie's education. She supported the Victorian belief that boys should be groomed for gentlemanly pursuits in later life, such as the Church, the law, the civil service or the army. Laurie was earmarked for the best education that money could buy and the adult life of a gentleman.

Initially he was given some rudimentary private tuition at home, though the results were disappointing. A little later young Laurie shared a governess at the home of neighbour, Patty Parker, and was groomed for his first proper school.

In late 1886, Laurie was enrolled at the private Dame School in Dealtry Road, within earshot of his Putney home. Shortly after, Dame School moved to Willington House, even closer to the Oates family home at 267 Upper Richmond Road, and became Willington School.[3]

Willington had been founded three years earlier by two resourceful Scottish spinsters, Annie and Ada Hale, who had turned their Putney home into a small school for well-to-do families in the area. The select handful of fee-paying pupils received firm but attentive instruction from the sisters and their lone assistant. It was a strict environment and the women set high standards, although one distinguished former pupil remembered that the sisters managed to make instruction a pleasure. Unusually for the Victorian period, he also recalled that there were rewards, but no punishments.[4]

Ada Hale, the younger of the two women, was a classical scholar who gave the pupils their early lessons in Greek and Latin, the bedrock of the Victorian public school syllabus. Improbably enough, she also doubled as cricket coach and part-time bowler as the school sought to widen the curriculum to accommodate the more active tastes of young boys.[5]

Annie Hale was the resolute headmistress who also taught English and the Scriptures. One old pupil remembered how she provided the school with an aura of 'benevolent austerity. . . (by the) skilful manipulation of her pince-nez'.[6] Violet Oates recalled the two women as 'daunting figures, wearing starched collars and with hair piled high'.[7]

William Oates had reservations about sending his eldest son to a school run by two women. He doubted whether it would be masculine or virile enough for Laurie. However, the far-sighted Hale women had clearly anticipated this potential problem and engaged the services of a retired army sergeant, who gave the pupils a daily Swedish military drill in the school garden. It was a timely move and the school's historian records that William Oates duly approved Laurie's enrolment after '. . . hearing the stentorian tones of the drill sergeant coming from the garden . . .'[8]

Laurie's three years of private tuition at Willington was the first clear-cut indication that he found school a major problem. He struggled to cope, especially with maths and the classics. In a private education system which deemed vocational training as unnecessary for future generations of generals, clerics or diplomats, there was precious little else for Laurie to learn and he soon fell behind the others.

The frequent interruptions caused by ill-health and the remedial trips abroad also made it difficult for the youngster. Laurie spent three successive winters in South Africa, where he learned more about the outdoor life than anything which could be found in books. Although his father was a willing amateur tutor, He was not an adequate replacement for the real thing. On his return to Willington, Laurie inevitably struggled and fell even further behind.

The school did its best to help him catch up. Willington's records show that one teacher, Mr Wolf, gave Laurie Oates 'special coaching' in subjects like Latin, algebra and geometry 'before he could reach the standard which the other boys had derived from the teaching of Miss Ada Hale'.[9] But the problem was not the lessons or the teaching.

What was not detected by anyone was that the child had some form of learning difficulty. It seems probable that Laurie was born with a form of dyslexia, which badly impaired his school progress and made it difficult for him to pass examinations. It also helped to shape his character.

Although somewhat fractured, young Laurie Oates enjoyed an especially privileged education for the period, which included three private schools, several years at a specialist 'crammer' and frequent and prolonged periods of one-to-one tuition. It is difficult to conceive a better education. However, even the most exclusive education of the Victorian age could not overcome his dyslexia.

Learning difficulties are more common than is generally appreciated and research has shown that up to one in ten people is affected by some form of dyslexia. Oates was in good company since some of the world's great figures have also had to battle against the same disability, including Leonardo da Vinci, Thomas Edison, Albert Einstein and Winston Churchill. They also shared the distinction that their disability was largely undetected.

Dyslexia was barely recognised in the late Victorian era and nothing was done in schools to combat the disability. In ignorance, children who were slow learners were frequently written off as simply dim or, at best, a pupil with a reading difficulty might be labelled 'word-blind'.[10]

A well-known modern writer glanced at some of Oates' letters in the 1980s and correctly observed that Oates wrote 'so ungrammatically and spelt so abominably as to be half illiterate', which was accurate. But it missed the point. Laurie Oates certainly possessed sound basic intelligence and solid good sense, as he would demonstrate in later life. He was not dim. But he struggled badly with words and numbers and had a frustrating time with formal examinations. His record was so unrelentingly abysmal that throughout his life he very rarely succeeded in passing any exam.

His obvious difficulty with the classics, which he first confronted at Willington, suggests he was suffering from one of the more common and highly frustrating symptoms of dyslexia – memory loss and lack of concentration. Many dyslexics find it extremely difficult to remember words and numbers on a page which they were reading only seconds earlier and this inevitably poses severe problems during examinations. Facts and figures can easily be lost in the brief moment between formulating the thought in the mind and writing it down on paper.

The repeated failure to cope with exams is not due solely to the inability to master the subject. But those with learning difficulties invariably take far longer to complete the exam papers and they frequently run out of time to finish the particular task. Failure was inevitable.

Short-term memory loss and lack of concentration will merely exacerbate the predicament and, of course, examiners at the time did not make allowance for weaknesses like poor handwriting or eccentric grammar. The struggle to cope merely adds to the stress and anxiety, making the task ever more difficult.

An interesting clue to his learning difficulties arose many years later in remarks made by Captain Robert Scott, who had asked Oates to tackle a fairly straightforward mathematical task, to log the feeding arrangements for the ponies on the South Pole expedition. Oates was a highly experienced manager of horseflesh and well capable of tending the needs of a few ponies. But columns of figures presented an unfathomable maze and Oates was simply unable to cope. Scott was puzzled at his fumbling attempt to handle the straightforward chore and after watching Oates struggling he wrote in his diary:

> 'I had intended Oates to superintend the forage arrangements but rows
> of figures, however simply configured, are too much for him. . .'[11]

Oates' inability to master columns of figures must have been starkly evident because, at this time, Scott was deeply embroiled in the final stages of detailed planning for his assault on the Pole. He was totally preoccupied with the logistics of transporting, feeding and sheltering sixteen men, ponies and dogs on a complex five-month journey across the most inhospitable terrain in the world. Amidst all this activity and preparation, it was the glaring failure of Oates to cope with simple sums which stood out and demanded comment from Scott.

Another member of Scott's last expedition, the biologist Dennis Lillie, recalled that Oates had a 'deliberate' way of writing, implying that he laboured over the task of putting pen to paper. Surviving copies of letters written by Oates show someone whose handwriting style was rather adolescent and elementary, while the grammar was often eccentric and the spelling erratic.

The privileged schooling did nothing to address his weakness. The spell at Willington was followed by a three-year period at the Remenham Place preparatory school, Henley-on-Thames, which merely confirmed his learning difficulties. His headmaster recalled that Master Oates was good at games, but a 'plodding kind of scholar'.

Dyslexics typically make up for their learning problems by focusing on other activities, such as arts or sport, where they invariably feel more comfortable. Laurie's likeness for sport was entirely predictable. He particularly enjoyed ball games like football and cricket, but had also developed a natural talent for boxing and as he approached his teens, was also beginning to indulge in his passion for horse riding.

Easy rider. Laurie (right) developed an early love of horses and is pictured on one of his first rides.

He was a popular child who made friends easily as he passed through school and was remembered fondly. From his earliest days, he was invariably nicknamed 'Titus' after the unscrupulous seventeenth-century anti-Catholic conspirator, Titus Oates.

However, the dyslexia was already beginning to leave its mark. It is likely that his confidence took a knock and at times he felt inhibited about expressing himself. He only came to life at games or other boisterous outdoor pursuits.

Oates enjoyed his own company as much as that of others and was an unusually quiet young man of few words. He developed a biting sardonic wit, but was otherwise a closed book. He never lacked friends but acquaintances remarked that he was never an easy person to get to know. By his early teenage years, Laurie Oates was already more introverted than extroverted. What is less clear is whether Laurie's difficulties in the classroom had any effect on his recurring health problems. It may be, however, that at least some of his early difficulties can be traced back to his dyslexia.

The classroom can be a cruel and humiliating experience for those struggling to overcome any disability and it is common for youngsters to develop psychosomatic disorders like imaginary headaches and inexplicable stomach pains to avoid attending school. It is also common for real ailments to be greatly exaggerated in an attempt to avoid the embarrassment of unmerciful classmates or the uneven battle with impenetrable scholarly subjects.

3

A place in the country

As Laurie was joining Remenham School, William and Caroline Oates had finally decided that it was time to escape the soot and smog of Victorian London and head to the countryside. Laurie's weak chest may have been the clinching factor, particularly for the ever-attentive Caroline. In the spring of 1891, William and Caroline arrived back in Putney to tell the children the gleeful news that they had found a new home.

It was Over Hall, a grand rambling property set in fifteen acres of gently rolling north Essex countryside, close to the border with Suffolk, in the quintessentially English village of Gestingthorpe. It was a spot very near to where earlier generations of the Oates family had lived at least 800 years earlier. One of the local estates took its name from John Otes, who with others held the manor of Little Laver at the time of Edward II in the late thirteenth or early fourteenth centuries.

The imposing property, which soon became known as Gestingthorpe Hall, suited the Oates family. It was the foundation that Caroline in particular was seeking and for William Oates, an estate in keeping with his social position. He had at last found his manorial home. They settled immediately and the Oates family would be associated with Gestingthorpe for almost 60 years.

Gestingthorpe Hall is believed to date originally from the seventeenth century or possibly earlier, though there have been substantial changes to the building over the years. A classic red-brick façade was added in the early eighteenth century and it now resembles a typical large Georgian manor house, although it probably predates this period by as much as 100 years.[1]

The area around Gestingthorpe has a long history, dating back at least to Saxon times under the general name of Laver. According to one historian, the village name itself was Saxon in origin:

'The name seems to be derived from three Saxon words: Gest, a stranger, a guest; Ing, a meadow or pasture; Torpe, a village.'[2]

Buying Gestingthorpe was a great adventure for the Oates family. Once inside the imposing house, they were greeted by a magnificent 40 ft (12 m) reception hall and a splendid array of accommodation, including an ornate drawing room and a billiard room which opened out to the vast garden. Up the sweeping staircase they found fourteen bedrooms, four bathrooms, a library and other assorted rooms. Outside they discovered a quaint two-bedroomed stable cottage, an abundance of trees, shrubbery, tennis courts, open fields and a nearby wood. They also found stables, which further encouraged Laurie to develop his burgeoning interest in horses.

However, Caroline Oates was unable to share the family's excitement with all four of her children. On the eve of the much-anticipated move to Gestingthorpe, she coldly banished Lillian, Violet and Bryan to faraway Whitby, presumably because she did not want the children under her feet during the move.

But the same concern did not apply to eleven-year-old Laurie, who was given the exclusive opportunity of sharing the thrills of the occasion with his

Home. The Oates family home at Gestingthorpe, Essex. William Oates bought the grand manor house in 1891 and it stayed in the family until 1947.(Michael Smith)

parents. Earlier biographers rightly concluded that Caroline Oates '. . . simply could not bear to be parted from him'.[3] It was another insensitive decision that must have wounded Lillian, Violet and Bryan, all of whom were at an impressionable age.

Laurie, the heir to the new estate, first saw Gestingthorpe in June 1891 when he travelled by train with his father from London's Liverpool Street Station to Sudbury. From Sudbury they took a pony-and-trap on the pleasant five-mile trip through the wooded and winding Essex lanes to the village of Gestingthorpe, then a modest secluded spot with a small collection of houses, assorted nearby farms and the delightful church of St Mary the Virgin, part of which dates back to the thirteenth century.

The Oates family quickly assumed their role as lords of the manor and established their place in the order of things. The villagers of Gestingthorpe had to doff their caps or curtsy as they passed a member of the family in the street. The mansion and sprawling estate provided welcome employment for a number of local people, but otherwise the villagers and lords of the manor accepted the medieval nature of things and led entirely separate lives.

In the house itself, Caroline Oates quickly imposed herself on proceedings by drawing up a list of stringent, slightly daunting rules for any visitors. The household regulations included such frosty directives as: 'Don't stay an awful time, ie. more than a week. . . Don't shiver. . . Don't ask what time the next meal is. . . Don't say 'What fish' when offered fish for breakfast.'

William Oates gave notice that he took his new family responsibilities seriously. In June 1891, as the family was preparing to move into Gestingthorpe, William Oates wrote his first will, leaving all his considerable wealth to Caroline.

Gestingthorpe was exactly what Caroline Oates had wanted. It gave her status and her first proper home since their marriage fourteen years earlier. It also allowed her to launch herself energetically into the local church, St Mary the Virgin, opposite the driveway into Gestingthorpe Hall.

The family was given an early opportunity to show their commitment to the community. Soon after moving in, they were asked to lend their support for essential restoration work at the church. Gestingthorpe's Rev C.T. Bromwich admitted the building was in an 'alarming condition' and launched an urgent appeal for cash. William and Caroline Oates were happy to oblige and became one of the earliest backers of the rebuilding fund, with William personally donating £200 (about £10,000 in today's terms).

Laurie Oates did not embrace religion with the same fervour as his parents and regarded going to church as an ordinary part of life's duties and no more.

However, Caroline Oates tried her best to encourage him and in August 1892, a year after moving to Essex, she bought Laurie a new Bible. On the flyleaf, the doting mother wrote the inscription:

'My son be wise & make my heart glad.'[4]

After a little over three undistinguished years at Remenham, the time had come for Laurie Oates to take a big step upwards in his education. In 1894, just before his fourteenth birthday, the young man was sent to Eton, another important stride towards the creation of an English gentleman.

The basic fees were around 150 guineas a year (£157.50 or about £8,500 at current purchasing value), although this took no account of additional extras for items like books, clothing and breakages. But money was not an issue for the Oates family and nothing was too much for Laurie.

Laurie Oates spent seven terms during his period of just over two years at Eton, arriving in January 1894 and leaving in the spring of 1896. But it was another mediocre scholarly interlude which achieved little for the young man. If William and Caroline Oates believed an expensive public school education could guarantee academic excellence, they were to be rudely awakened. The Eton experience was a grave academic disappointment.

Laurie and Eton were unsuited to each other. The school regime of the time was based on a well-established mixture of the classics, religion and games. But the keen focus on subjects like Greek and Latin was alien to Laurie and his learning difficulties left him trailing badly behind most pupils.

Even the benefit of the renowned Eton housemaster, Henry Rawlins, could do little for Laurie. Rawlins was something of an institution at Eton, an amiable and efficient teacher who spent over 30 years at the school and on at least two occasions narrowly failed to achieve the distinction of becoming head. But as the Willington and Remenham years had shown, young Laurie Oates was no scholar and Rawlins was unable to work any miracles.

The one bright spot for Laurie was that Eton placed great emphasis on robust games and hearty outdoor activities which were regarded as an essential element of character-building and developing team spirit for a later life in public office or on the battlefield. When mixed with the heavy doses of religious instruction, some called the regime muscular Christianity.

Unfortunately, young Laurie Oates failed to excel even in sports and he barely left his mark on the school's famous playing fields. One of his difficulties on the sports field was poor eyesight, which forced him to wear spectacles and in later life prompted him to seek specialist help. In his first year he managed a nominal

*England's finest. A slightly
uncomfortable looking Laurie at
Eton, the country's most
prestigious public school. The
photograph was taken around
1894.*

single run in the Junior House Cricket Cup and there were other doubtless
enjoyable but undistinguished attempts at games like football and athletics.

However, the major consolation was that he found it easy to fit in. As a member
of the landed gentry he was at home rubbing shoulders with the sons of
politicians, diplomats, bankers and generals who for centuries had been the raw
material of schools like Eton.

The most surprising omission from his Eton years is that he did not take the
obvious step of joining the Eton Volunteer Corps, the school's own private militia
founded a few years earlier by Edmond Warre, the headmaster during Oates'
time at the school.

Warre was a determined and influential Eton figure who epitomised the public
school ethic in the late Victorian age. He stood for wholesome outdoor games,
strong military values, duty and the supremacy of the British Empire. He also
believed that dying for one's country was the supreme sacrifice.[5]

It is little surprise, therefore, that Eton in the late Victorian age was a high-class
production line for future soldiers, many destined to provide the doomed officer

class for the British army in the trenches of the First World War. One informative study – undertaken in 1899 – charted the boys' careers after leaving Eton and showed that some 400 of the 1,400 pupils went straight into the army after leaving the school.

The Volunteer Corps was the first step on the road to a military career for many would-be soldiers at Eton, fitting in neatly with the underlying ethos of the school. The Corps and its clear path to the Army was also an obvious bolthole for the less gifted pupils who struggled to cope with the academic rigours of Greek and Latin. The Volunteer Corps was a welcome alternative to Homer or Horace for the less bookish types and Laurie Oates was definitely not bookish.

Moreover, the army was an attractive proposition at a time when Laurie's career prospects were narrowing. The traditional gentlemanly avenues of the law or civil service were closed off by his learning difficulties and the best options at this stage were probably limited to the clergy, farming or the army.

Laurie, even as a young man, relished a challenge and the reluctant worshipper showed little enthusiasm for joining the church. Nor was there much appetite for a slow-paced life on the land. The army was the obvious choice for anyone with an adventurous streak and the militia a promising first step. But illness again intervened before he could take even the initial move of joining the Eton Volunteer Corps.

Laurie caught a chill in the spring of 1896 while participating in the House sports event, probably because the spartan regime did not allow pupils to wear adequate clothing to combat the cold English damp. What was a relatively straightforward ailment suddenly deteriorated. The chill blossomed into a serious attack of pneumonia, which almost killed him. His concerned parents took him out of Eton at Easter 1896 and he never returned.

However, Laurie Oates' near-fatal illness did leave its mark on Eton. After his pneumonia, the school graciously allowed the Lower Boys to wear sweaters for outdoor games and a sensible new tradition was born.

While Eton had not been able to provide the young man with the full education his parents sought, it did leave him indelibly marked with some of the key characteristics of the English public school system. He emerged with a lasting belief in the code of duty and honour and the traditional values of hard work and a stiff upper lip.

But there was also the faint dislike of foreigners and the distinctive cold, unemotional face of the English gentleman schooled in the art of not displaying his emotions. Eton had also taught Laurie Oates that self-sacrifice was the supreme act.

*The young squire. Laurie
(right), photographed at
Gestingthorpe with his brother
Bryan. Within a few years he
would be titular head of the family.*

The abrupt end of his Eton schooling was a severe blow to his now growing ambition of forging a career in the army. Eton had been a key part of the plan, which would have taken him first to the Eton Volunteers, on to Oxford and subsequently a commission in the regular army.

His initial step was to earn a place at Oxford, which presented the immediate hurdle of passing the entrance exams. It was a formidable obstruction for which the young man was not prepared. Laurie's parents obviously recognised the problem and he was dispatched to a special 'crammer' school at Eastbourne on the south coast of England.

The South Lynn school, Eastbourne, operated under the private tutorship of the Reverend H. von Essen Scott, a devoted teacher and cricket-lover who was described as 'a born character-builder'. South Lynn, a large semi-castellated brick building on the very crest of a hill at the entrance to Eastbourne, was ideal for the young Laurie Oates. It was among the first buildings to be seen by visitors approaching Eastbourne and a contemporary commented that 'no healthier spot on the coast could have been chosen'.

The school was a haven for the struggling, less-gifted who laboured to fulfil the lofty ambitions of their titled and well-heeled parents. Fees were expensive and one former teacher gave an unflattering insight into Rev Scott's unfortunate charges. He wrote:

> 'His pupils, almost without exception, were public school failures; either the boy had failed with his school or the school had failed with the boy.'[6]

South Lynn had traditionally taken a large proportion of its pupils from Eton, mainly because of Rev Scott's long cricketing association with the school. It is likely a kindly master, perhaps Rawlins, had steered William and Caroline Oates towards South Lynn in the hope Rev Scott could work the education miracle impossible at Eton.

Laurie Oates found himself in familiar territory. South Lynn's pupils typically included the sons of diplomats and businessmen and, at one point, the grandson of the Prime Minister of Egypt. By coincidence, the school would later find another connection with Polar exploration. Emily Shackleton, the widow of Sir Ernest Shackleton, who lived in Eastbourne, was friendly with the head in the late 1920s and became an active supporter of the school.

The regime at Eastbourne was tough, starting with lessons before breakfast and followed by intensive studies throughout the morning. Scott was an accomplished all-round sportsman – cricketer, rugby player, golfer and oarsman – and ensured that the boys had ample time for more energetic pursuits which would balance their scholarly activities. He arranged sporting activities for most afternoons. But classes resumed immediately afterwards, often extending to nine or 10 pm at night.

Laurie was a long way off from being the finished article when he first came to South Lynn in 1896. But he was an engaging and popular personality. One of his teachers recalled:

> 'He came quite young, perhaps at fifteen, an Etonian of rough offhand manners. Gradually he grew into a sort of honest, great Newfoundland puppy. Hence, again, he developed into a grown-up tame Newfoundland, boisterous but kindly.'[7]

Oates spent much of the next four years at South Lynn, mostly engaged in the unequal struggle to overcome his learning difficulties. An earlier biographer recorded that he could never get over the conviction that reading was a waste of time, unless the books told of action.[8]

Once again, he compensated by plunging energetically into most sports and games, the rougher the better. He gamely tried most things, but became quite proficient at boxing and a teacher recalled:

> 'He was a fine middleweight boxer; the sergeant-instructor at the drill hall earned his bread, so far as Oates was concerned, with the sweat of his brow. On this account, and by reasons of sheer seniority, he was in later time the recognised cock-of-the-walk.'[9]

Shortly before he was sent off to Eastbourne, Laurie was given the welcome news that his father William wanted to take him on another trip to South Africa during the holidays. This time it was pleasure, not recuperation from illness. William Oates, though in his mid-50s, had lost none of his appetite for travel and exploration and wanted Laurie to accompany him in the summer of 1896. It would help make up for the disappointment of leaving Eton and offer an ideal opportunity for father and son to get to know each other.

But fate had other plans.

4

Lord of the Manor

Laurie Oates was dealt a severe blow even before he had time to prepare for the journey to South Africa. His father was taken ill and died suddenly on Good Friday, 1896.

William Oates had decided that, before Laurie started at South Lynn, the whole family would be taken to the sub-tropical Atlantic island of Madeira for Easter. In March they sailed to the capital, Funchal, with William full of hopes of a little time with his paints. But all plans were thrown into disarray shortly after landing when the island was hit by an outbreak of typhoid.

William Oates, the seasoned traveller in Africa, was aware that typhoid is normally caused by impure water or infected food and took immediate precautions, ordering the family to drink only boiled water. Ironically, he himself could not escape infection and before long was struck down. While typhoid today remains a highly dangerous disease, it is not necessarily fatal. But antibiotics were not discovered until the 1940s and William Oates was defenceless.

Caroline Oates watched in horror as her husband's condition quickly deteriorated from a chill, to a high fever and into the final fatal stages which bring internal bleeding and chronic pneumonia. She promptly packed the four children onto a ship bound for England and resumed a vigil at her dying husband's bedside. On 17 March – Laurie's sixteenth birthday – she had accepted the worst and wrote in her diary:

'I really believe my darling is sinking.'[1]

Less than three weeks later, on 3 April 1896, William Oates was dead. He was only 54 and like his brother and fellow traveller, Frank, had died of fever a long way from the comfort of home. Caroline Oates was devastated and her grief was exacerbated by the insistence of the Madeira authorities that William should be buried immediately because of the risk of infection. Almost before the awful reality had sunk in, Caroline had buried her husband in the Protestant cemetery at Funchal and was on board a passenger ship steaming back to England.

She was finally reunited with her children at London's Great Eastern Hotel, alongside Liverpool Street Station, shortly before they hurried back to Gestingthorpe by train. At Gestingthorpe, Caroline Oates closed the shutters on the outside world.

The death of William Oates had a profound impact. It was the start of an unrelenting period of mourning which lasted for the rest of her life and has inevitably aroused comparisons with Queen Victoria's intense grief for her dead husband, Albert. The women, by chance, had other things in common. Both had married their cousins and both husbands died from typhoid. Caroline donned black in 1896 after William's sudden death and was rarely, if ever, dressed in anything else until she died in 1937. Sadly for Caroline Oates, there was no John Brown figure, the Scottish gillie whose unorthodox attentions helped Victoria overcome her long period of mourning. Caroline Oates grieved alone.

The death of William Oates pitched the gauche, sixteen-year-old Laurie into the unexpected role of Lord of the Manor. Instead of the adventurous trip to the African interior with his father, Laurie suddenly found himself coming to terms with the responsibilities of being head of the household. However, he never assumed more than a notional supremacy, even in adulthood. The power on the Oates estate remained firmly and unequivocally in the grip of his formidable mother.

Mrs Oates exercised her authority through an inflexible mixture of strict maternal doctrine and rigid control of the family finances. William Oates left his wealth solely to his wife, thus securing the family's future. It also ensured that she was the undisputed head of the family.

His estate, largely property holdings and an extensive portfolio of shares, was valued at over £125,000, which in today's terms is worth nearly £7,000,000. She inherited a collection of cottages, offices, warehouses and workshops in the centre of Leeds which alone were valued at £8,981 (today: £495,000). In addition, she received an assortment of shares in a number of railway, canal and property companies, plus a small stake in Leeds General Cemetery. These holdings had a combined market value of almost £117,000 (today: nearly £6,500,000). At the time of his death, William was also owed another £1,083 (today: £60,000) in uncollected dividend cheques.[2] It was a safe, sensible package of investments, which brought a solid income and meant the family would never want.

The matriarch. Caroline Oates was a severe, profoundly religious woman who dominated the Oates family for half a century and continued to exert her influence long after her own death in 1937. (White Oates Museum)

The loss of her husband drew Caroline Oates even closer to her 'Baby Boy'. She confided in the young man, spent increasing amounts of time in his company and seemed to have fewer spare moments for Lillian and Violet, who were both still at Gestingthorpe. Laurie Oates, dutiful and considerate, was content to play a supporting role to his mother. He was far too immature to replace his father as head of the family and, in any event, there was no question of him standing up to his mother. She simply carried on running Gestingthorpe and the Oates estate, while always finding time to maintain her strong influence over the life of her eldest son.

The nearest Laurie came to independence at this time was to clarify his own ambitions to join the army. The only question was how to enlist. The Oxford entrance exams remained far beyond his abilities and he therefore decided to take the alternative route by joining the local militia. His father had been a long-standing member of the West York Militia in Yorkshire but Laurie chose a billet nearer to home. He joined the 2nd Volunteer Battalion of the Suffolk Regiment, not far from Gestingthorpe.

Although voluntary, the militia were frequently used effectively as reservists to support the standing army. It was a sizeable force, which in 1898 totalled 125,000 men. It was a collection of separate units and not an organised force ready to take the field. But the eager volunteers, who normally signed up for a term of six years, undertook regular training and were on standby for any national emergency.

In practice, the militia resembled a gentleman's club where would-be soldiers could keep their own civilian jobs and lifestyle, while meeting other like-minded souls with military ambitions. But for those with higher ambitions, the militia also represented a convenient entrée to the regular army, especially in times of war when they would be among the first summoned to the colours.

Laurie Oates blossomed in the strictly all-male environment, where customs and practice were an extension of the public school arena. After a short spell with the Suffolks, he graduated further by joining his father's old militia corps, the 3rd Battalion of the Prince of Wales' Own West Yorkshire Regiment, commanded by Colonel Sir George Hay. In December 1898 he was appointed second lieutenant.

Although progress in the militia was welcome, it was no substitute for the real thing and Oates still nurtured ambitions to become a full-time soldier. In the fond hope of surmounting the insurmountable Oxford entrance exams, he continued to slog unprofitably through dreary books at South Lynn and was even subjected to occasional doses of specialist one-to-one tuition. In his desperation, he enlisted the support of the most influential person in his life.

Oates wrote to his mother in 1899 urging her to persuade uncle Charles – his father's brother who still lived at Meanwood – to approach an acquaintance,

Henry Pelham, the President of Trinity College, Oxford. His ambitious plan was to avoid the entrance exams altogether. Laurie's clumsy and naïve stab at corruption was futile. Charles Oates politely declined to help.

Laurie sat the exam and had to endure a withering assessment from Pelham, who pronounced:

> 'Your papers are considerably below our standard and I do not think it would be worth your while to stand again in September, as only very few vacancies are left.'[3]

Oates had invested considerable time studying for the exams and was hurt and angry at his latest abject failure. He was so depressed by Oxford's rebuff that he considered abandoning his military ambitions. In a letter around this time, he wrote: '. . . I feel almost as if I could chuck the whole thing up, army and all, so bored am I with exams.' The problem, however, was that he had not developed an obvious alternative career.

After a while, Laurie came to terms with Pelham's blunt rejection and resolved to continue pursuing an army career, even exploring the possibility of approaching

*The Young Squire.
Laurie Oates
photographed around
the time he became
Lord of the Manor at
Gestingthorpe.*

43

a different college such as Merton or Oriel. The grinding struggle with education merely increased his appetite for outdoor pursuits and sports, especially if it involved horses. The listless, disgruntled scholar came to life on the playing fields or on horseback. They were the only places where he felt real fulfilment.

Oates had been introduced to riding at a very early age and by his late teens had become a first-class horseman. A few months after his twentieth birthday in 1900, he was among the 25 founder members of the East Essex Hunt Club and his range of riding activities also included polo, point-to-point and steeplechasing. Laurie Oates was known for his bravery in the saddle, even at an early age. He treated the odd tumble as a routine part of riding and was remembered as someone who knew no fear when on horseback.

Apart from horses, he had also taken a fancy to sailing. His father, who had owned a 40-ton yacht, *Curlew*, introduced him to sailing at a very young age and after his death, Laurie and Bryan bought their own vessel. It was an 18-ton sailing yacht, *Saunterer*, which became a firm favourite with the two brothers.

Laurie Oates approached sailing in the same fearless, devil-may-care manner as he did riding and, on his first trip, the *Saunterer* was piloted 200 miles along England's south coast from the Hamble River in Hampshire to Penzance Bay, Cornwall. Not everyone shared his sense of adventure and on one occasion Bryan refused to sail across the channel to Antwerp in a raging gale. Undeterred, Laurie reached Antwerp, but his crew of Cornish sailors followed Bryan's example and promptly deserted.

The active, outdoor life suited Oates and seems to have had a beneficial effect on his health. By now he had grown into a fine strapping character, who stood almost 5 ft 11 ins, weighed a shade over twelve stones and boasted an ample chest measurement of 38½ inches. The pallid, sickly boy who had been forced to leave Eton because of illness only a few years earlier had developed into a robust young man. It is not clear how he had overcome the recurring health problems of his childhood. It may be that at least some earlier ailments had been attention seeking, partly because of his learning difficulties and partly because of an over-powering mother.

But Caroline Oates could not fully accept the growing maturity of her eldest son. 'Baby Boy' still required special attention and she continued to exert her control, normally by keeping a tight rein on the family fortune. She knew money was power and the most effective way of controlling Laurie was through his allowance. She placed him on a drip-feed, never allowing him to take full charge of his own resources. She was not penny-pinching with her money, merely exercising her firm maternal rule.

The one-sided arrangement forced Laurie to conduct a continuous dialogue with his mother, begging and pleading for comparatively small sums of money to buy even personal items like cigarettes or to settle bar bills. Correspondence between the two is littered with Laurie's requests for money to buy anything from a new horse to a new pair of boots. She did not allow him to open his own bank account until he was well past his twentieth birthday and living in a different country.

Caroline Oates' generosity was never in doubt and she gave the four children a respectable annual allowance, which was frequently topped up with additional gifts of at least £50 (over £2,500 in today's terms). She also invested large sums in stocks and shares on their behalf. But, as both children and adults, Lillian, Violet and Bryan always received significantly smaller gifts and allowances than Laurie.

At a time when Laurie Oates was an adult earning his own living, his mother gave him regular allowances of between £500 and £900 a year (roughly £26,000 – £48,000 a year in today's terms). By contrast, Lillian and Violet were each awarded around £50 and Bryan between £250 and £500 a year. The one exception came in 1910 when Laurie was out of the country and Caroline Oates gave Bryan £1,000 (today: £47,000) to buy a farm.[4]

One explanation for her behaviour is that Laurie, the man who could not add up a column of figures, was poor with money. It is possible that she did not trust him to look after cash, even though her tight rein over the family purse sometimes angered her son. On one occasion, he bristled:

> 'I am rather insulted about you saying I am not good at accounts yet, as I have had nearly £100 (today: over £5,000) through my hands since the beginning of the training besides my own and I can account for every farthing of it.'[5]

Another more persuasive explanation is that Caroline Oates knew that money bought freedom and she simply could not bear to let him go.

5

A call to arms

Laurie Oates spent the summer of 1899 wrestling with yet more studies, punctuated by odd bursts of training at the militia barracks in York and an occasional visit to his uncle Charles at Meanwood. He also managed to take regular rides with a number of prominent hunts, including the long-established Quorn and the Pytchley.

South Lynn had become increasingly tiresome, partly because of the tedious slog and lack of progress and partly because he had outgrown school. He found it difficult to get along with some of his fellow pupils, particularly the younger ones. At nineteen, Oates was older than many of the others and by the middle of 1899 had concluded that South Lynn was 'a bad place'. In October he duly failed another of Oxford's entrance exams.

But events elsewhere were conspiring to make the torture of examinations unnecessary. In October 1899, as Oates was failing his latest attempt to enter Oxford, the Boer War broke out between Britain and the Afrikaner population in South Africa. It was the break that Oates needed.

With renewed vigour, he immediately set about the task of seeking promotion to the regular army. He calculated – correctly – that the army would bypass many of the formalities of entry to equip itself for the coming fight by calling up the militia. Oates was so confident he wrote home asking a member of the Gestingthorpe staff to clean his uniform.

However, it was not so straightforward and Colonel Hay of the West Yorkshire Militia was among those who warned that, regardless of the national requirements, he first needed to pass the standard school certificate, known as the PS.

To his utter frustration, Oates was again forced back into the unhappy arena of South Lynn. But he was more determined than ever and went as far as to attend night school. His anxiety was increased by the widespread belief in Britain that the war against the Boer upstarts would be over in a matter of months. Few gave the Boer irregulars any chance of defeating the might of the British Empire and Oates was concerned the fighting would be over by the time he graduated into the regular army.

He told his mother it was of the 'most vital importance that I get it (a commission) before the end of the war as there may never be another chance like it'. A little later he wrote:

> 'There is every prospect, I think, of the 3rd being called out as it will reassure the public, but I am afraid we shall not get out to South Africa.'[1]

Oates again turned to his mother for help, hoping the maternal touch might help bypass standard procedures and smooth the way to a commission. He asked her to speak to the wives of the generals at the War Office and drop a word in the right ears.

The war had gone badly for Britain from the very start and it was increasingly clear that the army would soon need to deploy reservists and militia officers. Oates was delighted, though like almost everyone in Britain he underestimated the enemy.

Victorian Britain, the most powerful nation on earth, began the war consumed with the arrogant self-belief that a bunch of irregular Afrikaner farmers would crumble at the mere sight of the highly-trained and battle-hardened British army. The familiar cry was the war would be wrapped up by Christmas.

It was a misplaced optimism. The historian, Thomas Pakenham, aptly described the Boer War as the longest, costliest, bloodiest and most humiliating conflict for Britain between 1815 and 1914. Kipling said the campaign gave Britain 'no end of a lesson'.

Britain had entered the war outnumbered, poorly prepared and ill-equipped even though the conflict itself had been coming for some time. The two Imperial powers, the British and Dutch, had found it impossible to co-exist alongside each other and jostled for power and influence from the time white settlers from Europe had reached the southern tip of Africa 250 years earlier. Britain was in the ascendancy for much of the nineteenth century and tensions increased after frontier farmers of mainly Dutch extraction, known as *trekboers* (Boers), poured across the Orange and Vaal rivers to escape Imperial dominance and establish the free state of Transvaal. Britain annexed the region following the Kimberley diamond rush of 1870–71 and Dutch settlers later rebelled against British rule, triggering the First Boer War of 1880–81. Britain suffered a wounding defeat at Majuba and Transvaal's independence was restored. Relations deteriorated further after the discovery of gold in the Witwatersrand in 1886, sparking a gold rush that brought thousands of eager prospectors flooding into the territory.

The Afrikaners resented the influx of *Uitlanders* – foreigners – and reacted by imposing tough new taxes and denying the newcomers basic civil and democratic rights. In retaliation, the British colonialist and financier, Cecil Rhodes, fermented a mini rebellion in the Transvaal in 1895 and his friend, Leander Starr Jameson, led a band of 600 armed insurgents in support of the *Uitlanders* in the unfortunate Jameson Raid. Jameson was defeated and captured and the two sides moved closer to war.

In 1899, the newly-appointed British Governor of the Cape Colony, Sir Alfred Milner, ordered a build-up of troops to defend Queen Victoria's interests. On 9 October 1899, Paul Kruger, President of Transvaal, issued an ultimatum demanding the withdrawal of British troops within 48 hours and war was officially declared on 11 October.

From the outset, the British army, under the leadership of Sir Redvers Buller, suffered humiliating defeats. Within days the Boers advanced deep into Natal, Orange Free State and Cape Colony and surrounded British troops at Kimberley and Mafeking.

Buller immediately sent fresh troops to relieve the besieged garrisons, but the Afrikaners inflicted heavy defeats on each of the relief columns. Victorian Britain, which ruled over 25 per cent of the globe, was dumbstruck by the disastrous news. It was known as 'Black Week' in Britain.

The immediate fall-out saw Buller replaced by Field Marshal Lord Frederick Roberts, the distinguished 67-year-old commander-in-chief of British forces in Ireland, who had served the Empire for over 40 years and became Lord Roberts of Kandahar and Waterford in recognition of his illustrious service. On the day he assumed command of British forces in South Africa, Roberts received news that his only son had been killed in the clashes of Black Week.

Roberts appointed the charismatic General Horatio Herbert Kitchener as his chief-of-staff and set about building up his forces, which included recruiting a mixture of regular troops, reservists and the militia. Buller, in one of his last orders, had asked for 8,000 mounted men to combat the more mobile horse-mounted Boer guerrillas.

It was the opportunity Oates had been seeking and, in early March, he wrote excitedly to his mother:

> 'Have you seen that they are going to give all qualified military officers commissions without any further exams so I am pretty safe I think.'[2]

His ambition was finally realised on 6 April 1900 when Oates was given a commission. Although not immediately assigned to a particular regiment, he was finally enlisted in the regular army. First, however, there was the small matter of passing the PS exam and the slight indignity of remaining in the 3rd West Yorkshire Militia until his full commission arrived. Oates somehow managed to pass the examination – a rare event in his life – in mid-May.

On 18 May, an explosion of national celebration greeted news that the town of Mafeking had been relieved after a Boer siege lasting 217 days. On 30 May Oates was formally gazetted into the 6th Inniskilling Dragoons.[3] It was not his first choice of regiment. Right up to the last moment before his posting came through, Oates had wanted to join the Greys.

The Inniskilling Dragoons were, in fact, one of the most distinguished regiments in the British Army and Oates had no reason to feel he had taken second best. The regiment was first raised in 1690 from around Enniskillen in the north of Ireland when Loyalist forces under William of Orange fought against James II and its baptism of fire came at the Battle of the Boyne. The Inniskillings fought at Waterloo in 1815 and formed part of the Heavy Brigade who charged the Russian guns at Balaclava in 1854. Now it was among the first regiments posted to South Africa to put down the Boer rebellion.[4]

Oates swallowed his disappointment and told his mother:

> 'I suppose you have seen that I am gazetted into the 6th Inniskilling Dragoons. I am very pleased about it as it is the best Heavy Cavalry regiment in the British Army which is saying a good deal when it has to compare with the Greys and Royals.'[5]

It is not clear just how much influence Caroline Oates had in getting her son into the Inniskillings, but it appears she did manage to pull some strings in his favour. The best clue to her manoeuvring behind the scenes comes in a letter which Oates wrote to his mother shortly after his appointment. It indicates she played a significant role and was vital to his enlistment. He wrote:

> 'I shall not try to thank you in writing for all you have done for me but what I say is this, that if it had not been for you I would still be rotting in the old 3rd and knowing how keen I was to get a commission you must if possible try to realise how grateful I am.'[6]

Caroline's influence over her twenty-year-old son now extended to her choice of his cavalry regiment.

6

A blast of war

Second-Lieutenant Lawrence Oates was posted to the regimental headquarters at the Curragh, the sprawling military camp in Kildare to the south-west of Dublin, in June 1900. It was an exciting moment of achievement for the young man, who had finally fulfilled his ambition of becoming a cavalry officer when for so long it had looked beyond his capacity.

Initially he was preoccupied with the thrill of getting kitted out in his new uniform, which ranged from drill tunics to polo whites and from braided mess kit to working overalls. He soon discovered being a member of an élite cavalry regiment was an expensive business and Oates immediately turned to his mother for help. Soon after landing in Ireland, he wrote home asking his mother for permission to open an account at Cox's, the regimental bankers, and added:

> 'If you could let me have £100 in there I could have it for subs and mess bills, etc. I should like to put it in as soon as convenient to you as you have to pay these things as soon as you are ordered.'[1]

Caroline Oates had little choice but to loosen her grip and provide him with at least some control over his own affairs. But it was only a partial relaxation since Mrs Oates retained overall power, making sure that she controlled the flows of money into his personal account.

The point was perfectly illustrated in September when Oates again wrote home asking for money to buy two horses. He faithfully promised:

> 'If you let me have the money for these horses I shall be very careful and live as cheaply as possible to the end of next year. I have got my £100 at Cox's which should see me alright.'[2]

When Caroline Oates duly obliged, Oates said the cheque gave him 'infinite joy' and he promptly bought a chestnut colt for £150. It was not enough to suit all his needs and within a fortnight he wrote again asking for more money to buy a pair of boxing gloves. Caroline Oates' strategy was working.

Oates was a consistent letter writer and he kept up a constant correspondence with his mother, often involving pleas for money or discussing a variety of military and personal affairs. But his letters were always rather formal as though he was addressing an unknown third party. He always addressed Caroline Oates as 'Dear Mother' and signed off with a detached, almost business-like, 'Yours affectionately, L.E.G. Oates.' There was no touch of warmth or feeling in his letters and it is strange that, even to his mother, Oates could not bring himself to use his Christian name.

The war, which had begun poorly for Britain, was now proceeding more predictably. Under the more decisive leadership of Roberts and Kitchener, the army made a remarkable recovery and by the middle of 1900, the tide had turned in Britain's favour. To great rejoicing at home, Ladysmith and Mafeking had been relieved and key towns like Bloemfontein and Johannesburg had fallen back into British hands.

The war, it seemed, was drawing to a close and Oates' main concern was that he might miss the fight, or as he put in one letter, 'the fun'. He may have been encouraged in his belief by Roberts, who in late 1900 rashly declared the war was all but over. In November he handed over command of the army in South Africa to Kitchener, who immediately changed tactics to a war of attrition. Kitchener went more firmly on the offensive, but the Boers, leaning heavily on tried and tested guerrilla tactics, regrouped and began to fight back. The war was far from over.

Rumours of extra forces being sent to the Cape circulated throughout the autumn and that the Inniskillings would form part of the new detachment to reinforce Kitchener's offensive. At the end of November, Oates learned he would be included in a group of three officers and over 50 Inniskilling troopers being sent to Cape Town under Captain Anstice.

The troopship *Idaho* sailed from Britain in mid-December and arrived at Cape Town in early January 1901 after an uncomfortable journey. Oates, who was used to a more luxurious style on family cruises to South Africa, caustically observed that the *Idaho* was a cattle boat and reported that the officers' quarters were 'very bad'.

Oates was in his element, despite the discomforts of his journey. The sense of adventure was enormous. Within days of arriving he was sleeping outdoors in pouring rain. At home, he conceded, such conditions would have meant a bout of pneumonia but Oates was now largely impervious to once life-threatening illnesses and cheerfully told his mother in a letter:

Anstice's contingent were soon attached to a larger force of around 250 under the command of Colonel Charles Parsons, who was tracking a band of guerrillas numbering up to 600 mounted men. After a few minor skirmishes, it became apparent the British were finding it difficult to pin down the highly mobile guerrillas, whose hit-and-run tactics tested and confused the more conventionally-led British. The mounted Boers rarely stayed around long enough to engage in the more typical face-to-face combat against the solid line formations and bayonet charges which had served the Empire for centuries.

The period of acclimatisation for the untried Inniskillings was brought to an abrupt halt in late January with the news that Queen Victoria had died. The loss of Victoria, who had reigned for almost 64 years, was a huge shock. Few Britons in 1901 could remember a time when she had not ruled.

Oates was an unalloyed monarchist with an unshakeable faith in its supremacy. To people like Oates, there was a reassuring permanence about Victoria and her death truly marked the end of an era. He admitted he and his colleagues were 'all very much cut up' about the Queen's death and commented:

'It is awfully sad and the worst thing that could happen to England.'[4]

Soon after, the unit again came into closer contact with the Boers about 30 miles east of Klaarstroom on the road to Willowmore, near the Swartberge range of mountains which cuts through the semi-arid scrubland of the Groot and Little Karoo in Cape Province. Miles away at the same time the first peace-feelers to end the fighting had come from Kitchener, who wanted to open negotiations with the Boer leader, General Louis Botha, to end a war which seemed likely to drag on for months, possibly years.

Oates' baptism of fire came in late February, as the first tentative peace talks were being held, at Middelburg in the eastern Transvaal. A small group of guerrillas attacked the British camp, an inconsequential little spat, typical of the tactics of harassment employed by the Boers. The sporadic exchanges of fire lasted almost three hours and Oates recalled:

'I got a shot with carbine at one of the blitters but I regret to say that I missed. If only I had a good long-range rifle with me I might have hit one.'[5]

After another minor affray, the Boers melted into the countryside and the Inniskillings broke camp and completed the march to Willowmore, where they were due for a breather. The troops had marched about 200 miles across the parched scrub of the Karoo in six days, interrupted by the two short encounters with the Boers. They were due a rest.

The first direct contact with the Boers had also exposed some tension between the officers and Oates soon discovered that the army was not the slick fighting unit he might have expected. After one dispute between officers over an unknown matter, Oates drily observed:

> 'If all the columns are run on the same lines as this, the war will go on forever.'[6]

Oates had discovered that, contrary to popular belief at home, the British army was no model of efficiency. As the Victorian age drew to a close, it was complacent, poorly-led and ruled by a mixture of strict discipline for the ranks and lavish self-indulgence for the gentlemen-officers.

Although the system of purchasing commissions had been ended almost 30 years earlier, private wealth and family connections were still highly important in gaining promotion. It was more important for an officer to act as a 'gentleman' than a good soldier, officer training was ineffectual, initiative stifled by protocol and officers devoted an absurd amount of time to games like polo and hunting.

On the surface, Oates was perfectly suited to the role of cavalry officer in the late Victorian age. He was rich, indulged and knew nothing different from the social codes which had served the landed gentry for so long. But he was different. Despite his upbringing, he disliked the rigid class system and possessed an untypical streak of egalitarianism. He did his best to treat all people fairly and equally and regarded professional duty as more important than petty rules and protocol. Oates was equally at ease in the company of generals or stable boys.

He particularly disliked snobbery and the exaggerated mannerisms of many of his contemporaries who owed so much to inherited wealth. Although accident of birth had bestowed much privilege on Oates, he once told his mother:

> 'They tell me you get such a good social position in the Army. Damn the social position say I.'[7]

Oates was also a man who held strong views, which he was never afraid to express. He readily criticised the officers who were leading the regiment's raw recruits into battle for the first time, despite his own obvious lack of fighting experience. Within days of landing at Cape Town, he wrote that the Captain who had brought the troops from England was 'not a popular man'. His fond hope was that, 'I am not under him if I go to the front'. Conveniently ignoring his own rawness, Oates said the Captain was 'perfectly hopeless on service' and several weeks later he dismissed his column commander, Colonel Parsons, as an 'awful old stick-in-the-mud'. In doing so, he planted the first seeds of disenchantment with an army career that had only just begun.

7

No surrender

The British column, led by Colonel Parsons, advanced on the small town of Aberdeen on 5 March 1901, where the guerrillas were reportedly operating. The British were chasing two groups led by Boer commandants, Gideon Scheepers and Willem Fouche. It was a typical Boer fighting force, an irregular but determined group who relied heavily on the simple combination of a good horse and a good rifle.

Boer troops were mainly hardened farmers who rarely fought hand-to-hand with fixed bayonets and preferred to keep their horses tethered nearby to cut and run if the battle was going badly. As inveterate hunters accustomed to living off the land, they were invariably skilled marksmen.

Parsons was intent on clearing them out of the area and engaged the commandoes at the earliest opportunity. After a short exchange of fire in the town, the Boers withdrew to the surrounding countryside and waited for the predictable response from Parsons to send out his patrols in search of the guerrillas. The ruse worked. Early next day, Parsons duly dispatched three patrols to explore the nearby hills and locate the Boers. At the head of one patrol of fifteen Inniskillings was Lt Oates, still eleven days away from his twenty-first birthday and for the first time in charge of a squad of men who were facing action.

The orders played into the hands of the Boers, who were waiting for the British. A group of fifteen was an awkward size, too small to put up a serious fight and too large to escape detection. The Boers quickly spotted the lines of men on the barren hillsides and immediately swung into action. What had begun as a routine series of patrols very quickly degenerated into a debâcle with near-disastrous consequences for the exposed and inexperienced British troops.

The first patrol, from the Imperial Yeomanry, ran into the Boers soon after leaving Aberdeen and promptly turned and fled back to the safety of the town. The hurried retreat only avoided serious casualties by the swift intervention of Captain Anstice from the Inniskillings, who rushed out of the town to defend the fleeing men. Anstice was wounded four times in the covering action but had succeeded in getting the men back to safety.

The second patrol, also from the Yeomanry, fared even worse. The men were caught in the open by the Boers and suffered the humiliation of being captured.

The third patrol, under Oates, spent two hours fruitlessly searching the hillsides for signs of the enemy. But it was the enemy that found them.

Oates was about six miles from Aberdeen and advancing towards a small river at around 7.30 am when the patrol came under fire for the first time. The Inniskillings were about 100 yards from the top of a small hill when the first shots rang out. Two men scouting at the head of the patrol were wounded in the opening exchange, with one pinned under his dead horse and the other captured by the Boers.

Oates quickly realised their vulnerability and calmly ordered an immediate retreat to safer ground down the hill. He took the patrol back to a dry river bed about a half mile away and began to cover the retreat of another three men who had been slightly wounded in the opening salvoes.

The party was in some disarray, fearing the worst from the numerically superior and buoyed up Boer force, which in a matter of hours had scored two notable victories against the British. The Boer forces were soon joined by the units which had routed the second Yeomanry patrol. A third triumph seemed certain.

Although outnumbered and cornered, Oates coolly assumed full command of the situation. He first ensured that the men in the river bed had sufficient cover and began plotting an orderly and secure retreat back to Aberdeen. He remained calmly resolute and disciplined, despite his inexperience. Oates was determined that the patrol would not be captured and as each soldier's ammunition ran out, he ordered them to creep back to the sanctuary of Aberdeen. Oates remained behind in the river bed with the three wounded men and four others to cover the retreat.

The Boers, some of whom crept as close as twenty yards to the beleaguered British stragglers, surprisingly, did not move in for the kill. In the face of overwhelming odds, it probably appeared foolish to continue fighting and perhaps the Boer commander wanted to avoid unnecessary bloodshed. Instead of annihilating the little cluster of troops, the Boers sent a note to the young lieutenant under a white flag asking him to surrender. The note, from Captain Fouche and written in English, was carried by the young Inniskilling trooper who had been captured at the start of the engagement. Oates bluntly refused the offer, saying he had decided to hold the ground he occupied.

A young Boer fighter delivered a second note at around 10.30 am, which indicated that the gracious Fouche recognised the gallantry of his opponents. Fouche promised to treat his prisoners fairly. The note, which Oates kept for posterity, read:

> 'Captain Fouche asks for an immediate surrender. Life and private property guaranteed.'[1]

However, a report from the Reuters news agency sent a day later from South Africa and picked up by the newspapers in London told an entirely different story, suggesting that the Boers were in uncompromising mood. The report claimed that Fouche's note included the words:

> '. . . all prisoners taken after refusal to surrender would be shot.'[2]

Oates' own account of the incident – he called it 'the scrap' – only mentions that Fouche promised to '. . . release me at once with my private property'.[3]

The Boers clearly felt that Oates had no option but to surrender and several guerrillas lying in nearby grass brazenly stood up and strolled slowly back up the hill to their positions, assuming the danger of being shot by the British had passed.

But Oates refused to budge and scribbled a defiant note to Captain Fouche:

> 'We came here to fight, not to surrender.'[4]

Unaccountably, the Boers still declined to move in for the kill. For reasons that remain unclear, Fouche decided that a fight was hardly worth the risk and around noon, the Boers suddenly decided to withdraw, satisfied that they had inflicted enough damage on Parsons' column that morning. The Boers rained down one final volley of shots towards Oates and prepared to leave the field. But unfortunately for Oates, one bullet found its mark, slicing through his left thigh and breaking the leg. Oates was in agony but still managed to order the fittest men to make their way back to Aberdeen while he remained behind with two troopers to cover the retreat and await his own rescue. He would have to wait a long time.

Confusion and indecision reigned at Aberdeen. As the men from Oates' patrol scrambled back to the town, the full-scale of the dangers facing the young lieutenant and the others were spelt out to the officers. But Parsons flatly refused to send a rescue party for Oates, insisting that he could not weaken the defences of the town for a handful of men.

The decision enraged some of the young Inniskillings. Oates was a popular soldier, both among the officers and men, and it went against the grain to leave wounded men unattended and exposed. Many years later the Inniskilling's historian recalled:

> 'The knowledge that the little party was in such straits caused great excitement all morning amongst the Inniskilliners in Aberdeen. . . .'[5]

The incident also sparked a minor mutiny among the Inniskillings, when two soldiers, in defiance of Parsons' orders, grabbed their horses and galloped off to launch their own rescue mission. The men were Lance-Corporal Malone, who was the son of the old regimental riding master and Private McConnell, Oates' servant.

Malone and McConnell were soon under heavy fire from marauding Boers in the hills and had to retreat to the safety of camp. In the melée Oates' charger, Mrs Butterwick, was badly wounded by a Boer bullet.

Rescue could not come soon enough for Oates, who was suffering badly in the sweltering heat and was in urgent need of medical attention. The jagged broken bone from his left femur had torn through the flesh and was causing great pain. He feared that he would bleed to death from his wound. He was also forced to lie in the burning sun without water or shade for over six hours before relief finally came.

Parsons had reluctantly given his permission to send out volunteers to rescue the Oates party. One of his friends, Herbert Dixon, promptly persuaded the regiment's Doctor Whyte to join him in the hunt for the stricken party.

The relief party finally reached Oates at around 6.30 pm. Dr Whyte gave him a glass of rum and water and said:

> '"I am afraid I have been a long time, Titus. Did you think I was never coming?"
> "I knew you would come," replied Titus.'[6]

Whyte promptly set the broken bone, although Oates had to endure the excruciating pain without anaesthetic. Makeshift splints were made from an old packing case found at a nearby farm and Oates then faced the ordeal of a six-mile trek back to Aberdeen, with the threat of more raids from the Boers always likely. Dixon, whose intervention had saved Oates from a night in the open, said that 'no words can describe what he must have suffered' on the tortuous overland journey. It was 10.30 pm when the badly wounded Oates was finally carried into Aberdeen, almost eleven hours after being shot. It was feared the wound was so serious he might lose his leg. But for the moment, Dr Whyte decided to leave the bullet lodged in his damaged thigh and see how the wound progressed.

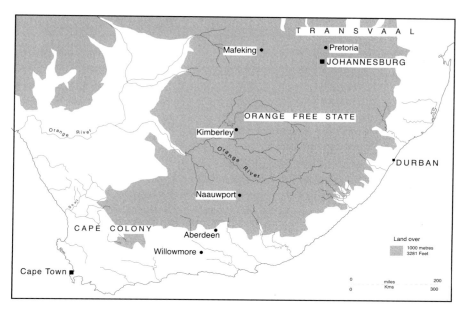

South Africa, 1900.

Oates, who had mastered the English art of stoicism and understatement, was almost dismissive of his injury. Lieutenant-Colonel O'Halloran, the column's chief medical officer, reported that he 'never uttered a murmur though he must have suffered considerable pain'. Indeed, Oates told O'Halloran there were others in more urgent need of help.

Oates was also concerned about his mother and felt that she should hear the news directly from him rather than indirectly through the newspapers. On 8 March, as the papers began to carry the first reports of the engagement, Caroline Oates received a brief telegram from her son which revealed:

'Wounded in the leg not dangerously.'[7]

Caroline, fraught with worry, cabled back to Oates demanding more details of the wound. Days later an equally terse reply arrived:

'Going on well, leg broken.'[8]

The day after being shot, Oates was well enough to write a fuller account of the incident. It was written in a shaky hand because he had to scratch away while lying prone on his back and still in considerable pain. Anxious not to cause undue concern to his mother, he deliberately underestimated the scale of his wound and likely speed of his recovery. He wrote:

'You may well have heard about my wound and I shall be well again before you get this.

I got in rather a hot corner with only seven men, two of which were wounded and we were attacked by about 170 Boers. They summoned us to surrender twice but we refused and when they attacked us we beat them off. We were fighting about 5½ hours.

I was struck just at the end by a sniper who broke my thigh. This happened yesterday. This morning the Colonels commanding the Column came to see me and said I had done very well and my men had fought very gallantly.

I am now encased in splints in a private house. The lady who owns it is very good to me. I expect I shall be here about six weeks and I shall get sent home.'[9]

The brave story of Lt Oates' defiant stand against overwhelming enemy odds soon spread through the column. It was at this point that the Inniskilling regiment acquired a new hero who, until this very day, is known by the sobriquet of 'No Surrender Oates'. When his squad rejoined their regiment they were instantly called 'Lieutenant Oates' No Surrender Draft'.[10]

However, the heroics of 'No Surrender Oates' received only meagre recognition from the top, even when the story reached the pages of newspapers who were always keen to report tales of heroism from the front. A local English-language South African newspaper reported 'A case of conspicuous bravery on the part of Lieutenant Oates' and suggested that the Boers had only withdrawn from the fight 'out of respect for the gallantry'.

Many felt that Oates deserved considerably more recognition and he was recommended for the highest military honour for valour, the Victoria Cross. But it never came. In the event Oates was rewarded with the perfunctory 'Mention in Dispatches' and the award of the Queen's Medal.

There was a considerable sense of injustice within the regiment. A contemporary told an earlier biographer of Oates of the strong feeling in the regiment for many years afterwards that his gallantry was 'inadequately rewarded'.[11] It was a belief shared elsewhere and years later the regimental journal recorded that Oates' bravery was 'acknowledged, one cannot say rewarded'.[12]

It may be that the lack of recognition owed something to the unfortunately long drawn out rescue, which if exposed to public scrutiny would leave the officers open to charges that they had abandoned Oates to the Boers. A citation for the Victoria Cross would have thrown an unwelcome spotlight on the critical question of why it had taken so long to send a rescue party for the injured officer. There was also the risk of shedding light on the embarrassing episode of the high-spirited men who disobeyed orders and took the matter into their own hands.

More important for the eager young lieutenant was that his wound had brought an abrupt end to his war. The regiment was moving on in pursuit of the Boer commandoes and there was no choice but to leave the wounded behind.

The withdrawal from the action was almost as painful to Oates as the wound itself. He had been desperate to join the fight and felt 'useless' at being left behind. His impatience was compounded by the need to lie flat on his back for endless hours and he became depressed by the long, monotonous hours of recovery. One night he dreamt he was home in England drinking beer and added: '. . . (I) woke up crying.'

What he did not know was that Botha had rejected the British peace terms and both sides prepared for a new intensity in the increasingly bitter struggle. Kitchener moved to break the deadlock, sweeping the countryside clean of anything which might sustain enemy troops like horses and cattle and by burning crops. He also ruthlessly ordered wholesale rounding up of women and children from the land into special encampments – concentration camps.

Oates was slightly cheered by a welcome change of scenery on 25 March when he was shipped off to a railway halt 25 miles away, which would take him to hospital at Naauwport in the north of Cape Colony, close to the border with the Orange Free State. It was another appalling journey, starting with a bumpy ride in bullock wagons to the rail line and followed by a three-day nightmare in the oppressive heat of a tin baggage van with only canned milk and chicken to eat. The ordeal by train, he recalled, 'nearly rattled your teeth out'.

The bumpy journey to hospital coincided with his growing realisation that the injury would take far longer to heal than he had anticipated. It was another depressing blow and he wrote to his mother:

'I am afraid the war will be over before I am well again.'[13]

Oates was allowed the luxury of chloroform shortly afterwards when surgeons finally removed the bullet in his thigh. The bullet hole, he reported, was 'not very big' but he soon discovered that he would carry a permanent reminder of 'the scrap' with the Boers. He informed his mother:

'I am afraid I shall have rather a limp even after I am well again as my left leg is a good deal shorter than my right.'[14]

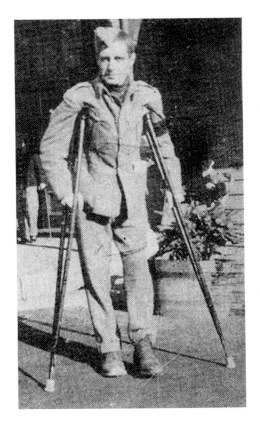

*Walking wounded. A rare photograph of
Oates pictured at a hospital in Naauwport,
South Africa, where he was recovering
from the bullet wound sustained during the
fighting at Aberdeen. The incident earned
him the name 'No Surrender Oates' and a
recommendation for the Victoria Cross.*

In fact, the bullet from the Boer sniper had clipped at least one inch from his left leg. In modern times, the injury would be treated with a combination of traction or a metal pin to the broken bone. For Oates, the Boer bullet left a legacy which caused considerable discomfort for the rest of his life.

But the stoic English gentleman, who had learned not to show his feelings, never complained about the disability.

8

The bells of St Mary's

Oates was not a good patient. He was dreadfully bored and unused to spending so much time stuck in bed. He also suffered minor bouts of depression and had lost a considerable amount of weight, which made him feel weak. In addition, he also developed irritating sores on his back and buttocks through lying in the same position for days on end. Oates felt sorry for himself and gloomily recalled that on the day he had been shot, he had never felt better in his life.

The dark mood only began to lift as his strength slowly returned and he learned how to cope with crutches. He was also cheered by the companionship of fellow patient Captain Anstice. However, after a few weeks at Naauwport he received the sad news that Private McConnell, who had unsuccessfully tried to rescue him at Aberdeen, had died from typhoid.

With his strength returning, the good news arrived that Oates was going home. In early May 1901, the young lieutenant was given six months' leave to recover from his wounds and shortly afterwards, shipped off to Cape Town where he boarded the *Bavarian* for the 6,000-mile trip back to England.

Oates arrived home to find himself something of a local hero. His exploits had reached the columns of the British press and Gestingthorpe was preparing itself to celebrate the return of the young squire. But the celebrations were abruptly put on ice when Caroline Oates, the real lord of the manor, saw her son for the first time. She was shocked. He was limping heavily under the burden of his crutches and looked pale and thin after losing so much weight. She ordered immediate rest before facing the well-wishing crowds. She also wanted her son to herself for a while.

After several weeks of privacy and recuperation, Caroline Oates generously threw a party for the entire village. She also found time for another kind gesture.

Quietly, without fuss, she sent the Aberdeen bookkeeper, Charles Harvey, a set of silver teaspoons in gratitude for allowing her son to recover in his home.

The local newspaper reported that Gestingthorpe turned out '*en fête*' for the day of celebration, with most houses in the village flying flags, bands playing and everyone in festive mood. About 100 children were given tea in the schoolroom and allowed to play on swings and roundabouts which Mrs Oates had ordered to be set up. A little later, a sizeable throng of 270 adults sat down to a lavish meal. Bryan Oates travelled up from Eton and Lillian and Violet sat dutifully alongside, once again watching their brother as the centre of attention.

The occasion was essentially feudal and Oates, as notional lord of the manor, did his bit by handing out packets of tobacco to the menfolk of Gestingthorpe. It was a microcosm of the ordered English Edwardian society where everyone across the social divide knew their places. But the event was a coming of age for Oates, who had more than lived up to the role as Gestingthorpe's manorial figurehead. He had done his duty, served the country and even acquired the trophy of a wound. The young man, who arrived in Gestingthorpe as the privileged and gangly heir to the estate, was now a figure to be respected and admired in his own right.

The parish vicar, Reverend C.T. Bromwich, told the cheering crowd that Lt Oates had proved himself to be a 'genuine soldier, a true Englishman, loyal to his King and to his country'.[1] In one short, but memorable passage, Rev Bromwich gave a near-perfect description of character which, even many years later, would be not be out of place. He said that Oates had '. . . done his duty with no swagger and no fuss, but in that simple way, natural way as if he were doing something in the ordinary events of everyday life'.[2]

It was a proud moment for Caroline Oates. Soon after the ceremonies, she paid her own unique gesture of thanks for her son's homecoming: she paid for the aged and cracked fifth and sixth bells at St Mary's church to be re-cast and re-hung. The fifth bell, which originally dated from 1581, was inscribed with the simple message:

'In gratitude to God for the safe return with honour of my beloved son, Lawrence E.G. Oates from the dangers of war in South Africa.'[3]

Oates spent the next few months quietly, regaining his strength and learning to walk without the aid of crutches. He wore a built-up inner-sole in his left shoe as a hidden concession to the limp. He also began to involve himself in the work of the Gestingthorpe estate, particularly the stables. He purchased new horses from Yorkshire, but the quiet life held no attraction. At the back of his mind was the overwhelming desire to get back to the war in South Africa. In his impatience

*Convalescence. Laurie pictured with his elder sister, Lillian, recovering from his wounds in the
grounds of Gestingthorpe during the summer of 1901.*

to rejoin his regiment, Oates contemplated surrendering part of his six months
leave and returning early to the Cape.

Oates undoubtedly felt more comfortable in uniform than he did at
Gestingthorpe, where his mother's constant attention and the stuffiness of the
drawing room were now strangely foreign to him. He had much enjoyed his
freedom away from home and the enforced convalescence only reminded him
why he now valued it so highly. But the 21-year-old solider and war hero was still
not entirely his own man and knew he could do nothing without his mother's
approval. Caroline Oates' emotional grip on her son remained as firm as ever and
in one revealing letter at the time, he wrote:

> 'I am nearly great fit for work and it would do me good at the WO
> (War Office) if I give up some of my leave. However I will not do
> anything until after I have had a conflab with you.'[4]

It is not clear whether Mrs Oates intervened to sabotage his bid to make an
early return to South Africa but Oates served his full penance and officially

67

rejoined the regiment in November 1901, exactly six months after being shipped home.

Oates sailed back to the war when the British public was growing increasingly unhappy at the prolonged conflict. Even some pro-war MPs questioned a continuation and both sides had begun exploring how best to extricate themselves from the struggle.

On the last day of 1901, Oates finally caught up with an active unit when he and 60 Inniskillings were ordered to join a column led by Lieutenant-Colonel Michael Rimington near Villiersdorp, a few miles to the east of Cape Town.

Rimington was one of Kitchener's four élite commanders appointed to take the war to the enemy. He deployed a 9,000-strong force of mounted troops stretched over a line 54 miles long, who drove the Boers towards the line of British blockhouses – small, heavily-armed fortresses – like a hammer against an anvil. Rimington, an experienced cavalryman, was an unorthodox and highly energetic character whose tactics were to chase and harry the Boers in a relentless fashion designed to wear down their resistance. In one daring assault he came close to capturing the Boer commander, General Botha.

The return to battle was not without mishaps, however. On one occasion Oates narrowly survived a near fatal accident, when he came close to being a victim of 'friendly fire'. As orderly officer of the day, he was posting a line of eight, closely spaced sentries on the perimeter of the camp to guard against stray Boer insurgents. It was a routine exercise and alongside Oates was a young servant who carried his gun. The inner circle of sentries suddenly became nervous when they spotted two dark shapes looming out of the blackness and as the figures came closer, the panicky sergeant ordered the pickets to open fire. A volley of shots crashed through the darkness and one of the figures dropped like a stone. The other, who sat motionless on his horse, blithely shouted in familiar tones that the sentries would waken the whole camp. A contemporary remembered:

> 'It was Oates with his black boy who had lost their way and wandered
> to the front of the outpost line. At the sound of the volley the black boy
> had simply tumbled off his horse through fright, as the bullets had
> gone high, a lucky illustration Oates pointed out, of the justice of the
> old musketry proverb, "Lights down, sights down".'[5]

Soon afterwards on 2 February 1902, Oates was promoted to the rank of First Lieutenant, although there is no evidence that the two events were linked.

Away from the war, Oates had officially become a man of property. In January 1902, while Oates was getting reacquainted with South Africa, his uncle Charles had died at the age of 57. Charles Oates had never married and he bequeathed the Meanwood estate in Leeds to trustees for his nephews, Laurie and Bryan Oates.

Oates' army promotion came just as the Boer War was drawing to a close. Both sides were exhausted and had suffered heavier than expected casualties in a bitter struggle in which concentration camps, barbed wire and heavy civilian casualties heralded a grim foretaste of far bigger conflicts later in the century.

The initial peace initiatives emerged in late March and on 31 May 1902 the Treaty of Vereeniging, which brought an end to hostilities, was signed. Although the treaty would lead to eventual self-government for the Orange Free State and the Transvaal as British colonies, the price of peace was heavy.

For Britain, the cost of upholding the Empire against the Afrikaner farmers was the loss of 22,000 men from the contingent of around 400,000 troops sent to South Africa to quell the revolt. The Royal Commission on the war also noted that over 400,000 horses and mules were 'expended' during the fighting and the bill for the British taxpayer was put at £201 million (over £10 billion in today's terms).

The Boers lost an estimated 7,000 of their 87,000 soldiers in battle and at least another 20,000 civilian men, women and children who died away from the battlefields in British concentration camps. Approximately 12,000 black Africans are also thought to have died, though their records were incomplete and it was never possible to calculate the real cost in lives.

South Africa delivered its own parting shot to Oates. As the fighting reached its final days, he was struck down by typhoid, the disease which had claimed his father only six years earlier. Typhoid was an affliction with a special resonance for the British army, which suffered more deaths from the disease than to enemy guns. Fortunately, Oates had a less virulent dose and recovered sufficiently finally to leave South Africa on 21 June 1902.

The news of his homecoming was again the cause of celebration in Gestingthorpe, where Caroline Oates ordered the newly-restored bells of St Mary's to be rung in honour of her son. But Oates was in no mood to celebrate.

9

A piece of flotsam

O ates returned to Ireland and the familiar surroundings of the Inniskilling's regimental headquarters at the Curragh in October 1902. He would spend over three years posted in Ireland, either at the Curragh's Ponsonby Barracks, Marlborough Barracks, Dublin or briefly at Ballincollig near Cork. While at Ballincollig in 1906 he wrote his will, leaving everything to his younger brother Bryan.

It should have been a welcome return but Oates' three and a half years in Ireland were characterised by a growing unhappiness and an increasing sense that his life was going nowhere. On the surface, he should have been perfectly content. His reputation had been firmly established as an accomplished officer of great bravery and the Curragh at the turn of the twentieth century was made for a typical English gentleman officer. 'I fairly love the Curragh,' he wrote soon after reaching Ireland. But his mood quickly changed.

The Curragh Camp, the Aldershot of Ireland, lies on a bleak, open, grassy plain in County Kildare. It was the British army's largest military station in occupied Ireland, resembling a large town. The permanent population of 5,000 was swollen to between 10,000 and 15,000 during the peak summer months when soldiers flocked to the camp for training and manoeuvres. The camp, a self-contained enclave for the British abroad, included churches, hospitals, libraries, swimming pools, shops and an abattoir. [1]

Oates would have found the area around the Curragh as recognisable as the English countryside of his upbringing. It was a bustling gentrified spot where English and Irish country gentlemen could hunt, play polo or join shooting parties during the day and mingle socially in the evening at the unremitting round of parties, seasonal balls, concerts and less formal gatherings in the mess.

British officers abroad on Imperial duty rarely strayed out of their class and did little to establish close links with the local communities around them. One nobleman said the main characteristic of the British officer at this time was 'his exclusiveness'. Another contemporary observed that the cavalry from their 'superior heights looked down on everybody'.

Ireland was different, helped by the common language and the common social status of the local landed gentry, many of whom had served in the British army and had strong family associations with Britain. The area around the Curragh attracted Ireland's gentrified and wealthy landowners, many of whom first settled in the seventeenth century and now included several earls and a sprinkling of lords and ladies who ranked as equals with the English officer class.

English and Irish gentlemen rubbed along easily together and mingled freely at local social activities. The nearby Kildare Hunt became especially popular for

Oates spent over three years in Ireland. Here he is pictured at the Curragh military camp in 1904 alongside other officers from the 6th Inniskilling Dragoons. Oates stands at the rear (back row fifth from the left). Also pictured is the celebrated soldier and founder of the Boy Scout movement, Capt. Baden-Powell (middle row, second right). (Royal Dragoon Guards)

visiting officers, who made up a substantial slice of the club membership. Racing at venues like Punchestown became notable dates in the social diary, regularly attracting visits from members of the British Royal Family.

The early Edwardian years were a comparatively peaceful period in the long and fractured relationship between Britain and Ireland. This partly reflected the first of the two historic Land Purchase Acts in 1903 and 1909 which transferred the ownership of vast tracts of land to Irish farmers and took the urgency out of the more emotive nationalist campaign for independence.

But even the comfortable surroundings of the Curragh could not disguise Oates' growing unhappiness with the army. Not long after reaching Ireland, he wrote a revealing letter to his mother:

> 'It is beastly here but will improve when the regiment comes home. It will not take long to sicken me of soldiering at home and then the fun will begin.'[2]

The seeds of discontent were probably sown from the start of his army career. He had been plunged into active service almost from the moment he joined the Inniskillings. Oates could not come to terms with the inevitable inactivity of peacetime. As old soldiers will testify, military life is frequently made up of long periods of routine and boredom, interspersed with short frantic bursts of activity and extreme danger.

Oates signalled the depth of his discontent shortly after moving into the Curragh when he applied for a posting to Swaziland, which would have taken him back to southern Africa and close to the area where his father and uncle Frank had explored 30 years earlier. A little later he pondered running his own farm. But nothing came of either plan, like so many of his fruitless attempts to get away from the service.

His uneasiness simmered throughout his time at the Curragh and was only interrupted by his increasing reliance on gentlemanly sports like hunting and steeplechasing, which had replaced the excitement of active service. Oates wanted adventure and without a proper war, he was forced to compensate through an *ersatz* existence of manoeuvres and games where, for example, hunting foxes across the plains of Kildare replaced the genuine article.

Oates was the consummate English gentleman officer during his time in Ireland, indulging himself to the full, running with the hounds and racing over the fences at various military and local meetings. He also found time for the occasional visit to Dublin Bay to sail his yacht, *Saunterer*.

A highly capable rider, he rose to the racing challenge with great distinction and clinched some notable prizes during his posting in Ireland. He won the Military Cup at Dundalk in 1904 and 1905, St Stephen's Plate at Leopardstown in 1904 and the Irish Grand Military Cup at Punchestown in 1905. In 1904 he took time off from his own racing to pop across the Irish Sea and attend the Grand National at Aintree. Horseracing became increasingly important. At one meeting at Punchestown the normally unemotional young lieutenant broke down in tears after a triumphant ride. His success on the track also propelled him into the highest circles, bumping into people like King Edward and Queen Alexandra and the Duke of Connaught in the paddock or at some post-meet function.

His personal stables of horses soon grew to seven mounts and Oates was forced to turn to his mother to finance his habit. Caroline Oates saw no harm in her son's increasing fondness for the horses and she readily gave him £100 (the equivalent of nearly £5,000 at today's values) to buy another. Other payments followed as he built up his stables.

Oates was fairly well off, earning his army pay and picking up an annual allowance of at least £500 (today: £25,000) from his doting mother. In addition she regularly topped up his income with extra dollops of money for items like new boots or yet another horse. But she could never cure his failure to manage his affairs and he once admitted:

> 'I think I am spending too much on horses but it would be dull without them.'[3]

Horses, in fact, had assumed disproportionate importance in his life. In the absence of adventure or a military challenge, they were the only things which mattered. Oates was torn between his two separate lives, the uneasy mixture of professional soldier and idle gentleman. On the one hand, he was the resourceful, courageous hero who yearned for adventure and a sense of purpose to his life. He also craved, like so many products of the Victorian age, for a chance to serve the Empire. Oates felt a burning need to make a proper contribution and one colleague remembered:

> 'Oates worshipped duty; it was his religion.'[4]

On the other hand, there was the privileged, self-indulgent member of the landed gentry who wasted much of his adult life racing horses or ritualistically slaughtering foxes for fun. He also belied his otherwise professional approach to the military by objecting to any demands from the army which might interfere with his social activities.

On one occasion, he arrogantly refused to attend the special cavalry school at Netheravon because it would obstruct the hunting season. A little later he found it a 'great nuisance' to be sent to the Musketry School at Hythe and while stationed at the Curragh he complained that it was 'very difficult to get any hunting done with the present Colonel'. When finally ordered for musketry practice, a superior officer sarcastically asked Oates if the posting 'fits in with your plans'. Oates responded by declaring: 'It suits me admirably.'

Part of the problem lay in the changing nature of the army itself. The army of the Edwardian era was in transition from a largely amateur-led to a more professional fighting unit, but traditionalists like Oates found the changes difficult to accept. Oates was determinedly old school and opposed the reforms, especially if the challenges of modern warfare meant dismantling the cavalry. The courtesies and etiquette of the old-style of war appealed to Oates, but he saw little appeal in heavy artillery bombardment or the merciless efficiency of the newly-emerging machine guns.

On one manoeuvre, Oates had been placed in charge of a field gun. At a post-operations conference, the General pointedly asked Oates where he would recommend placing the gun. With a glint in his eye, Oates replied:

'I should have it lashed broadside across the road in order to close it to cavalry.'[5]

Even practical and sensible measures, such as the widespread introduction of khaki uniforms for soldiers in the field, upset him. He once moaned to his mother:

'You will be sorry to hear that the whole of the British army is going to wear karki (sic) in the spring. It is a great shame I think as they will never be able to recognise us from the Hussars or Dragoon Guards.'[6]

Oates was suited to a more chivalrous and honourable age of battle. His style was more that of a medieval knight than a soldier of the industrialised age of warfare. But his glaring weakness was that he struggled to recognise that the tide of change was to change things forever.

Oates may not have welcomed the army reforms but, as ever, he did not have an obvious alternative career in mind. Oates had the energy, but he lacked the inspiration or the ambition to make a radical change in his life and was incapable of saving money to pay for any new venture.

It was an unsettling time and in May 1903 – exactly three years after securing his commission in the Inniskillings – he bluntly told his mother that he was so fed up he would leave the army immediately if he had somewhere else to go. His discontent also spilled over into bitterness about the army's modernisation and he added:

> 'The annoying thing is the War Office does not mind us going as they want to get rid of people who are soldiering for amusement and trying to get people who do not play polo, etc.'[7]

During a term at Marlborough Barracks, Dublin in February, 1904 he announced: 'This is a beastly place and I am thoroughly sick of it already. I wish I could make up my mind to clear out.' On another occasion, he wondered why he was not on the other side of the world fighting in the war which had broken out between Japan and Russia. By the middle of 1904, Oates had decided it would be his 'last winter in Ireland, in the service'.

Over the next few months he vaguely contemplated buying a farm near the Curragh Camp and even applied to learn Japanese in the hope of getting shipped out to the Far East to play some undetermined role in the war with Russia. Sensibly enough, he later conceded that mastering the Japanese alphabet was probably beyond his capabilities.

It was also clear by 1905 that Oates felt he stood little chance of gaining significant advancement through promotion, probably because he would have to overcome more exams. He was now drifting like a piece of flotsam and explained to his mother:

> 'I should like to point out to you that I do not want to leave solely because I do not like it: there are various reasons but the chief one is that I am neither doing myself nor anyone any good.'[8]

Oates at this time lacked a mentor, a more senior character who could advise and support him. What he needed was a father figure. But his father had been dead for around ten years and his brother Bryan was not mature enough to act as counsellor. Most of his fellow officers were from the same peer group with the same reservations and gripes about the army and it appears there was never a suitable guiding hand among the higher-ranking officers.

Nor was Oates capable of developing a serious relationship with women. The only woman in his life was his mother. But a stable and meaningful relationship with a woman would have tempered his mood and provided stability and a different purpose to life which was clearly lacking at this stage. In the event none ever materialised. Indeed there is little evidence to suggest that he ever conducted a lasting association with any woman, apart from his mother.

Caroline Oates always indulged Laurie, even in later life. Here he is pictured with brother Bryan examining his new motorbike, a gift from his mother for his twenty-sixth birthday in 1906.

There are no suggestions that Oates was homosexual in spite of a life spent predominantly in an all-male environment of public schools and army barracks. There were suggestions that, if anything, Oates was frequently celibate, while one writer rashly declared that Oates died a virgin without ever being in a position to prove or disprove it.

Oates was a tall, good-looking man with a strong personality and a complete lack of vanity, who undoubtedly attracted women. But he was also shy and dyslexia had made him an introverted wallflower who preferred to remain out of the spotlight. There was a practised air of mystery about Oates. He was a loner but those who persevered found him immensely likeable and a strong character with hidden depths.

Very little is known about Oates' sexual activities, largely because the bulk of the correspondence that survives to this day are letters to his mother and Caroline Oates was certainly not the sort of person to discuss these matters with. His letters contain few, if any, remarks on the subject of women.

His known associations with women are few. On a holiday with his mother to the Caribbean island of Barbados in early 1899, he became friendly with the two daughters of a fellow traveller, Sir Gibson Craig, and kept in touch with one of the women for some years afterwards.

Another promising relationship with Florence Chambers in Leeds came to an abrupt stop when her protective aunt refused to allow the couple to see each other. Oates wrote to the young woman as 'Your Ardent Admirer' to avoid detection by her aunt. Chambers said Oates was 'one of my first sweethearts' and it was said he carried a photograph of her in his wallet for the rest of his life.

But the enduring impression is that Oates was uncomfortable with women and always struggled to understand the opposite sex. To hide his discomfort, he adopted the pose of casual indifference.

Army colleagues observed that he never joined the other officers on nightly tours of the flesh-spots while the regiment was stationed overseas. The Curragh, in particular, offered ample opportunity for female company, mainly through the scores of prostitutes who camped in the furze bushes on the outskirts of the camp and provided a brisk business for idle troops.

After suffering a bout of smallpox in 1908, his regimental doctor quietly reassured his mother that his 'very healthy life and steady habits' would help him to recover quickly, which suggests that he was free from any of the sexually transmitted diseases so familiar to many soldiers of the time.

Oates' self-imposed chastity also suited the army of the day, which did not encourage young officers to marry too young. The rule of thumb was that junior officers *may not* marry, captains *might* marry, majors *should* marry and lieutenant-colonels *must* marry. It was a culture which inadvertently helped reinforce his own doubts and uncertainties about women.

He also rejected the loathsome custom of other officers seeking suitable husbands for their daughters by dragging them onto the army's merry-go-round of parties and other social functions in search of a suitable mate. Oates saw it as like taking cattle to market and the girls, he once told his mother, are 'touted round in the most barefaced way'. His stern disapproval must have delighted Caroline Oates.

The approval of Mrs Oates in any liaison was crucial and it must have been profoundly difficult for Oates to form close relationships while always asking the question of whether his mother might approve or not. It was understandable if he compared all women with his mother.

However, there were other matters weighing on his mind, particularly money. His grasp of basic husbandry was appalling and he continued to live far beyond his means. By his own account, he was spending around £800 a year (almost £40,000 at today's prices) and was repeatedly forced to turn to his mother for help. In one letter he reminded her of what she already knew when he wrote:

On duty. Oates (right), the stiff-backed cavalry officer, photographed during the period when he became disenchanted with army life.

'If you were in the same way with money as I am with mine, we should be in the soup.'[9]

Unable to find a way out of the turmoil, he sank even deeper into sports, the only thing which kept him sane. Caroline Oates indulged him further when she bought him a motorbike for his twenty-sixth birthday.

Then, to his own surprise, Oates passed a veterinary exam. This time there were no problems with his dyslexia because it was a practical exam designed to help officers deal with illnesses in their horses. For the first time in his life he found a test 'rather easy'. Simple or not, the result alerted the army hierarchy to Oates and in April 1906 he was unexpectedly offered the rôle of adjutant.

The offer caught him on the hop because he was still looking for a way out of the service. Oates had also lost his ambition and it may be that he was afraid of responsibility. But he did not lack self-confidence. His passive, introverted nature might have been interpreted as insecurity or lack of drive. But he found passion and commitment when it mattered. The prospect of additional responsibility only complicated matters. It also threw up the grim prospect of passing more written tests, which would be more demanding than the practical veterinary exam. But, as he observed in one letter, '. . . some awful fools are passing, so why not I?'

In desperation he again turned to his mother, writing a long, rambling letter which was as much a plea for help as a request for parental guidance. He wrote:

> 'It seems to me that my friends and relatives wish me to continue soldiering; this wish does not make me think any more highly of the intelligence of my friends and relatives. However, secondly, there is a slight increase in pay and it may lead to something better; thirdly, if I soldier at all, I may as well do it properly.
>
> Against this it would be a great nuisance and take up a lot of my spare time, also it would cost a good deal as I should have to buy a lot of new clothes and kit. I should also have to work with a crammer as I have not passed for promotion. What I propose is that I tell the Colonel I will take it and that you should increase my allowance by £100 in the event of my being made adjutant. If you think my allowance is already large enough, please say so and I shan't be too upset.'[10]

Before Caroline Oates had time to respond, orders came through that the regiment was being dispatched to Egypt. Oates was suddenly jubilant, casting off the gloom and depression of wasted years in Ireland and looking forward to travel and the potential for more adventure far afield.

In the rush to leave Ireland, he overlooked settling the debts which had piled up. Once again, he threw himself on the mercy of his indulgent mother, emphasising rather indignantly that some creditors 'seem to think me capable of going without paying them'. The reality was that Caroline Oates would pay the debts, not the debtor himself.

Oates, who was still waiting to learn if he had been appointed adjutant, sailed from the Irish port of Queenstown (now Cobh) in May 1906 and arrived at Alexandria, Egypt three weeks later. It was a sizeable landing party of more than 500 men, women and children, plus 346 horses, who survived the uncomfortable journey without suffering any casualties. The regiment moved to Abbassia, Cairo, and within six weeks of their arrival Oates was duly installed as adjutant.

The Inniskillings had been sent to Egypt as part of a flag-waving exercise and show of strength against the differing threats posed by the rival imperial interests of France and Turkey and the nationalistic ambitions of the local Egyptians. There had been some territorial differences with Turkey in the Sinai and local factions were stoking up hostility against the British presence in the country. Almost inevitably, it was a recipe for tragedy and controversy.

In one incident, a column of soldiers had been sent from Alexandria on the coast through the Nile delta to Cairo in an exercise to remind the locals of British military presence in the area. Some officers ill-advisedly went pigeon shooting close to the village of Denishwai and soon found themselves surrounded by an angry anti-British mob. In the struggle, the protesters grabbed the rifle of a young lieutenant, which went off and wounded four people, including a woman. The crowd attacked the troops and all but one managed to scramble back to the main body of the column. Captain Bull, who had sailed from Queenstown with Oates, was caught by the rabble and suffered a serious beating. He died the following evening.

Oates was called upon to help supervise the typically swift and brutal justice meted out by the British authorities. Some 75 locals were arrested, four were hanged in public and 21 were flogged and sentenced to lengthy periods of imprisonment.

The incident at Denishwai remained one of the few moments of note during his spell in the Middle East, which was characterised by a series of dreary military manoeuvres, frequent bouts of polo and other sports and ample spells of sight-seeing. He managed to visit the ancient cities of Damascus and Jerusalem but succumbed to a touch of malaria while passing through Port Said on the Suez Canal and ended up in hospital.

The change of scenery did little to change his mind about soldiering. Resignation was again in the air and he drew little satisfaction from the decision in November 1906 to elevate him to the rank of captain. In the absence of an obvious alternative, he soldiered on at a higher rank.

Oates' departure from the service was postponed yet again when he learned in 1907 that the regiment was soon to be posted to India. As ever, he was at the mercy of events and with nothing better to do, he prepared to follow the regiment eastwards. India, like Egypt, was another routine exercise for the Inniskillings, who were deployed largely to demonstrate Imperial power in the region and deal with any local disturbances.

After landing at Bombay in the Autumn of 1908, the regiment made the day-long journey inland by train to Mhow, a few miles south of the large city of Indore in the Madhya Pradesh region. The town had an English feel about it, with its church steeple, theatre and clusters of pleasant, stone bungalows. Oates and his fellow officers were billeted in the neat rows of bungalows and sought to establish a home-away-from-home. He shared a bungalow with his friend, Fergus Nixon, and found time to develop his garden, helped by a small army of willing local hands who cut the grass and planted bulbs in return for a pittance.

Soon after arriving in India, Oates gathered a pack of dogs and became the local Master of the Hounds. It was a long way from the lush green fields of Essex or the plains of Kildare, but the principle was the same.

Mhow was another boring, largely uneventful posting. It was a small military station, a backwater consisting of one cavalry regiment, one battery of horse artillery and two battalions of Indian infantry. There was little action, apart from playing games or hunting. Most officers slept in the afternoon to avoid the worst of the heat and in the evening, congregated in the clubhouse, played bridge and drank too much whisky and soda.

The posting represented everything from which he wanted to escape. It was dull, meaningless and unfulfilling and to compound the misery Oates was struck down by smallpox, which left his face permanently scarred. Fortunately it was a mild bout, though the mystery remains as to how a senior officer had escaped the army's routine anti-smallpox vaccination.

Oates returned home for a lengthy four-month spell of leave in May 1909, an interlude which allowed him the rare luxury of a summer at Gestingthorpe. He took *Saunterer* out for a run across the Channel and purchased a new pack of hounds, which he arranged to be shipped out to India.

The leave also allowed him to catch up on family developments, where marriage was in the air. Lillian had married Frederick Ranalow, an accomplished singer, in

*Home-from-home. Oates (centre) rides with the hounds during his tour of duty in India.
(Royal Dragoon Guards)*

January 1909 and before long Bryan announced his engagement to Alma Kirby, the eldest daughter of Augustus Kirby, vicar of nearby South Weald, Essex.

He also discovered that Caroline Oates had lost none of her crustiness. Mrs Oates doubted whether Ranalow could keep Lillian in the style to which she had become accustomed. When told how much the singer earned, Mrs Oates' icy response was that Lillian 'spends that much on hats each year'. She later warmed to her son-in-law and in 1910 ensured that Ranalow was awarded the honour of singing three songs – including Mendelssohn's *O God Have Mercy* – at the dedication ceremony for a new organ at St Mary's, Gestingthorpe.

Oates was slightly bemused by all the romantic activity, saying he was 'wildly surprised' at Bryan's sudden engagement and wondered how long Violet would remain single. He had been away from Essex for long periods and for the first time felt something of an outsider, even in the familiar surroundings of his home. 'I feel quite out of it,' he confessed at the time.

But, like his ambition to leave the army, Oates had done little to secure a new rôle in life or follow his brother and sister down the aisle. He remained casually detached from both possibilities.

By chance, while he was passing time at Gestingthorpe, the opportunity he had been seeking for years suddenly emerged.

10

The great escape

The unexpected escape route from the army was Antarctica, the most remote, inhospitable and then unexplored region on earth. For reasons that remain unclear to this day, Oates suddenly applied to join Captain Robert Scott's British Antarctic Expedition, which was launching a bid to reach the South Pole for the first time.

There was no disguising his eagerness to join Scott, even if his initial motives remain blurred. Oates wrote offering to serve Scott in any capacity and to make a substantial personal donation to the expedition's funds. He also declined any rank or responsibility and promised not to draw a penny in salary for the duration of the trip. It was a calculated act of generosity driven by desperation.

Oates was an attractive proposition to Scott, even without the welcome financial inducements. His *curriculum vitae* made impressive reading. He came from a respectable family, had the benefit of a public school education at Eton and was an experienced cavalry captain and war hero. His considerable knowledge of dogs and horses was also crucial.

Scott, of course, knew nothing about the learning difficulties or his profound disenchantment with the army, and had to rely heavily on the simply written application and the testimony of people who knew him. But Oates stood out, even among the deluge of 8,000 personal applications to join the expedition.

The clinching factor was undoubtedly his skill and experience with horses. Transport was to be the key to reaching the South Pole and Scott was planning to deploy hardened Siberian or Manchurian ponies to carry essential supplies on the trek across the ice of Antarctica. The ponies were central to his plans, although the expedition would also include teams of dogs and three motorised tractors. But Scott was sceptical about the value of dogs and the tractors, whose heavy wheel-tracks gave them the appearance of an early version of the tank, were at an experimental stage and could not be relied upon. The ponies would be vital until men began to man-haul their own sledges.

Scott was following the lead of his rival, Ernest Shackleton, in taking horses to the South. Shackleton had taken a handful of Manchurian ponies on the *Nimrod* expedition in 1907–09 when he successfully blazed a trail across the 400-mile Ross Ice Barrier and climbed the unexplored Beardmore Glacier onto the previously unknown Polar Plateau.

However, both Scott and Shackleton seemed unaware that horses are unsuited for travel across the ice. The weight of their heavy hoof invariably breaks through soft terrain and they sink deep into the snow like someone wading through water. Their sheer bulk also makes them hard to manage. Nor could horses live off the bleak Antarctic landscape so every morsel of fodder had to be carried on the expedition ship and on the march across the ice fields. Scott's animals were supposed to carry tons of supplies and equipment on the first leg across the Ross Ice Barrier, leaving the explorers almost halfway to the Pole itself.

Scott, a career naval officer, was particularly ill-suited to manage horses. He had little or no grasp of animals after a lifetime at sea and most of the other men on the expedition were either sailors or scientists who, like Scott, had no knowledge or experience of handling horses. Expertise would be vital and Oates fitted the bill.

But there was another diverting consideration. The Royal Navy had traditionally dominated most British expeditions to the Arctic and Antarctic regions in the nineteenth and twentieth centuries. Scott, with a cavalry captain at his disposal, considered it appropriate for the army to be represented in the venture. Oates, therefore, suited both purposes: he was the ideal horseman and an acceptable token worth taking along.

What is not fully understood is why Oates chose Scott's expedition as the route out of the army. He had, after all, been actively contemplating his resignation for several years without ever taking positive steps to fashion an alternative career and had never displayed any interest in the exploration of the Polar regions. It seems likely that the idleness of army life and the depressing prospect of middle age indolence were the catalyst which finally galvanised him into action. Violet Oates recalled that 'inactivity galled him as nothing else did' and added:

'He seemed to be searching for something really worthwhile to lend his talents to – perhaps he found it in the expedition.'[1]

It was certainly not unpopularity that drove Oates from the army. He was liked and respected by both fellow officers and men from the ranks. The regimental journal reported that he had 'courage, initiative and dogged determination which always commanded respect.' The point was emphasised when he surrendered his post as adjutant in August 1909. In his confidential report, his commanding officer declared:

> 'His action and energetic character speak for themselves. I have no hesitation in saying he is the most popular and generally respected and esteemed officer the regiment has in the present generation.'[2]

He was also popular with men in the lower ranks, who respected his undemonstrative, professional approach to soldiering and the easy way he mixed with people from all walks of life. The men playfully called him 'Leggy' after the initials of his first three names, Lawrence Edward Grace.

Headley Bennett, an old soldier who served with Oates at Mhow, recalled many years later how much respect the men had for their captain. Bennett, speaking in 1984, remembered:

> 'Oates was always breezy, very alive and full of pep. We rankers never knew him that personally of course, but he certainly was a man to look up to.'[3]

The venture to Antarctica probably appealed to Oates' well-honed sporting instincts. The concept of exploration as a game fascinated the Victorians and Edwardians, who regarded it as a necessary means of expanding and demonstrating the superiority of the Empire itself. The South Pole, the last major unclaimed geographical prize, was a bauble to be won by the boldest and bravest, a challenge that appealed to Oates.

The expedition also provided him with his first real opportunity to strike out on his own. Oates was 29 years of age when he applied to join Scott's expedition and had been a member of one institution or another since his earliest days, either at public schools or soldiering. In the background was his ubiquitous mother on whom he still relied to buy new boots or settle mess drinks bills. Independence was long overdue. To emphasise the point, he deliberately chose not to consult his mother about the Antarctic expedition, perhaps the only time in his life he took a major decision without first seeking her blessing.

It was no oversight. Oates was fired up by the thought of joining Scott. The once drifting, lethargic character had the bit between his teeth and the more he learned, the more he was determined to play a meaningful role in the campaign. He had developed an ambition to stand at the Pole itself. He confided his objective to a regimental colleague, Colonel Yardley. Oates told Yardley he had every intention of being in the final party of men which struck out for the South Pole. Yardley recalled the conversation:

> 'I (Oates) told Scott that I had no intention of being left at the base and that I should want to be in the party to make the dash for the Pole.'[4]

Timing was also a key factor in persuading Oates to join Scott. Dissatisfaction with the army life had reached a new intensity in 1909 as he approached the milestone of his thirtieth birthday. He had become increasingly embittered with his life in uniform. When the Army Council decided to recruit more working-class men – 'poor men with brains' – to overcome a critical shortage of cavalry officers, Oates responded by saying: '...a man with brains knows too much to join the service.'

A contemporary also recalled a conversation which took place shortly before Oates left India for the last time:

> 'I don't think he was bored with India. He wanted something that would require a good deal of sacrifice on his part. He wanted adventure and he wanted something that would be a tough proposition. He didn't think he was doing enough for his country enjoying life in India.'[5]

Oates almost certainly first heard about Scott's plans while at home on leave in the summer of 1909. The South Pole was on everyone's lips that summer after Shackleton made a triumphal return to London with the astonishing news that he had struggled to within 97 miles of the Pole before being forced to turn back. Shackleton had arrived back in London on 14 June – only a few weeks after Oates came home on leave from India – and the heroic episode generated huge public interest. It also aroused feverish speculation that Scott would launch a new expedition to finish the job and reach the Pole.

Public enthusiasm had been further whipped up in September by the equally dramatic news that two celebrated American explorers – Robert Peary and Dr Frederick Cook – each claimed to have reached the North Pole. Only the South Pole remained unconquered. It was the last great terrestrial journey of exploration and Oates had suddenly found a new goal in life.

Scott had been quietly planning to return to Antarctica ever since his three-year spell on the 1901–04 *Discovery* expedition and Shackleton's near-miss was the catalyst he needed. The speculation came to an end on 13 September 1909 when Scott announced the official launch of the British Antarctic Expedition.

The mood of the occasion also captured the imagination. Britain had assumed a proprietorial right over Antarctica, her resolve stiffened by the Scott and

Shackleton expeditions. It was unthinkable that any other nation should lay claim to the region. Had there been an indigenous population, Britain would have annexed the continent, sent in a few warships and installed a civil service.

There was talk of an American or Japanese expedition and even the Germans were said to be planning a dash to the Pole. No one mentioned the Norwegians, the most accomplished Polar travellers.

Scott stoked the jingoistic fires by declaring that he wanted to reach the Pole for the honour of the Empire. Leonard Darwin, President of the Royal Geographical Society, said Scott was 'going to prove once again that the manhood of the nation is not dead'.

There were more personal considerations for Oates. The decision to join Scott probably meant leaving the army. The outline scheme indicated he would be gone for up to two years and there was no guarantee the army would grant such a lengthy leave of absence. Without official approval he would be forced resign his commission and a determined Oates was in the mood to resign. The prospect of going back to the tedious, unfulfilling routine after an adventurous two years with Scott was improbable.

The other unresolved issue was how to tell his mother. Although there were flickering signs of a new found streak of independence, Oates was not entirely free of the maternal apron strings and at some point he would have to secure her approval. In the event, he waited until the last minute before delivering the news. Instead of seeking her permission, he simply told her that he had made up his mind to volunteer and hoped she would not object too much.

Oates broke the news in cautious, almost apologetic fashion, writing a long letter from his hospital bed in Delhi where he was laid up with food poisoning. Oates appeared more like a contrite sinner giving confession than an upbeat, ambitious explorer optimistically looking forward to the great challenge of treading virgin territory. His letter also displayed a touching naïvety about the rigours he faced in Antarctica. He told his mother:

> 'I have a great confession to make. I offered my services to the Antarctic Expedition which starts this summer from home under Scott. They wrote and told me to produce my references and they appear to have been so flattering that I have been practically accepted.
>
>   Now I don't know whether you will approve or not but I feel that I ought to have consulted you before I sent my name. I did not want to do so as I thought there was very little chance of being taken (as cavalry officers are not generally taken for these shows) and I wanted to have something to go on.

Scott, however, appears to be a man who can make up his mind and having decided he told me so at once which was the first intimation I had I was likely to go.

Points in favour of going. It will help me professionally as in the Army if they want a man to wash the labels off bottles they would sooner employ a man who had been to the North Pole than one who only got as far as the Mile End Road. The job is most suitable to my tastes. Scott is almost certain to get to the Pole and it is something to say you were with the first party.

The climate is very healthy although inclined to be cold. I shall get home twice within the next 3 years whereas if I stay here I shall only get one.

Now the points against. I shall be out of touch for some considerable time. It will require a goodish £1,500 as I have offered to subscribe to the funds.

Let me know what you think about the affair but I think it had better be kept a secret until it is decided that I go because if you say I am going on a show like that and then don't go, people put their tongues in their cheeks and laugh. But consult anyone you like.'[6]

The application to join Scott came in a typically simple and undemonstrative note sent to the expedition's offices in London's Victoria Street. Lieutenant Teddy Evans, Scott's second-in-command, described it as a 'straightforward note'. When Scott asked for his qualifications, Oates replied that he had considerable knowledge and experience of dogs and horses. Oates then surprised Scott by revealing that he was prepared to pay around £1,000 (about £47,000 at today's prices) to join the expedition.

The money was especially important for Scott, who badly needed the funds. But Scott, who was well versed in social climbing, also liked the sound of the gentleman cavalry officer. He was also impressed that one of his referees was Algernon Rayner-Wood, a teacher of the classics and French and German at Eton. What Scott probably did not know was that Rayner-Wood was a cousin of Oates.

Scott spoke directly to Rayner-Wood about the suitability of Oates and Evans recalled that '. . .we could hear nothing but praise for our volunteer.'[7] Scott also checked him out with others who knew him and was happy to discover that they, too, shared a high opinion of the officer. Evans disclosed:

> 'We learnt from several sources that Oates was a man of fine physique, full of pluck, energy and spirit.'[8]

The biggest immediate hurdle was getting the necessary permission from Lieutenant Colonel Frederick Fryer, Oates' commanding officer at Mhow. It was no easy task. Fryer was vehemently opposed to the move. He was particularly irritated that Scott, a naval officer, had gone over his head and appealed directly to the War Office in London for Oates to join the expedition. He was furious at the poor timing. Scott's formal request for Oates' services – deliberately or by chance – arrived while he was away from Mhow. Fryer smelt a rat.

Oates anticipated problems with his commanding officer, telling his mother that Fryer would be 'pretty upset' when he discovered the news. Fryer's anger intensified when he returned to Mhow to discover how far the matter had progressed and he launched a last-ditch attempt to scupper Oates' plans. He wrote a stiff letter of protest to the Commander-in-Chief, India, demanding that the secondment of Oates should be cancelled because it would leave him short of experienced officers. Fryer forcibly pointed out three other officers of similar rank had left the regiment in the previous few months. He warned that the 'whole of the squadron commanders of this regiment would have left almost at once' and argued that the regiment could not afford to lose its experienced men.[9]

Unknown to Fryer, the War Office in London had already recommended that Oates should be allowed to join Scott and were not prepared to change their mind. Conditional approval was granted on 8 March 1910 while Fryer was still away from Mhow and unaware the die had been cast. The War Office did wring suitable concessions from Oates, insisting their approval was conditional. The War Office, after lengthy consideration, decided Oates would not be paid while away from the regiment and his pension entitlement would be diluted by his term of secondment.

Oates was also asked to pay his own fare from India to London and that of Lt A.R. Moncrief, the officer who was sent from Britain to replace him. The War Office reasoned that since Oates had volunteered for the enterprise, he would be prepared to accept the loss of wages and cited several examples of other officers who had taken unpaid leave to join various expeditions.

A flurry of cables went back and forth between Oates in Mhow and the War Office in London as they haggled over the trivial matters like the cost of the sea passage home. But on 17 March, the War Office sent a brief cable to the C-in-C India declaring:

'Oates accepts – proceed at once.'[10]

It was Oates' thirtieth birthday.

Fryer was enraged and confronted Oates twice in the space of 24 hours in a final attempt to block his departure. Fryer again insisted that Oates would not be allowed to leave if he could prevent it. Oates was equally determined and said the outcome of the impasse depended on 'who is the most pig-headed'.

The War Office would probably have been more sympathetic to Fryer's case if his protest had reached London a little earlier. Fryer had a reasonable point about the loss of experienced officers and it is tempting to speculate that Oates may have been refused permission to join Scott if the strong objections from Mhow had been lodged sooner. Or if Fryer had not been away from Mhow.

The War Office resolutely refused to change their minds and Oates duly won his battle with the disgruntled Fryer. On 26 March 1910, Captain Lawrence Oates was officially seconded for 'extra regimental employment' with Scott's expedition to the Antarctic.

After a series of hurried arrangements – including selling his pack of hounds to a fellow officer – Oates left his unit for the last time on 24 March. He travelled south to Bombay where he boarded the liner, *India*, for the long trip home and a new life outside the army.

A number of Inniskilling officers were uneasy about Oates' plans to explore Antarctica and tried to persuade him to abandon the project. They probably recognised Oates' army career would inevitably come to an end if he sailed with Scott. One of his closest friends, Captain C.R. Terrot, launched a spirited attempt to dissuade him. Terrot's daughter remembered:

'Father (Capt. Terrot) told me he sat up in the early hours trying to persuade him not to go on Scott's expedition. He thought it wasn't properly organised, and besides they were short of staff officers and didn't want him to go.'[11]

But Oates had finally taken a positive decision in his life.

11

Terra Incognita

Antarctica is not designed for humans. Yet the continent has always held a special place in the imagination. It is the fifth largest continent, with a landmass of 5,400,000 million square miles, larger than Europe or the United States, and represents about ten per cent of earth's landmass. It is an island continent cut off from the inhabited world by the violent, treacherous Southern Ocean. The tip of South America is about 600 miles away and it is more than 1,500 miles to Australia and New Zealand.

The continent is also the world's most inhospitable place. Over 99 per cent of the land is permanently covered in ice and wind speeds have been known to reach nearly 200 mph (320 kph). Antarctica has also produced the lowest temperature ever recorded on earth – minus 129.3°F (–89.6°C). Only a tiny proportion of the sun's heat actually reaches the continent because most is reflected back into the atmosphere by the perpetual covering blanket of snow and ice. For many months of the year, Antarctica is either plunged into total darkness or total daylight for 24 hours a day.

Antarctica was thought to exist many thousands of years before humans confirmed its presence in the early nineteenth century. The Greek mathematician Pythagoras postulated that the earth was round as long ago as the sixth century BC and reasoned that it was necessary to have land in the south of the planet to counter-balance the known populated areas of the northern hemisphere. Without a counter-balance, it was said, the earth would have tipped over. The unseen continent was known as Terra Australis Incognita – the 'Unknown Southern Land'.

As the Northern Hemisphere lay under the easily recognisable stellar constellation of Arktos (the Bear), the mysterious land to the south became known as the opposite to the Bear – Antartiktos.

In 1840 a party under James Clark Ross, a veteran of Arctic exploration, penetrated the encircling pack ice and sailed alongside the frozen Antarctic continent for the first time, giving his name to the Ross Sea.

After the exploits of Ross in the 1840s, British interest in Antarctica lay dormant for several decades until the emergence of the remarkable ex-naval character, Sir Clements Markham.

Markham, the son of a Yorkshire vicar who enlisted in the navy at fourteen, spent a short time in the Arctic during the early 1850s searching for Sir John Franklin's lost expedition. Three decades later, almost single-handedly, he led the campaign to switch British attention from the north to the south and he became the powerful driving force behind successive attempts to reach the South Pole.

A crusty, bewhiskered figure, Markham spent about fifteen years plotting and out-manoeuvring his political and scientific opponents before launching the British National Antarctic Expedition in 1901, the largest and best-equipped party ever sent south.

The 71-year-old was an uncompromising character whose dictatorial style left little room for discussion of the important advances in Polar techniques which had been successfully adopted by others, notably the Americans and Norwegians. Nearer to home, Markham also blindly ignored the achievements of the redoubtable Scottish doctor, John Rae, in the Arctic.

Rae was among the first British explorers to demonstrate that Europeans could survive the hostile Polar climate if they adopted the native Inuit methods. Rae proved conclusively that men should understand more about the environment and adapt to their surroundings. He travelled prodigious distances over the ice and most notably discovered vital relics which helped solve the mystery of Franklin's disappearance. But Rae, an unorthodox loner, was not a naval man and establishment figures like Markham kept him at arm's length. Vital lessons – such as why the Inuits did not suffer from the dread of scurvy which ravaged English explorers – were blindly ignored.

Rae's abilities were, however, fully recognised by the next generation of Polar explorers, such as the Norwegians Fridtjof Nansen and Otto Sverdrup and the American, Robert Peary. By the 1890s they had embraced many Inuit practices, fashioning new lighter sledges, wearing more efficient fur clothing and using quicker, more effective forms of travel with skis and dogs.

A classic image was created a little later by Roald Amundsen, the most proficient of all Polar explorers. During his epic voyage through the North West Passage in 1904, Amundsen spent months on King William Island with a local Netsilik Eskimo tribe studying their customs and practices and absorbing fundamental lessons about survival. Only 100 miles away was the scene of Franklin's disastrous expedition, where 129 men perished in an area where Netsiliks had quietly existed for generations. Where the British contrived a terrible death, the Norwegians had learned to live.

The lessons brought back by Nansen, Peary and the others were freely available to those with open minds. But Markham, misguided and blinkered, blithely discounted progress and sowed the seeds of ruin which would eventually bring catastrophe to British Polar exploration.

Markham's principal blind spot was animals. While innovative ice travellers like the Norwegians routinely employed well-trained dogs and skis to cross the snow and ice, Markham held steadfastly to the belief that explorers should be yoked in harnesses to haul their own sledges. Dogs, he once said, were useful only to foreigners like Siberians or Greenlanders. The implication was that there was nothing a 'primitive' race could teach the English.

Dogs are better suited to Polar travel than any other animal and in the extreme can be slaughtered to provide food for both men and dogs to prolong journeys. Markham stuck with the sentimental British attitude that dogs should be pampered as pets and believed it was cruel to deploy animals dragging sledges or to feed each other. Men, he insisted, should be their own beasts of burden.

Markham passed on his ignorance in full measure to the malleable and ambitious Scott and the *Discovery* expedition became the apprenticeship of looming failure. Scott, like most of the men on the *Discovery*, lacked any experience of the ice and was hopelessly unprepared for the task which lay ahead. Few of the 45-strong shore party had been to the ice before and Scott freely admitted that he had 'no predilection for Polar exploration'.

Discovery's overall achievements were modest and the party notably failed to learn important lessons about key issues of countering the environment, such as an effective diet which would stave off the effects of scurvy. Scott did succeed in penetrating about 300 miles into the interior of Antarctica and establishing a new record 'furthest south'. But the journey almost ended in disaster and the three-man party – Scott, Edward Wilson and Ernest Shackleton – was lucky to escape with their lives. In 1909, Shackleton was knighted for his effort in getting to within 97 miles of the South Pole. Scott, eager to eclipse his rival, readily took up the challenge.

Initially the biggest hurdle for Scott's second attempt at the Pole was to raise £40,000 (£1,900,000 today) to finance the expedition. Although the venture generated considerable public interest, getting people to part with money was a different matter. Scott found it difficult to find substantial backers.

Asquith's Liberal Government donated half the funds – £20,000 (£950,000) – but Scott was forced to go cap in hand in search of the other £20,000. He collected some modest handouts from a few wealthy individuals, raised a little more by selling the publishing and photography rights and went on a whistlestop tour of the country to drum up money from public subscriptions.

Scott dipped into his own limited personal resources and schools around the country were recruited to help generate badly needed support, raising small sums to sponsor essential equipment for the explorers. A pony could be sponsored for as little as £5. Oates' sleeping bag was bought from money donated by Trafalgar House, Winchester, the country's oldest public school, while Eton was among the other notable schools and colleges which made generous donations to buy sledges, tents, sleeping bags, a dog or a pony.

Oates emerged as one the largest private supporters of the expedition. His personal donation of £1,000 (£47,000 at today's prices) represented a little over two per cent of the project's entire funding, or five pence in every £ raised from private sources. It is also clear that Oates was prepared to make an even larger contribution and at one stage he told his mother that he was willing to donate £1,500 (over £70,000 today) to secure a place on the expedition.

Oates' generosity dwarfed the money provided from more familiar official sources. Despite the national appeal of the venture, the Royal Society and Royal Geographical Society, who had sponsored the *Discovery* expedition, provided limited backing. The RGS gave only £500 (£23,500) and Markham, whose early ambition had fuelled the dash to the Pole, donated just £100 (£4,700).

Another problem was finding a ship capable of getting through the pack ice to the Antarctic continent itself. The natural choice was *Discovery* but by 1909 the vessel was on charter to the Hudson Bay Company of Canada and unavailable. In desperation, Scott turned to an old Dundee whaler, the *Terra Nova*, which was bought for £12,500 (almost £590,000).

Terra Nova was not ideal. She was old, expensive to run and needed much work to make her seaworthy for the long and hazardous trip across the fearsome Southern Ocean. But she had a distinct pedigree from 30 years in the whaling fleet and had been south before, having taken part in the rescue of *Discovery* in 1904. *Terra Nova*, at least, was a known quantity.

12

A fatal mistake

Lawrence Oates' first contribution to the great adventure was to do the thing he hated most in life – he went back to the classroom. Soon after Scott secured War Office approval for his secondment, Oates was asked to take a crash course in surveying and map making at the Royal Geographical Society in London.

The course, conducted by E.A. Reeves, the Map Curator and Instructor at the RGS, was designed to provide explorers with a basic grasp of map-making techniques. Scott believed it would be useful to add the cavalry officer to the expedition's surveying resource, although there is no evidence that Oates' newly-acquired skills were ever employed on the expedition.

However, Oates did make a big impression when he first met the other expedition members at South-West India Docks on the Thames, where the *Terra Nova* was undergoing intensive preparations. Oates was the first soldier to serve on a Polar expedition of the time and his appointment aroused great interest from the largely naval crew on board *Terra Nova*, who were mostly hardened veterans of the sea and doubtless eager to indulge in bawdy inter-service banter.

Oates' rank and élite regiment conjured up images of a swaggering, impeccably smart cavalry officer with a flowing moustache. Even the experienced sailors were amazed at the sight that greeted them striding up the gangplank in May 1909. Oates, perhaps deliberately, chose to dress down for the occasion. The clean-shaven, weatherbeaten figure walked with a slight limp, wore a shabby Aquascutum raincoat buttoned up to the neck and a bowler hat was perched jauntily on the back of his head. 'I'm Oates,' he announced to the surprised seamen.[1]

Petty Officer Tom Crean, one of the most experienced seamen on deck that day, remembered the occasion:

'We could none of us make out who or what he was when he came on board – we never for a moment thought he was an officer for they were so usually smart! We made up our minds that he was a farmer, he was always so nice and friendly, just like one of ourselves, but oh! He was a gentleman, quite a gentleman and always a gentleman.'[2]

The incident is typically Oates. In one simple act he had disarmed potential sceptics and demonstrated that he could move effortlessly through the ranks, casually indifferent to status. It was a popular move and the men on board *Terra Nova* warmed to their new recruit.

Teddy Evans remembered his 'kindly brown eyes (as) indicative of his fine personality'. The seamen cheerfully called him the 'Dragoon Rigger'.

Terra Nova was a hive of frantic activity as the ship prepared to set sail and one visitor reported men darting about like 'busy ants' in an attempt to make the vessel presentable and ready for the long voyage south. The modest, unkempt 749-ton ship was overshadowed by the impressive passenger liners and stout cargo vessels which all jostled for space in the cramped confinement of London's busy docks. By coincidence the distinguished *Discovery* was berthed nearby.

Terra Nova was a grubby relic of her long history in the whaling fleet and Evans said he blushed when navy admirals came on board because she was so dirty. The stench of whale oil and seal blubber was overpowering. But experienced seamen said the 187-ft vessel, which was built in 1874 at Alexander Stephens yard, Dundee, was an 'easy ship'.

Geoffrey Herringham, a fellow Inniskilling officer, dropped by to meet Oates on the dockside and confessed to being 'horrified at the smallness' of the vessel as she prepared to cross the globe. Herringham, who was accustomed to the ample living quarters for officers, was particularly astonished at the poky sleeping arrangements on board but reported Oates as 'cheery as possible'.

The ship was also dangerously overloaded with stores and supplies for the proposed two-year mission and Evans craftily painted out the Plimsoll line round the hull to avoid the prying eyes of the authorities, who might have prevented the unseaworthy ship from sailing. As a further precaution, *Terra Nova* was quietly registered as a yacht to avoid potentially troublesome merchant shipping regulations.

Oates was immediately put to work on a variety of tasks, including fitting out the *Terra Nova* which involved a visit to a nearby furniture dealer to choose 'serviceable but not very ornamental' fittings for the wardroom, warrant-officers' mess and the cabins. He also revealed a considerable experience of the sea and surprised his new colleagues with his ability to climb aloft. The time on *Saunterer* was now paying dividends.

It was soon apparent that Oates was an unobtrusive character who preferred the shadows to the spotlight. Evans recalled that Oates was a quiet man who rarely said much, but his 'dry old remarks' were always to the point. He was immediately popular and quite soon the naval contingent began to call him by the new nickname of 'Soldier'. The name stuck and for the rest of the expedition he was known by either his more common sobriquet of 'Titus', or 'Soldier'.

Oates had created an immediate impression among his new colleagues, partly because of his willingness to work on even the most menial tasks and partly because he was happy to accept orders from naval officers. He seemed to relish the freedom from the familiar, dull army routine and cheerfully threw himself into a range of wholly unfamiliar and mundane tasks like shifting cargo boxes or painting whale boats.

Indirectly, however, Oates' eagerness to help encouraged Scott to make a serious blunder which would have far-reaching implications for the expedition. The misjudgement arose over buying the horses which were vital to the success of the expedition. Oates, the expert, fully expected to be sent to the Far East to buy the hardened Siberian or Manchurian ponies on which so much rested.

But Evans and the First Mate, Lieutenant Victor Campbell, persuaded Scott not to send Oates. The well-meaning Evans and Campbell convinced Scott that Oates would be better employed in London as an ordinary seaman helping to fit out the *Terra Nova*. Scott agreed. It was a fatal mistake which had profound consequences.

Instead, Scott asked another expedition member, Cecil Meares, to travel east and buy the ponies. Meares was already scheduled to make the long trip to Manchuria to buy sledge dogs and Scott casually asked him to extend his journey and pick up the required number of ponies. Meares, an experienced Far-Eastern traveller with considerable knowledge of China and Russia, had good experience of handling dogs and was well suited to that part of his task. He had driven dog teams in remote spots like Kamchatka and spoke Russian and a little Chinese. But he knew nothing about horses.

As a result, a man with no knowledge of horses was sent to the other side of the globe to choose an essential component of the expedition's transportation and Oates, the acknowledged authority, was humping boxes around the decks of *Terra Nova* like a menial docker. It was no careless oversight.

Meares hurried to join the Trans-Siberian Railway for the exhausting overland journey to the Far East and on 31 May Oates was officially installed as a midshipman at the princely wage of 1s a month (5p or £2.35 at today's prices).

The day before formally assuming his new role, Oates took time off from the hubbub of the London docks and dashed to the small Essex village of Pebmarsh to act as best man at the wedding of his brother Bryan to Alma Kirby. The pair had always enjoyed a fairly close relationship even though they were temperamentally very different.

Laurie Oates was steady, disciplined and even-tempered. In contrast, Bryan was a more lively but moody character who would later gain an unfortunate reputation for arrogance and undisciplined behaviour. When Britain was desperate to enrol officers for the war in 1914, Bryan Oates' behaviour had become so unreliable that his commanding officer denounced him as being 'unfit to hold a commission in any branch of the service'.[3]

Oates gave the newly-weds a canteen of silver and rushed back to London to take up his new posting on *Terra Nova*. It was his final act of family duty.

Terra Nova began her long journey south at around 5 pm on the evening of 1 June 1910. As the heavily-laden ship moved slowly out onto the Thames, guests on board were struck by the coincidence that Britain was again mourning the loss of a monarch on the eve of a major Polar expedition. *Discovery* had slipped out of the same London Docks in the summer of 1901 while the nation was still coming to terms with the death of Queen Victoria and the funeral of her successor, King Edward VII, had taken place only ten days before *Terra Nova* sailed for the Antarctic.

Terra Nova headed down the Thames to Greenhithe, on to Portsmouth and later to Cardiff, which was an unusual choice as the final departure point for the expedition. But the venture had caught the imagination of the Welsh and the

Oates (right) stands alongside Scott's wife, Kathleen, on board Terra Nova *shortly before the expedition's departure to the Antarctic in 1910. Also pictured (left) is Henry 'Birdie' Bowers, who was also destined to die.*

largest single donation from public subscription came from the generous people of Cardiff. *Terra Nova* was given free docking facilities, supplies of coal and the use of an office and staff to help with the last minute administrative details.

A seemingly endless line of enthusiastic visitors swarmed over the little ship and Oates, who was rarely at ease in large formal gatherings, found it all rather tiresome. The arch conservative was also uneasy about the cluster of local Labour councillors from staunchly socialist Cardiff. He called them a 'mob'. According to an irascible Oates, the only gentleman to come on board was the telephone operator.

To relieve himself of the glad-handing, Oates took himself off to Chepstow for a few days with his old army colleague, Colonel Herbert. But even in the rural retreat of Herbert's home, Oates could not escape from the near celebrity status which the expedition conferred on its members. Herbert's children wanted to know whether Oates had left the army to become a pirate.

After a few days of receptions and preparation, the *Terra Nova* was finally prepared to cast off on 15 June 1910. Large crowds of animated well-wishers gathered to see the expedition depart and the Cardiff Artillery Band blasted out a rousing rendition of *Auld Lang Syne* as the ship lumbered slowly and inelegantly out to sea.

One significant omission from the noisy ranks of well-wishers was Caroline Oates, who had decided not to venture to the dockside to see her son off in person. Mother and son said their goodbyes in private a little earlier, which suited Oates. Shortly before departure, he told her:

> 'I am glad you are not going to see me off: I hate those awful goodbyes.'[4]

Caroline Oates had by no means forgotten her son and on 13 June, shortly before *Terra Nova* steamed into Cardiff, she gave him a parting gift of £50 (today: almost £2,500) to take on the expedition. Even though there was little opportunity to spend in the wastelands of Antarctica, Oates could be relied upon to let money slip through his fingers and her gift was well meant.

Another insight into the occasionally quirky Oates' character emerged a few days after leaving Cardiff when he called on the officers and gentlemen scientists to drink the health of Napoleon. Oates admired and respected Napoleon, whom he believed to be the greatest of all soldiers. He developed a curious fascination with Napoleon and regarded his hero as the 'high priest of his religion' – the religion of duty. A friend, William King, had given him a portrait of Napoleon to take on the expedition and he also took a small bust of the Frenchman. One of the few books he packed for the trip was Napier's *History of the War in the Peninsula* chronicling Napoleon's lengthy campaign in Spain and Portugal a century earlier.

Oates had picked an odd day to toast his health – 18 June, the ninety-fifth anniversary of Waterloo, Napoleon's greatest and final defeat. But in the face of good-natured teasing from comrades around the dinner table, Oates stood his ground.

Oates' colleagues on the expedition were drawn from all walks of life, though like Scott's earlier expedition on *Discovery*, there was a large presence of naval men. But, unlike the *Discovery,* the starched naval influence would be diluted by a larger number of civilian scientists, adventurers and even a famous photographer.

Scott, now 42, had joined the Royal Naval College, Dartmouth as a cadet at the age of thirteen and spent the rest of his life in service. He had been largely anonymous until picked by Markham to lead the *Discovery* expedition in 1901. Scott probably recognised the Antarctic as a golden opportunity for promotion, a trend established in the nineteenth century when Arctic exploration had helped many ambitious young naval officers achieve fame and advancement. To friends he was known as Con, but to the men on *Terra Nova* he was The Owner, a traditional naval term for a ship's captain.

Scott's official second-in-command was the 29-year-old Edward Ratcliffe Garth Russell Evans, an ambitious and energetic naval lieutenant, who had been south before on the mission to rescue Scott's *Discovery* a few years earlier. Evans had wanted to launch his own expedition to the Antarctic before agreeing to sail with Scott. However, the pair were unsuited and found it increasingly difficult to rub along together. Scott soon lost confidence in his deputy and their relationship deteriorated badly as the expedition reached its critical stages. Evans, widely known as Teddy, would later become the life peer, Lord Mountevans.

The effective second-in-command was the multi-talented Edward Wilson, a zoologist, doctor and gifted artist who had travelled with Scott on *Discovery* and was his closest friend. The 38-year-old Wilson was a kindly and deeply spiritual figure to whom many people turned for guidance, solace and judgement. Wilson was perhaps Scott's only confidante. His family called him Ted, but his colleagues affectionately knew him as 'Uncle Bill' and the biographer, Roland Huntford, aptly described Wilson as the Sancho Panza to Scott's Don Quixote.

Wilson was head of a large scientific team, which included two Australian geologists, Frank Debenham and Thomas Griffith Taylor, and a wealthy, indolent marine biologist, Edward Nelson. The meteorologist was a solemn 32-year-old George Simpson who was mocked as 'Sunny Jim' and the physicist was a hearty 23-year-old Canadian, Charles Wright. Wilson's eager assistant was a 24-year-old short-sighted Oxford graduate, Apsley Cherry-Garrard. Like Oates, 'Cherry' made a personal donation of £1,000 to expedition funds and would later write a memorable book about the enterprise, *The Worst Journey in the World*.

The backbone of the expedition was provided by tough, resourceful naval petty officers, Tom Crean and Edgar 'Taff' Evans, and the veteran stoker, Bill Lashly, who were all well known to Scott. They were hugely experienced and formidable characters who had distinguished themselves on *Discovery*. Scott recognised that these were men for a tight spot and after his near fatal 'furthest south' journey in 1902–03, Scott never undertook a major sledging mission without one of the three stalwarts in harness alongside him. Together the three formed the engine room of the expedition.

Crean, a 33-year-old straight-talking Irishman from Kerry, had run away from home to join the navy at the age of fifteen and proved to be an indestructible figure on three of the four British expeditions during the Heroic Age of Polar exploration. He was one of the few who served both Scott and Shackleton and he outlived them both, retiring to Ireland to open a pub.

Evans, who hailed from the Gower Peninsula in Wales, was a powerful, boisterous man who represented what Scott regarded as the finest qualities of the British bluejacket. Hampshire-born Lashly was a quiet, imperturbable figure with formidable strength. At 42 years of age, he commanded enormous respect and, unusually among seamen, he neither smoked nor drank.

Scott's gamble with the motorised tractors was the responsibility of a 26-year-old mechanic, Bernard Day, who had travelled south with Shackleton on the *Nimrod* expedition and was gleefully described as a 'cynic and philosopher'. Cecil Meares, who had mistakenly been assigned to buy the ponies, was one of life's wanderers, who had fought in the Boer War and never lost his taste for adventure. Although only 33, he had travelled extensively, especially in the vast and remote expanses of China and Russia.

Scott chose the much-admired and pioneering photographer, Herbert Ponting, to record the expedition, which he did with a remarkable series of incomparable still and moving images that impress to this day. Ponting, at 40, was older than most of the men on *Terra Nova*. But he had distinguished himself in a rich and varied career that ranged from war correspondent during the Russo-Japanese and Spanish-American wars, cattle ranching in the American West and regular travel to then largely unknown places like Japan. Ponting saw himself as more than a simple photographer and preferred to be known as a 'camera artist'.

Scott was also looking for someone to teach his men the art of skiing and on the advice of the legendary Norwegian explorer, Fridtjof Nansen, he agreed to take the 21-year-old Tryggve Gran. He was another who had nursed ambitions of organising his own Antarctic expedition and leapt at the chance to join Scott.

One of the resident doctors was Edward Atkinson, a quiet, reflective 28-year-old naval surgeon who was known as 'Atch'. Atkinson developed a close friendship with Oates, two of the expedition's quiet men.

Scott also agreed to take Henry Robertson Bowers, a small, squat man with a 40-inch chest and a huge beak-like nose which earned him the inevitable nickname of 'Birdie'. Bowers, aged 27, was an adaptable and prodigious worker who had progressed from naval cadet to merchant midshipman, before joining the Royal Indian Marines where he was appointed lieutenant and hunted gun-running dhows up the Irrawaddy. Bowers possessed superhuman strength and strong religious convictions, but never overcame a terror of spiders.

Scott had appointed Victor Campbell, a cultured unassuming man, to lead a smaller six-man party to explore an unknown King Edward VII area of the continent. Campbell, known as the 'Wicked Mate', also took along a young geologist, Raymond Priestley, and an experienced naval surgeon, Murray Levick, who would later write the standard work on Antarctic penguins even though he was no scientist.

Scott was not on board *Terra Nova* as the party made their way slowly away from Britain and towards the Atlantic island of Madeira, which Oates had last visited fifteen years earlier on his father's last ill-fated trip. Scott, still at home arranging the expedition finances, planned to join the ship in South Africa.

Madeira was especially poignant for Oates, who took the opportunity to visit his father's grave in the cemetery at Funchal. He reported it 'quite tidy' but noted the lillies were a little faded and the roses had finished blooming. 'It was most quiet and nice,' he added.

13

A race for the Pole

*T*erra Nova pressed on slowly for a stopover at Cape Town, enabling Oates to make the transformation from sailor back to horseman. Soon after landing, he returned to familiar territory when he took Atkinson, Bowers and Cherry-Garrard to the hills around Wynberg for a spot of riding and hunting.

The brief excursion to the countryside was a welcome relief to Oates, who was uncomfortable with the receptions and public relations duties of the expedition. He particularly disliked dressing up in stiff collars and pressed suits to attend stiffly formal cocktail parties, which were an unhappy reminder of the army's dreary social routine now left behind. He lampooned the swarms of well-wishing socialites as 'nibs, nobs and snobs' and said they always forgot to bring important items for the men like the mail and bottles of beer.

Despite the irritating social intrusions, Oates was happier than he had been in years. He relished the change of life and enjoyed the hard work. He gladly accepted orders as any ordinary seamen and all talk of rank was superfluous. He told an army friend that he was enjoying himself 'immensely' and another that he was having a 'top hole time'. The initial experience on *Terra Nova* strengthened the belief Oates had left the army for good. Although he never formally resigned his commission, Oates liked what he saw and was evidently contemplating a new rôle in life.

Bowers had broached the possibility of some exploration up the Amazon after returning from the Antarctic and Campbell wanted Oates to accompany him on a trip to the remote, game-rich Novaya Zemlya islands in the Arctic Ocean. Oates was impressed with the various ideas and even tried to recruit his friend and former Inniskilling officer, King, to join the would-be adventurers.

Oates and King were similar characters, both unhappy with the routine of army life and anxious to find more excitement and fulfilment. King had left the regiment first and Oates saw an opportunity to team up again. In doing so, he gave King a clear indication that he was contemplating resigning from the army, declaring:

> 'I don't suppose I shall do much soldiering after this.'[1]

Oates had been even more quiet and introverted than usual when he first joined *Terra Nova*, probably because of the unfamiliarity of the surroundings and a hint of shyness. Others on board found it difficult to get a word out of him, perhaps because he felt out of place in the overwhelmingly naval setting. But he slowly began to emerge from the shadows as his contentment grew. Oates found his feet and a fortnight after sailing from Cardiff, Wilson observed that Oates was 'just beginning to come out'. He reported a 'delightful suppressed geniality' about the man's character.

Oates fitted in well and enthusiastically shared in the friendly horseplay amongst those on board when the *Terra Nova* crossed the Equator. He was centre stage for the extravagant initiation ceremony – a ritualistic shaving and ducking – for those, especially the young scientists, who were 'crossing the line' for the first time. Oates took on the unlikely role as one of the four 'sea bears' who unceremoniously ducked the unfortunate victims. On another occasion, the normally non-musical Oates surprised everyone by suddenly breaking into song with a cheery rendition of 'The Fly on the Turnip'.

However, proceedings took on a more serious note on 2 September when Scott joined the *Terra Nova* in South Africa. Most realised that, from this moment, things would be more business-like and Oates informed his mother:

> 'The Skipper has decided to come on the ship to Melbourne with us,
> this is not a very popular move but in a way I think it is a good thing
> as he gets to know the people better and we get to know him.'[2]

The one area of discontent was the slow-moving *Terra Nova*, which he described as a 'frightfully dirty ship'. *Terra Nova*, he said, sailed and steamed 'very badly' and had only two speeds – 'one is slow and the other is slower'. He reckoned his own yacht, *Saunterer*, would 'knock her head off' in a sailing match.

Terra Nova duly crossed the Indian Ocean and sailed into Melbourne Harbour on 12 October where a great shock greeted the expedition. Waiting for Scott among the mails was an abrupt telegram which read: 'Beg leave to inform you, *Fram* proceeding Antarctic. Amundsen.' The most chronicled race in history was under way.

Roald Amundsen was the greatest of all Polar explorers and his challenge to Scott was a stunning threat. While the British under Scott were essentially well-intentioned but amateur explorers, Amundsen was the consummate single-minded and ruthlessly ambitious professional. From the moment that Amundsen challenged Scott in the race for the South Pole, there would be only one victor.

Amundsen, who came from a seafaring family, aspired to be a Polar explorer from his earliest days. As a young man, he slept with his bedroom windows open during the freezing Norwegian winter nights to help toughen himself for the rigours ahead. In 1897–98, he was a member of the *Belgica* party which spent the first ever winter in Antarctica. His next momentous achievement came between 1903 and 1906 when his tiny 47-ton ship, *Gjoa*, made the historic first trip through the North West Passage. It was a goal that had defeated a succession of sailors and navigators, particularly the English, for over 300 years. Amundsen succeeded at his first attempt.

Following the triumph of *Gjoa*, Amundsen set himself the task of being the first man to reach the North Pole. But in 1909 he learned that the Americans, Peary and Cook, were claiming to have reached the Pole and he promptly switched his attention to the South Pole.

There was a stark contrast between the two enterprises. Scott planned to mix the serious business of exploration with a large and diverse scientific programme, which was admirable but added to the complexities of planning and preparation. It inevitably meant that he could not focus solely on the principal task of reaching the South Pole.

Scott's party, including the crew of *Terra Nova*, numbered 65 men and organising the landing party of 31 assorted officers, seamen and scientists was a major logistical challenge. More important, the vast majority of Scott's expedition had no experience of the ice. Among the leadership, only Scott and Wilson had travelled on the ice. The rigid constraints of the British class system ensured that the experienced men from the engine room – Crean, Evans and Lashly – were not involved with the key decision-making process and were barely even consulted.

Scott planned to use four separate means of transport: men in harness hauling their own sledges, teams of dogs, horses to haul heavier sledges and the experimental motor tractors. On paper this covered every eventuality, but in reality it confused things and meant, for example, that each form of transport travelled at different speeds across the ice and each demanded different skills of leadership.

In contrast, Amundsen had no intention of confusing the issue. His expedition had one simple goal – to reach the South Pole. His ship, the *Fram* – the English translation is Forwards – sailed south with a total complement of nineteen, with only nine hand-picked men in the landing party. Any scientific work was secondary and would not divert attention from the main task ahead. He would use only two simple means of transportation: skis and dogs.

While the British party was largely untried and inexperienced, the Norwegians were in their natural environment. The ice held no terrors. Teddy Evans once applauded the Norwegians as 'princes of ice and the sea'. Each of the men in Amundsen's landing party had considerable experience of the ice and was an expert in his field.

Dogs were central to Amundsen's assault on the Pole and he recruited Helmer Hanssen, a renowned dog driver, ice-traveller and navigator who had accompanied him on the memorable first journey through the North West Passage. He was a durable, dependable character who was born inside the Arctic Circle and knew the ice better than most. Amundsen, who was normally grudging in his praise, said Hanssen was the most efficient dog driver he had ever met.

He also took Sverre Hassel, another specialist with dogs who had been in the Arctic with Sverdrup a decade earlier and Oscar Wisting, an adaptable and resourceful character who had seen service as a whaler in Icelandic waters. Amundsen went to the very top of the profession to recruit Olav Bjaaland, a Nordic ski champion from Telemark, the birthplace of modern skiing. Even the expedition cook and handyman, Adolf Lindstrom – who was destined to remain behind at base camp while Amundsen rushed to the Pole – had spent years in the ice and was a member of *Gjoa's* North West Passage party.

These men, professional to the core, would form the team for Norway's expedition. Or, as someone later remarked, a Viking raid on the Pole.

Amundsen was a driven man who could not tolerate failure and deliberately kept his South Pole plans under close wraps. He kept the truth from both his financial backers and even the small band of men who accompanied him southwards. Even his departure from Norway was kept a secret, possibly to avoid detection from his creditors. He waited for darkness before slipping out of Christiania – now called Oslo – around midnight on 6 June 1910. By an odd coincidence, 6 June was Scott's birthday.

He borrowed the purpose-built ice-ship, *Fram*, from Nansen on the pretence, that he was heading north into Arctic waters and only revealed his true plans when the expedition was under way. On a brief stop at Madeira, Amundsen summoned the men on deck and coolly showed them a map of the southern hemisphere. Most still thought they were heading north but Amundsen asked them one by one if they were prepared to accompany him to the South Pole.

Everyone said yes. Amundsen urged the men to go below quickly and write letters home, informing their families that they were going to the South Pole. He added that it was now a question of racing the English and Bjaaland, the ski champion accustomed to winning trophies, retorted: 'That means we'll get there first.'

Amundsen's brother, Leon, sent the fateful telegram informing Scott of the Norwegian's intentions as the slow-moving *Terra Nova* was struggling across the Indian Ocean. Amundsen himself was out of touch, in the middle of a non-stop 14,000-mile journey in the *Fram* from Madeira to the Antarctic coast. Both *Terra Nova* and *Fram* were heading for much the same area at the same time.

Scott's proposal was to return to the McMurdo Sound area near Ross Island on the edge of the vast Ross Ice Barrier, near the former base camp on the earlier *Discovery* expedition. His plan was to follow Shackleton's route across the Barrier, up the newly-discovered Beardmore Glacier to the Polar Plateau and then to the Pole.

Amundsen was heading for the Bay of Whales, first discovered by Shackleton in 1908 and about 400 miles along the coast from McMurdo Sound. Although this meant finding a completely new route up the Trans-Antarctic Mountains to the Polar Plateau, Amundsen was confident his dogs were equal to the task. He was also intending to drive the dogs to the limit, ruthlessly shooting the weaker animals to feed the stronger beasts.

The base camp, called Framheim, would be located on the Ice Barrier itself, a vast floating mass of sea ice. While Shackleton and others were concerned about the calving icebergs breaking off from the Barrier, Amundsen noted that this particular area had remained intact since Ross had sailed alongside 70 years earlier in 1841. He reasoned – correctly as it later emerged – that the Barrier at this point was anchored by an unseen chunk of land. The land, which was not discovered until 1934, was later named Roosevelt Island.

It was an inspirational choice which positioned Amundsen 60 miles nearer the Pole than Scott – a valuable 120-mile saving on the round trip. Amundsen was in the lead even before the race had begun.

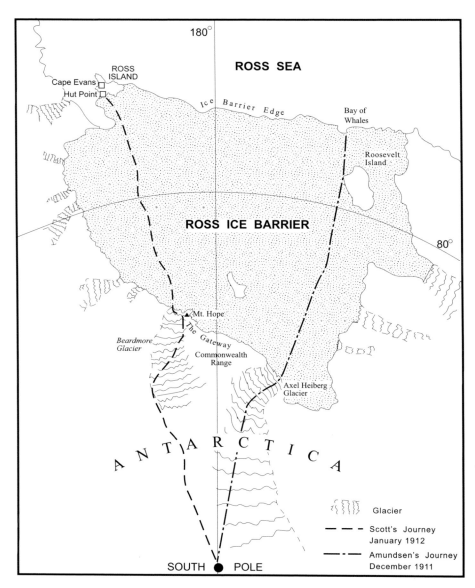

The route to the Pole.

14

A load of crocks

News of Amundsen's dramatic intervention filtered slowly through to members of Scott's expedition. Scott himself stoically refused to be depressed by the news and tried to carry on as though nothing had changed. The brief telegram was a little ambiguous and did not spell out Amundsen's real plans. But there was little doubt the message contained a major threat to Scott's ambitions.

Oates was philosophical about the Norwegian expedition. He was aware that expectations in Britain were very high after the public fanfare surrounding the expedition. He told a friend that the 'b _____ y Norskies coming down south is bit of shock' and added:

> 'I only hope they don't get there first. It will make us look pretty foolish after all the noise we have made.'[1]

Oates felt that the high profile of the expedition left Scott's party a hostage to fortune. He also had a sneaking regard for Amundsen's low key and unobtrusive approach, which was more suited to his style. He told his mother in a letter:

> 'I must say we have made far too much noise about ourselves, all the photographing, cheering, steaming through the fleet, etc, etc, is rot and if we fail it will only make us look more foolish. They say that Amundsen has been underhand the way he has gone about it, but I personally don't see it as underhand to keep your mouth shut.'[2]

While some in the expedition were furious about Amundsen, Oates took a more considered view and dismissed the temptation to write off the Norwegians. Oates, the professional soldier, recognised a fellow professional in Amundsen. He also knew about the reputation of the Norwegians as tough, resourceful explorers and questioned the wisdom of matching untried horses and man-hauling parties against the more proficient skis and dog teams. He commented:

> 'I myself think these Norskies are a very tough lot, they have 200 dogs and Yohandsen[3] is with them and he is not exactly a child, also they are very good ski-runners while we can only walk, if Scott does anything silly such as underfeeding his ponies he will be beaten as sure as death.'[4]

It was not the widely-held view about Amundsen, whose intrusion offended the proprietorial British attitude towards Antarctica. At home, the combustible Markham dismissed the Norwegian as a 'blackguard'.

Oates was already beginning to develop his reputation as an outsider on the expedition, someone who preferred to make up his own mind about issues and who rejected convention. Two minor incidents in Australia summed up his idiosyncratic behaviour and aversion to custom.

Against his better instincts, Oates was dragged to another tiresome dinner at Melbourne's smartest venue, the Menzies Hotel. It was a formal function for the entire party but Oates turned up late and was a model of studied scruffiness. Dressed in shabby work clothes and hobnailed boots, Oates was challenged by the porters as soon as he entered the hotel lobby. They did not recognise the unkempt figure in front of them and diplomatically explained that, perhaps, the swanky hotel might not suit his taste. Oates shrugged off the porters and strode triumphantly into the dining room to be warmly welcomed by ranks of chuckling shipmates.

A day at Sydney races, an important event in the social calendar, held a particular memory for Scott's wife, Kathleen, who was taken aback by the cavalry officer's scruffy appearance. Oates had pointedly chosen to ignore the etiquette of the occasion and she recorded in her diary:

> 'In the midst of a most brilliant and over-dressed crowd, I suddenly espied the Soldier in Norfolk jacket, such boots and marvellous trousers and an indescribable hat, quite unconscious, I think, that he hadn't a top hat and morning jacket!'[5]

A few days later the expedition travelled to Lyttelton, on New Zealand's South Island, the traditional embarkation point for explorers to the south ever since Ross had visited Antarctica decades earlier. Lyttelton is the port of nearby Christchurch, whose name is derived from Christ Church College, Oxford, and is regarded as the most English of New Zealand's cities. Appropriately enough, it was the last opportunity for the largely English party to feel the grass beneath their feet.

It was also the moment when Oates completed his thoroughly enjoyable duties as a midshipman on board *Terra Nova* and assumed his main responsibility, the stewardship of the ponies. Initially this involved building fifteen special stalls on the forecastle deck and four more outside to accommodate the nineteen animals on the hazardous crossing of the Southern Ocean to the Antarctic coast.

Oates' main concern was how to squeeze the animals into the tiny space allocated on the hopelessly overcrowded little ship. He took his responsibilities very seriously and told his mother he was 'sick with anxiety' about the animals.

Meares had arrived in Lyttelton with the cavalcade of dogs and ponies ahead of the *Terra Nova*, having completed a remarkable overland and sea journey which had taken him over halfway round the world.

After leaving the expedition headquarters in London, he had taken the Trans-Siberian Railway on the long overland trip to the remote river port of Khabarovsk, almost 400 miles north of Vladivostok. From there he travelled another 400 miles northwards by horse-drawn sledge along the frozen River Amur to Nikolayevsk, an isolated port on the Sea of Okhotsk.

He first bought 33 dogs and put them on a train heading south to Vladivostok before turning to the more pressing matter of the ponies. Meares accepted his limited knowledge of horseflesh and asked an acquaintance to buy the animals at a fair in Harbin, a bustling city on the Songhua River in the heart of Manchuria. It was another tough journey of around 850 miles.

Harbin was a fast growing trading centre, which in under two decades had been transformed from a small fishing village by the development of railways that now linked into the mighty Trans-Siberian Railroad. The flourishing city became Russia's military base during the Russo-Japanese War in 1904–5 and its new rail and navigable waterways made Harbin a natural meeting point for merchants and travellers.

However, Scott's instructions, conveyed to Meares and then onto the unnamed associate, effectively hobbled the buyers. Scott emphasised that the darker ponies on Shackleton's *Nimrod* expedition had died before the white-coated animals. Meares therefore travelled east with explicit orders to buy only white horses.

Unfortunately, less than one in five of the ponies on sale at Harbin's markets were white and Meares' friend bought what he regarded as the best of the remaining bunch. To help with the deal, Meares' chum had taken along a Russian, Anton Omelchenko, a jockey and someone who understood horses. Anton, who stood barely 4 ft 10 ins and was later to join the expedition as groom, remembered that the man who sold the horses went away with a 'plenty big smile' after the deal was clinched.[6] Meares had been sold a 'pup'.

Meares had originally wanted twenty ponies, but when the animals were eventually lined up for inspection on the quayside at Vladivostok, one was suspected of having glanders, a highly unpleasant and contagious disease which can afflict both horses and humans. The pony had been tested for the disease but Meares could not a take a chance and the animal was left behind at the docks.

Meares admitted that acquiring the dogs and ponies was a 'very big contract indeed' and was hopeful, rather than optimistic, about shipping the animals to Antarctica in one piece. 'I hope that they will get down all right,' he told his father.[7]

It was an enormous task for one man to ship the menagerie of nineteen ponies and 33 dogs from Asia to the Antarctic and Scott arranged for Wilfred Bruce, his ineffectual brother-in-law, to assist with the sea journey to New Zealand where they were due to meet up with the *Terra Nova*. The pair also recruited Anton and another Russian, Dimitri Gerov, as dog driver.

It was a fraught exercise for Meares and Bruce, who struggled with the troublesome animals in torrential rain on the sodden quayside at Vladivostok. The jetty was two feet deep in mud and manure and it took almost eight hours of toil to load the animals onto the small Japanese steamer, *Tategami Maru*. To add to the strain, two of the ponies broke free and had to be recaptured.

Unfortunately, the work-shy Bruce proved to be of little value to Meares, who rose each day at 5.30 am to begin tending the animals and soon found himself doing all the work. Although Bruce was an experienced merchant navy officer with the P&O line, Meares was unimpressed and wrote:

> 'Quite one of the boys, but a bit too kid glovey for this job, he stands
> on the upper deck and looks on instead of taking off his coat when
> there is a job of work, so it keeps me pretty busy.'[8]

Bruce, who had given Kathleen Scott away at her wedding to Scott, was equally unimpressed with Meares. He observed that passengers were unhappy about Meares' unshaven, tattered appearance. Bruce, who was more familiar with wealthy cruise liner passengers, said he 'wasn't a bit my style'.

From Vladivostok, the Meares caravan went to Kobe in Japan, where they picked up a German vessel, the *Prinz Waldemar*, because they could not find a British ship that would carry the troublesome cargo. The ship took them on a convoluted procession around the Pacific to Hong Kong, Manila, New Guinea, Rockhampton, Brisbane and finally to Sydney.

The long, sweaty journey was an ordeal for the animals and they became ferociously bad-tempered. Hackenschmidt, a particularly vicious beast, bit an old man standing on the quay at Sydney Harbour and Meares and Bruce struggled to keep the animals from snapping at anyone who came near.

The horses were transferred to a New Zealand steamer, *Moana*, for the next leg of the trip to Wellington. On arrival they changed ships once more, putting the weary animals on the *Maori* for the final lap of the tortuous journey to the port of Lyttelton. The circus eventually reached Lyttelton on 15 September, seven weeks after leaving Vladivostok and well ahead of *Terra Nova's* anticipated arrival. Miraculously, Meares had not lost a single animal during the journey, though the ponies had been on their feet without a break for the entire trip. But Bruce did not escape lightly and reached Lyttelton with two black eyes and a swollen nose after a bruising encounter with one obstreperous beast.

The ponies, which Scott called Siberian, were mostly from Manchuria. Only two, the biggest, were Siberian. The animals were probably too large to be called ponies, standing between fourteen and fifteen hands high compared with the conventional classification that a pony measures less than 14.2 hands.[9]

Meares and Bruce took the two sets of animals to Quail Island, a little spot about five miles out into Lyttelton Bay where they were quarantined and inoculated. After a total of 52 days on their feet, the animals were also able to lie down for the first time.

Scott duly arrived at Quail Island some weeks later and announced that he was 'greatly pleased' with the animals. Oates was horrified. Fully aware that the ponies were vitally important to the expedition, he was astounded at the inadequate squad of feeble crocks which stood before him. To his experienced eye, it was abundantly clear that Meares had bought badly. More seriously, it was too late to do anything about the blunder.

Oates inspected the animals and gloomily jotted down a private assessment in his diary. It was a depressing catalogue of deficiencies, which included remarks such as:

> 'Victor. . . Narrow chest, knock knees. . . suffers with his eyes. Aged windsucker.
> Snippets. . . Bad wind sucker. Doubtful back tendons off fore legs.
> Pigeon toes. Aged.
> James Pigg. . . Sand crack near hind. Aged.
> Bones. . . Aged.
> Snatcher. . . Black marks under eye. Aged.

Chinaman. . . Has ringworm just above the coronet on near fore. I
think the oldest pony of the lot which is saying a good deal.
Christopher. . . Aged. Ringbone off fore. Slightly lame off fore.
Jehu. . . Aged. Suffering from debility and worn out.
Nobby. . . Aged. Goes with stiff hocks. Spavin near hind. Best pony we
have.
Michael. . . Lame near hind. Ringbone. Aged.

In mentioning the ponies' blemishes I have only mentioned those
which appear to actively interfere with their work or for identification.'[10]

He gave a shorter, but equally dismissive judgement on the condition of the
ponies in a letter to a friend and was so depressed by the initial inspection that
he promised to have a 'skinful of beer' to drown his sorrows. He explained:

*A load of crocks. Oates and Scott get a first sight of the ponies regarded as crucial to the
success of the expedition. Oates (third left wearing bowler hat) dismissed the animals as a
'wretched load of crocks'. Scott (fourth left) stands next to photographer, Herbert Ponting (fifth
left) and aside from his wife, Kathleen. (SPRI)*

'I took over the ponies the other day and am not impressed with them. They are very old for a job of this sort and four of them are unsound. However, we shall have to make the best of them.'[11]

Oates, never a man to equivocate, gave Scott his own damning assessment of the animals but was surprised to receive an almost dismissive, offhand response. Instead of taking Oates' professional judgement at face value, the over-sensitive Scott took the comments personally. He did not like being told that he had made a grave mistake and he interpreted Oates' caustic opinions on the ponies as a direct attack on his leadership and judgement.

Scott was a novice on the subject of animals and refused to concede that Oates knew more. Scott was also overly sentimental towards animals and found it hard to take cool unemotional decisions about them. He dismissed Oates as a 'cheery old pessimist', which totally missed the point.

Oates found it hard to understand Scott's attitude, particularly as he had been recruited specifically for his expertise and to deliver the very type of judgement he was now imparting. Oates rightly asked: What was the point of employing an expert if you did not listen to his advice? It was the moment when, for the first time, Oates began to question Scott's abilities as a leader. It was also the moment which marked the beginning of a rapid deterioration in their relationship.

However, the one person he did not wish to worry over the mediocre state of the ponies was his mother. Oates deliberately played down their poor condition, telling her in one letter:

'The ponies themselves are first class but all the feeding I have been stuffing them with has made them fairly festive and there may be trouble.'[12]

He also gave her a further reminder of his customary financial shortcomings when he asked her to send £20 to his bank. It was the last time he asked for money, explaining:

'I find I have run things rather fine and that will give me a margin. . .'[13]

Oates moved to Quail Island to be nearer his charges in the final days before the ship's departure. While there he gave the ponies some rudimentary training in how to draw a sledge and became acquainted with the expedition's latest recruits, Anton and Dimitri.

Oates was in his element, once again working closely with horses and impressed with the willing support of the two Russians. He found Quail Island a charming, tranquil haven after the hustle and bustle of the crowded uncomfortable ship and he was rarely happier. But his contentment was soon disrupted by another clash with Scott over the ponies.

Scott was desperately concerned about the heavily over-laden *Terra Nova*, particularly as the ship faced the testing ordeal of crossing the Southern Ocean, where hurricanes and mountainous seas present a formidable barrier to seafarers. Bowers, who had assumed responsibility for storing and packing supplies and equipment, had worked flat out to stow as much as possible. Every inch of the ship, above and below decks, had been utilised and *Terra Nova* was groaning under the weight of the coal and other equipment needed to sustain the large expedition for at least two years. Scott believed that something had to give.

Under pressure to cut back where he could, Scott arbitrarily and irrationally decided that Oates could manage on 30 tons of pony forage. Oates, who understood the risks, warned against the dangers of under-feeding horses in cold weather and insisted that 45 tons would be necessary to keep the animals fit and well for the rigours of their intended job.

Oates was again upset that Scott questioned his judgement on a subject he knew nothing about. The pair argued for an hour before Scott finally backed down and agreed to take extra feed at the expense of some sacks of coal. Oates told his mother about the little skirmish:

> 'I have had a great struggle with Scott about the horse forage. He told me I was a "something" nuisance. He has given way which shows he is open to reason, but they will have to leave some coal behind to get the extra forage in. I have told him that we shall have all our ponies by the time we start laying depots. I had to say this to get my argument about the forage but it has increased my anxiety.'[14]

In fact, Oates had also managed to smuggle an extra two tons of forage on board, generously paid for out of his own pocket. He also recruited the help of Bowers, whose role in skilfully supervising the storing of supplies in the cramped confines of the *Terra Nova's* decks and holds had taken on Herculean proportions.

Scott was still anxious about cash and wanted to buy a cheaper compressed variety of horse fodder. Oates, looking for the best feed in the cold environment, demanded the more expensive linseed meal and Bowers remembered:

> 'When my opinion was asked (knowing nothing of horse fodder) I got a wink from Oates and I said I was sure nothing could equal the linseed meal and to O's great delight the motion was carried on the spot.'[15]

On board *Terra Nova*, the scene was one of frantic activity and last minute preparation, intermingled with a constant flow of well wishers and visitors all eager to get a last look at the explorers. The expedition was a major public event and the people of New Zealand were especially generous, lavishing the party with gifts ranging from free coal to frozen chunks of choice lamb. Some visitors left an indelible mark by scratching their names on the ship's paintwork, which a tetchy Oates found 'rather sickening.'

However, there were also under-currents of tension and Scott's favourite bluejacket, Petty Officer Taff Evans, went on a heavy drinking bout, fell in the harbour and had to be rescued. Elsewhere, there was a noisy clash of personalities involving Mrs Kathleen Scott, Teddy Evans' wife, Hilda, and Wilson's wife, Oriana.

Oates was an amused spectator and chronicled the minor fracas in the style of a newspaper report on a boxing match, though using his own inimitable grammar and spelling. He wrote:

> 'Mrs Scott and Mrs Evans have had a magnificent battle, they tell me it was a draw after fifteen rounds. Mrs Wilson flung herself into the fight after the tenth round and there was more blood and hair flying about the hotel than you see in a Chicargo (*sic*) slaughter house in a month, the husbands got a bit of the backwash and there is a certain amount of coolness which I hope they won't bring into the hut with them, however it won't hurt me even if they do.'[16]

Soon, however, it was time for more important matters and with preparations complete it was time for the *Terra Nova* to head south. The great adventure, the reason Oates had ditched his army career, was finally under way in earnest.

15

Footprints in the snow

*T*erra Nova eased slowly out of Lyttelton and went down the coast to Port Chalmers where she picked up the last few sacks of coal that could be stowed on the teeming decks. Shortly before 3 pm on 29 November 1910 the little ship sailed sluggishly towards the Southern Ocean, the most dangerous waters on earth. Crowds lined the quays to bid an enthusiastic last farewell and the hopes of all those on board were high.

Terra Nova resembled a floating farmyard. On deck the chained dogs yelped and the ponies, encased in their tight stalls, presented a sorrowful picture as they struggled to keep their feet in the rolling seas. All around bags of coal were stacked and every available space above and below decks was utilised to accommodate vital supplies and equipment.

Oates had placed fifteen of the animals under the forecastle and the remaining four on the port side of the forehatch. Alongside the makeshift stables were four or five tons of fodder, where Tom Crean had mischievously smuggled aboard and hidden a pet rabbit. The rabbit later surprised everyone by giving birth to seventeen young ones. Crean only added to the surprise of the occasion by promising 22 different people that they could each have a pet rabbit.

Many of the men, especially Ponting and the young scientists who had not yet gained their sea-legs, suffered badly from seasickness in the choppy waters and could barely move from their bunks. There was scarcely enough room below decks for the jumble of officers, sailors, scientists and adventurers who were jammed together cheek by jowl. Some 24 officers from the landing and ship's party were squeezed into the modest wardroom and the seamen had to share hammocks, one man climbing in as another left for his watch. The discomfort was made worse because the ponies' stalls had been built directly above their quarters and the animals' foul-smelling urine seeped through the leaky decks onto their clothing and hammocks.

However, the immediate concern was the seaworthiness of the ship. Campbell, an experienced seafarer, said 'we must hope for a fine passage' and Gran, a newcomer to the sea, prayed '. . . let's hope we don't run into bad weather'.

Oates, who understood and respected the sea, was primarily concerned with the safety of the ponies and knew that the rough waters of the Southern Ocean posed a serious threat. In his last letter to his mother from New Zealand he had written:

'I only pray we don't have any heavy weather going south, or there is bound to be trouble.' [1]

Dedication. Oates took personal charge of the nineteen ponies on the Terra Nova's *perilous journey to the ice. During the hurricane which threatened to sink the ship, Oates stayed on duty for 60 hours without a break. (SPRI)*

The concern was well placed and less than 48 hours out of New Zealand, *Terra Nova* ran into a full-blown gale which threatened to send the entire expedition to the bottom of the ocean. As the barometer sank, the winds roared to Force 10, between 55 and 63 mph on the Beaufort Scale or just below hurricane force. The ship became increasingly unstable as screaming gusts of wind whipped up the seas, sending tons of water pouring over the sides. *Terra Nova* was soon at the full mercy of the Southern Ocean, occasionally toppling over at the crazy angle of 40° under the onslaught.

At one point about ten precious coal sacks on deck broke adrift and threatened to damage some cans of petrol. There was no option but to dump the stray bags overboard, even though it represented a serious loss to *Terra Nova's* steaming capacity.

The ponies suffered badly in the tumult and found it difficult to stay upright in the rolling, pitching seas which sent them crashing back and forth into the sides of their stalls. The dogs, chained up in the middle of the ship, were drenched and forlorn and their long pathetic whines could be heard over the roaring winds. In one miraculous moment, the force of the seas snapped the chain holding one of the dogs and swept him overboard. Seconds later another wave washed the hapless animal back on board.

Oates, ably assisted by the willing Atkinson, faced a daunting task to save the ponies, staying in the bow of the ship throughout the crisis at risk to his own life. Anton, the groom, was horribly seasick and barely capable of helping.

Waves of 35 ft battered the ship as Oates fought a desperate battle to keep the ponies on their feet. Evans recalled seeing his 'strong brown face illuminated by a swinging lamp' and that he seemed to be physically lifting the wretched ponies to their feet as the ship lurched heavily. One pony slipped over eight times at the height of the storm, but was somehow restored to its feet. Another sank to the floor and had to be winched up on all fours using a large canvas sling. Oates was amazed that any of the ponies remained upright for more than five minutes at a time and as the storm intensified, he feared the worst.

Bowers recalled that Oates and Atkinson 'worked like Trojans' but could not prevent one of the ponies slipping over and breaking its leg. Even Bowers, an irrepressible optimist, concluded that the dogs '. . . looked finished and the ponies were finishing'. Evans, in awe at the huge efforts made by Oates to save the ponies, wrote:

> 'One felt somehow, glancing into the ponies' stalls, which Captain
> Scott and I frequently visited together, that Oates' very strength itself

123

inspired his animals with confidence. He himself appeared quite unconscious of any personal suffering, although his hands and feet must have been absolutely numbed by the cold and wet.'[2]

Water continued to pour in and many on board feared that the ship might founder when the bilge pumps became clogged with coal dust and stopped working, filling the holds with freezing water. In desperation, the men grabbed buckets and anything else which would carry water. A human chain was quickly formed and they baled for their lives.

Williams, the ship's engineer, and Davies, the carpenter, managed to cut a hole in the engine-room bulkhead to gain access to the blocked pump. Bowers and Evans, two of the smallest men on board, crawled through the tiny gap and, standing up to their necks in icy cold water, finally cleared the blockage.

The pumps began shifting water again and the worst of the crisis had passed. Happily for the stricken vessel, the gale also began to ease after a relentless hammering, which had lasted almost 48 hours. But a second pony succumbed after falling so badly that Oates was unable to get the beast upright again. In the black humour of sailors, the two dead ponies were quickly named Davy and Jones.

Oates, not given to exaggeration, confessed that he 'could not remember having a worse time' during the storm. Ponting recalled that it was 'rather too close a call for all of us' and Debenham said that at the height of the storm, 'our chances were 100 to 1 in favour of foundering'. Scott, ignoring the fearsome reputation of the Southern Ocean, felt it was 'bad luck' to strike a gale in these seas. But he conceded that another gale soon after would have 'disastrous results'.

He also reasoned that the ponies' suffering could not be judged by human standards. He believed, for example, that ponies were the type of animal that did not need to lie down because they have especially tough ligaments in their legs which take their weight 'without strain'. It is not known where Scott had gained his knowledge of horses but he was badly mistaken because horses far prefer to sleep lying down, although they will adapt and sleep standing for short periods, resting their feet alternately.

As the winds dropped off and the seas grew calmer, Oates began the unhappy task of hoisting two dead ponies through the forecastle skylight and into their watery graves. He then climbed into his bunk, which was soaking wet from the deluge, for a few hours well-earned sleep. Oates had been on his feet for 60 hours. It was a memorable act of endurance and fortitude which, more than anything, earned him the lasting admiration of his colleagues and finally dismissed any lingering doubts about the calibre of the quiet, unassuming cavalry officer.

The storm had left its mark on the expedition and there was little doubt that they had been lucky to escape with their lives. They had lost two ponies, one dog, about ten tons of coal, 65 gallons of petrol and a case of biologists' spirits. It could have been far worse.

A few days later, in calmer seas, the men saw their first iceberg and on 9 December, the *Terra Nova* entered the 400-mile wide pack-ice which encircles the Antarctic Continent like a girdle. In the early hours of 10 December, the ship crossed the Antarctic Circle (66° 33') and they sensed at last that the expedition was really under way.

Terra Nova made painfully slow progress through the pack, a mixture of open water and floating ice, which is constantly on the move at the behest of ocean currents and winds. The ship stuttered backwards and forwards for about three

Outsider. Oates, a member of the landed gentry and a professional soldier, was an outsider among the sailors and scientists crammed into the wardroom of Terra Nova *as the expedition headed south in 1910. Oates (standing second right) is watched by Scott, sitting rear centre. The expedition's other outsider, Cecil Meares, is also standing (fourth right). (SPRI)*

weeks in the hope of finding a suitable route through the maze in search of open seas.

The delay enabled the men to get off the ship, stretch their legs on the surrounding ice floes and to try out their skis. True to type, the sporty Oates, stripped to the waist, donned ski goggles and was among the first to try skiing under the expert eye of Gran. On one occasion he fell through the ice and had to be hauled out, though he was none the worse for his first icy ducking. However, he never quite mastered the art and found skis more a cumbersome irritant than a vital aid to travel on the ice.

The lull gave Scott time to assess the condition of the ponies. The storm had demonstrated their vulnerability to bad weather and Scott, who knew that conditions in the south were significantly worse, wrote in his diary:

'. . . I'm anxious, anxious about these animals of ours.'[3]

While he confided his fears to his diary, Scott was unable to convey a similar message to Oates, the person who was best placed to understand and deal with the inadequacies of the animals. The problem lay in the personalities, with Scott a complex person who found it difficult to confide in others and Oates a straightforward man of few words who was curt and sardonic. Their most common shared trait was introversion. The two introverts found it increasingly difficult to communicate and the more strained the relationship became, the harder they found it to reach the same wavelength.

Another breakdown in communications arose a little later when one of the weaker ponies collapsed and was brought out onto the deck for some fresh air and exercise. Scott wondered why Oates had not taken the opportunity of exercising all the ponies while the *Terra Nova* was stationary in the pack ice. But he did not appear to have mentioned his concerns to the person in charge of the animals. He simply wrote in his diary:

'Oates is unremitting in his attention and care of the animals, but I don't think he quite realises that whilst in the pack the ship must remain steady and that, therefore, a certain limited scope for movement and exercise is afforded by the open deck on which the sick animal now stands.'[4]

Oates took the initiative a few days later on 2 January and moved five of the ponies out their stalls for the first time in 38 days. It was an opportunity for the poor beasts to stretch their legs and for Oates and Anton to shovel away the 3-ft pile of rotting manure which had accumulated in each stall. A clean-up was

essential since the foul combination of urine and excreta had infected the horses'
feet with a complaint commonly called thrush. It may also have contributed to
lameness which afflicted some animals later in the expedition.

After almost three weeks tip-toeing through the labyrinth of the pack ice,
Terra Nova finally emerged into open seas and resumed her journey to the
Antarctic coastline, finally reached on 3 January 1911. Initially, Scott had
planned to land at Cape Crozier, which lies on the eastern extremity of Ross
Island, close to where the Great Ice Barrier meets the Ross Sea. *Terra Nova* was
brought close to the edge of the barrier and the imposing white cliffs which
towered over the ship.

A boat was lowered to find a suitable landing place and Oates joined Scott,
Wilson, Campbell and others on the brief reconnoitre of the locality. But heavy
seas made a landing impossible and the men in the whaler had their doubts
confirmed when a large chunk of ice broke off from the cliff-face a few hundred
yards away and plunged into the sea with a resounding crash.

Hopes of landing at Cape Crozier were promptly abandoned and *Terra Nova*
turned west towards McMurdo Sound on the other side of the island, near to
where *Discovery* had berthed ten years earlier. A day later, the ship steamed
alongside the rocky western shore of the island to a headland originally found by
the *Discovery* party, which had been dubbed The Skuary because flocks of the
hawk-like skua birds had colonised the site.

The tongue of land had been formed by old lava from the nearby Mount Erebus
and although covered with loose cinders, it was frozen solid a few inches below
the surface. Scott decided it was a suitably stable spot for a base camp and named
the headland Cape Evans after his second-in-command.

Cape Evans, Ross Island, sits beneath the smouldering slopes of the world's
most southerly volcano, Mount Erebus, the smoking beacon which rises to
12,400 ft (3,3779 m). The island is jammed against the Great Ice Barrier, the vast
triangular-shaped floating sheet of ice surrounded by land and covering an area
larger than France. In a warmer climate, it would be an enormous bay. The Barrier,
today called the Ross Ice Shelf after its discoverer, Sir James Clark Ross, is a flat,
featureless gateway to the Transantarctic Mountains, which lead up to 10,000 ft,
(over 3,000 m), to the Polar Plateau and South Pole itself.

Work began immediately to unload the animals and equipment and, most
important of all, to build a hut for the 25 men who would spend winter at Cape
Evans before setting out for the Pole the following spring. Speed was essential
because tons of supplies and equipment had to be dumped onto the Barrier in
preparation for the following year's journey to the Pole. But this had to be

completed before winter darkness descended in mid-April and temperatures plummeted.

Under the watchful, paternalistic eye of Oates, the seventeen surviving ponies were among the first items to be offloaded. Each animal was ushered into a horsebox by a mixture of shoves and pushes and Oates' gentle persuasion before being lowered onto the ice by block and tackle which was hung from the yardarm.

The animals had suffered badly from the ordeal of the trip across the Southern Ocean, but relished their new-found freedom and were soon rolling about in the snow and kicking their legs in the air. However, the skittish behaviour could not disguise a worrying decline in their condition. All seventeen had grown thin, their hair was falling out and some had been attacked by a nasty skin irritation, which explained why they were so eager to scratch themselves by rolling in the snow.

The men worked flat out to unload supplies before the *Terra Nova* was forced to escape the ice and depart for New Zealand. They rose at 5 am and kept up a constant procession between the ship and the fast-emerging hut. Debenham estimated he travelled over 25 miles a day on the ice in a series of round-trips to the ship.

Oates released less than half the ponies to the operation, each hauling sledges laden with up to 1,100 lbs (500 kgs) of supplies. Five of the animals were not considered fit enough, two regarded as too weak and three required some 'breaking in' before being put to work. Oates felt that some ponies, who were used to firmer surfaces at home, were particularly nervous about keeping their footing on the slippery ice. The working ponies performed creditably and Scott conceded that he was 'astonished' at the strength of the beasts, which helped to ease his underlying fears about the effectiveness of the animals.

In contrast, the dogs struggled, partly because they were badly out of condition after the sea journey and partly because – Meares and Dimitri aside – the other drivers lacked the necessary skill or experience to handle a team. Handling dog teams requires practice and patience but no one had thought of instructing the men who would be driving dogs before *Terra Nova* departed. Commands to the dogs, for example, had to be delivered in Russian and Scott freely admitted that he frequently forgot the correct words at the crucial moment.

The motorised tractors, spluttering along at a pedestrian 3 mph, were a disappointment and suffered many irritating breakdowns. On 8 January calamity struck. The third tractor was moving slowly away from the ship when it suddenly crashed through weak ice and sank without trace in over 700 ft of water. Scott said it was a 'day of disaster'. With the dogs and two other tractors not performing as well as expected, it also meant that Scott would now have to rely even more heavily on Oates' poor squad of ponies to carry vital supplies and equipment. It was not a cheerful prospect.

The hut was erected just two weeks after landing at Cape Evans and made habitable for the 25 men who would spend a long winter incarcerated in the frail-looking 50 ft × 25 ft (15 m × 7.5 m) wooden building. The hut was insulated with layers of dry seaweed in quilted sacks, while outside the pony fodder was stacked against the building to provide another barrier against the hostile winter. Stables were erected outside on the north-west side by piling up 6-ft walls of fodder and attaching a roof of rafters and tarpaulins.

A few home comforts were quickly installed, including a gramophone, which brought an immediate and welcome touch of home to the desolate scene. Before long, the cold air around Cape Evans was punctured with the metallic crackle of Dame Nellie Melba, Harry Lauder and Enrico Caruso echoing across the icy landscape.

Scott was undoubtedly impressed with Oates' skill in handling the frequently difficult ponies. After so long in confinement and suddenly being forced into the hard labour of dragging heavy loads on slippery ice, it was no surprise that the animals were unpredictable and high-spirited. Several bolted, scattering their loads across the ice, while others kicked and tried to bite anyone who came near. Oates described them as a 'fairly rough and obstreperous lot'. But Scott admitted:

'Oates is splendid with them – I do not know what we should do without him.'[5]

It was also evident the ponies were an uneven lot with widely different strengths and weakness. Blossom, Blucher and Jehu struggled to keep up and had clearly taken a fearful battering from the long sea journey. Punch and Nobby were regarded as good workers, while Christopher and Hackenschmidt – named after a famous wrestler of the day – were vicious, dangerous beasts capable of taking a bite out of anyone who strayed too close.

Cherry-Garrard said Christopher had come south to initiate the inhabitants into 'all the vices of civilisation'. He felt that Oates' management of the animals 'might have proved a model to any governor of a lunatic asylum'.

Oates reached a more pertinent judgement. To the privacy of his own notebook, Oates damned the ponies and on the eve of their first proper journey he delivered a brief but withering verdict on their suitability. He wrote:

'A more unpromising lot of ponies to start a journey such as ours it would be almost impossible to conceive.'[6]

The journey in question was a vital one to lay down depots for the march to the Pole the following year. The trip, which had to be completed before winter darkness enveloped Cape Evans, would be built around fifteen of the seventeen ponies. The two remaining animals had been given to Campbell for his proposed journey to King Edward VII Land. The two remaining tractors, which constantly broke down and were clearly unsuitable for the terrain, would be left behind. The experiment with motors had failed before it started.

The depot-laying journey was a vital part of Scott's plan for the Pole. The aim was to carry well over one ton of supplies to two depots on the Barrier. The first, called Corner Camp, would be placed about 45 miles from Cape Evans at the point where sledging parties turned due south away from the land for the march over the Barrier to the mountains and on to the Pole.

The second, to be called One Ton Depot, was due to be built approximately 160 miles (180 statute miles) out onto the Barrier at 80° and was reckoned to be as far south as the expedition would be able to take supplies in the first year. The more food and fuel the men could leave on the autumn trek, the less they would have to carry over the ice on the main journey the following spring.

Scott, too, had serious misgivings about the ponies but he chose not to discuss them with the men, least of all Oates. He recorded in his diary:

> 'Some of the ponies are not turning out so well as I expected; they are slow walkers and must inevitably impede the faster ones. Two of the best have been told off for Campbell by Oates, but I must alter the arrangement. Then I am not quite sure they are going to stand the cold well and on this first (depot-laying) journey they may have to face pretty severe conditions. Then of course there is danger of losing them on thin ice or by injury sustained in rough places. Although we have fifteen now, it is by no means certain that we shall have such a number when the main journey is undertaken next season. One can only be careful and hope for the best.'[7]

Oates also had severe reservations about the travel arrangements. He confessed that 'things are not as rosy as they might be'. Far from being a vital cog in the expedition's transport system, Oates knew the animals were a liability. He pointed the finger of blame at Scott. In a letter to his mother, which probably understated his depth of feelings because he did not wish to alarm her, Oates wrote:

> 'Scott and Evans boss the show pretty well and their ignorance about marching with animals is colossal. On several fronts Scott is going on

lines contrary to what I have suggested. However, if I can only persuade him to take a pony himself he will learn a lot this autumn.'[8]

Oates was especially concerned only he and Meares had any real knowledge of handling animals and Meares was fully occupied with the demands of his dog teams. He was also worried that the lines of communication to Scott were unnecessarily complicated. Oates was used to formal chains of command in the army but moaned that running the pony teams was difficult '. . . as there are three people over me to give orders'. In a landing party of only 25 men, he correctly expected far shorter channels of communication with the top.

Oates had begun to develop a severe dislike of Scott, a feeling which had intensified since the party landed at Cape Evans because they inevitably spent more time together than on board ship. Oates saw things as simply black-and-white, while Scott was more cautious and as leader was naturally concerned with the wider issues affecting the expedition. Inevitably he was often called upon to hedge his bets and prioritise decisions. But the intolerant and one-dimensional Oates failed to appreciate that the animals were not the only issue confronting Scott. Oates gave Scott very little slack.

There was a streak of bitterness in Oates which prompted him to question all forms of authority. Right from the start he had been critical of his superiors in the army and his growing misgivings over Scott's leadership were entirely predictable. Oates was not a man who suffered fools gladly and he never sought to ingratiate himself with people he did not respect. He was intolerant of incompetence and inefficiency and could be very blunt with those who fell short of his standards.

He had a strong point with Scott, even if he often neglected to appreciate the bigger picture. Oates was particularly irritated that Scott appeared to ignore his advice and failed to ask for guidance on matters on which Oates was undoubtedly an authority. Scott's weak management left Oates feeling excluded, which grated.

Oates had other reservations. After only a brief time on the ice, Oates was able to spot that the expedition was handicapped by the 'lack of experience in trekking'. Scott, he maintained, had spent 'too much of his time in an office' and added:

'. . . he would 50 times sooner stay in the hut seeing how a pair of Foxs spiral puttees suited him than come out and look at the ponies' legs or a dog's feet – however I suppose I think too much of this having come strate (sic) from a regiment where horses were the first and only real consideration.'[9]

The value of Oates to the expedition was well understood by the more discerning members of the team. Evans, who was having his own problems with Scott, wrote:

> 'No man in our expedition had more common sense than Oates; his whole work was marked with the stamp of thoroughness and reliability, and his field training made him a most welcome tent mate.'[10]

Debenham put his finger on the clash of personalities many years later when he wrote a carefully considered judgement on the pair:

> 'Between Oates, dry and caustic, humorous, objective in his outlook – Scott shy and moody, temperamental and sensitive, quick in mind as in action, with the soul of a poet – there can have been little in common. Their natures jarred on one another.'[11]

Scott had not singled out Oates for special treatment. He was highly-strung and short-tempered and his inability to communicate frustrated many of his colleagues. Scott was no natural leader of men, although strangely he managed to inspire tremendous loyalty in people as diverse as Wilson, Bowers, Crean and Lashly.

Scott was ill-suited to the more intimate confines of a small expedition, where men are clustered together in overcrowded little ships or cramped huts. He was far more comfortable with the relative anonymity of large naval battleships where he could lose himself among hundreds of other officers and seamen.

Scott's sole confidant was Wilson, a slightly unworldly individual who had effectively replaced Evans as Scott's second-in-command. But even Wilson was not privy to all his thoughts. Oates observed that there was 'considerable friction' between Scott and Evans which, he suggested, might make the environment 'uncomfortable' in the crowded, claustrophobic atmosphere of the hut during the long, dark Antarctic winter.

The differences with Scott also prompted Oates to examine his future commitment to the expedition. Only three weeks after reaching Cape Evans, the first doubts about the mission had arisen and the early optimism shown on board *Terra Nova* had evaporated. Oates was no longer sure he wanted to remain in the party a second year if Scott failed to reach the Pole at the first attempt.

Scott had built a contingency against first-time failure to conquer the Pole. Plans had been laid for a second attack in the following Antarctic spring, starting in late 1912 to reach the Pole in early 1913. Oates would be a key figure on any second attempt since Scott would need a new team of ponies to make the march across the Barrier and Oates would be required to repeat his efforts of 1911 with fresh animals.

Oates, to his credit, did not let his differences with Scott affect his judgement over the animals and he took immediate steps to ensure the expedition was equipped with a better team for the second assault on the Pole. Oates was worried that, left to his own devices, Scott might pick another poor team of horses and 'get stuck as he did with this lot'.

Oates' recommendation was that Scott abandon his fascination with white-coated Siberian ponies and switch to Indian mules for the next attempt to reach the Pole. Oates had seen the mules perform on a trip to Tibet and was impressed. He wrote to his old friend, Colonel Haig at Mhow, asking for him to put in a good word with his famous uncle, General Sir Douglas Haig, then head of the British army in India.

Haig agreed to Scott's request for help and sent word to his transport department at Simla to select seven mules for the expedition. After some rudimentary training in hauling sledges, the animals were scheduled to join the Union Steamship Company's liner, *Aparima*, at Calcutta in August in time to meet *Terra Nova* in New Zealand.

But Oates was not sure he would be around to handle the mules when they arrived on the returning *Terra Nova* early in 1912. He confided to Haig:

> 'I am very doubtful myself about staying a second winter and shall come back to the regiment as soon as you have room for me.'[12]

He repeated his doubts to his mother, saying that he did not know whether he would stay a second season and would wait until seeing next year's mail before making a final decision. These comments are contrary to the hints Oates had dropped at around the time of joining the expedition and clearly reflect his disenchantment with Scott. But, as if to contradict himself further, Oates also told his mother and Haig that he was having a 'first class' time with the expedition.

His contradictions went further. Despite his reservations about Scott's leadership qualities, Oates somehow remained optimistic about the venture and even retained a touching faith in Scott's abilities to reach the Pole. In a prophetic note shortly before leaving on the depot-laying journey, he wrote to his mother:

> 'Don't think from what I say that Scott is likely to endanger anyone, it is quite the reverse. . .'[13]

16

The seeds of destruction

T he depot-laying journey, a vital component in Scott's planned conquest of the South Pole, began in a muddle and degenerated into near disaster. It was to have serious implications for Oates and his companions.

In essence, Polar travel of the age was a vicious circle in which men could travel only as far as the weight of food and fuel they could carry. The more they carried, the slower they travelled and the less they carried the shorter distance they would be able to cover. To extend travelling time, supply depots were placed at strategic spots along the route to provide necessary food and fuel for the return leg of the long journey. Right from the start, the journey was plagued with difficulties.

Scott's plan was to move the supplies from the hut at Cape Evans onto the Barrier, dropping off one load at Corner Camp about 45 miles away and then pushing on to One Ton Camp at 80° S, over 160 miles from base camp. Right from the start, the journey was plagued with difficulties.

The obvious route of travelling overland across Ross Island to the Barrier's edge was made difficult by glaciers and icefalls, so Scott decided to move the party over the sheets of sea ice which cling to the foreshore for part of the year. But the ice was breaking up in the Antarctic summer and it was soon clear that this route to the Barrier would be highly dangerous.

Scott opted to move before the ice broke up even more, bringing forward the start day by 24 hours and shifting all the heavy equipment back on board *Terra Nova*. While some men made their way across the sea ice with the ponies, the ship would dump the laden sledges on the Barrier's edge.

The last minute change of plan brought a flurry of activity, with loaded sledges and the dogs laboriously taken back to the ship they had left only three weeks earlier. It needed another exhausting Herculean effort by Bowers, who had now fully assumed the role of quartermaster general. Men worked through the night transferring supplies and Bowers had no sleep for 72 hours in the frantic rush to get under way.

It was a disorderly mess and the party, Cherry-Garrard said, finally left the camp in 'a state of hurry bordering upon panic'.[1]

Terra Nova dropped off the supplies a little nearer to the Barrier at Glacier Tongue, about five miles south of Cape Evans and close to the old *Discovery* hut at Hut Point on the southernmost tip of the island. The men then spent a tiring four days humping boxes and sledging supplies to Safety Camp, about two miles out onto the Barrier, a site chosen because there was no danger of it breaking off into the sea.

The short trip from Cape Evans confirmed the inadequacies of the ponies. The animals, struggling in the soft snow and slushy sea ice, found the going very hard. They frequently sank deep into the snow and often broke through the fragile layers of ice near the Barrier edge. They also suffered badly from the penetrating cold.

At one point, Oates told Cherry-Garrard that he would 'sit down and cry' if another pony fell into one of the gaping holes in the ice and within minutes, Guts was wallowing in a mess of brash ice and snow, with only its head and forelegs visible. Oates supervised the hurried rescue and held back his tears.

Two days later on 28 January, the depot-laying party of twelve men, eight ponies and 26 dogs finally managed to get away. It was a monumental task, with the party carrying close to 2½ tons (2,400 kgms) of supplies, including fourteen weeks food and fuel for the men. Oates, Bowers, Cherry-Garrard, Gran, Atkinson, Crean, Forde and Keohane each led a pony and the two dog teams were under Scott and Wilson, and Meares and Teddy Evans.

The inexperience of the party was readily apparent, despite the previous few weeks of activity shifting supplies back and forth between the *Terra Nova* and the hut. Only Scott, Wilson and Crean of the twelve had any sledging mileage under their belts, although Gran was an experienced skier and Meares had driven dogs.

In addition, the men were physically tired, having worked flat out offloading supplies and erecting the hut since the *Terra Nova* sailed into McMurdo Sound three weeks earlier. The last-minute change of plan added to the workload at a time when they should have been resting before the exertions of the coming journey. The men frequently turned in at midnight, too tired even to remove their clothes and considered themselves lucky if they slept until 5 am.

Unfortunately, lacking in experience, Atkinson carelessly developed snow-blindness and a bad blister on his heel, which soon began to suppurate. Temperatures dropped as soon as the party headed south over the Barrier and Gran cheerfully recorded that 'It isn't funny to be ill here'. Atkinson could not travel any further and with his options limited, Scott ordered the experienced and dependable Crean to remain behind to look after him, thus removing one of the few seasoned ice travellers from the assignment.

After a quick reorganisation, the depleted group moved south again on 2 February, travelling by night because the surfaces were firmer in the lower temperatures which made it a shade easier for the ponies. It also allowed the ponies to rest in the daytime when the marginally higher temperatures brought a little welcome relief to the animals.

Nevertheless, the ponies, who started hauling loads of between 800 and 900 lbs (360–400 kgs), struggled and were plainly not up to the task. Jimmy Pigg, the pony led by Irishman Patsy Keohane, went lame on the first day and Bowers' animal, Uncle Bill, was reported 'weak in the foreleg'. A few days later, the ponies were overwhelmed by their first encounter with an Antarctic blizzard. Scott said

First steps to disaster. Members of the depot-laying party pictured on 26 January 1911. Oates (second right) clashed with Scott (sixth right) over the positioning of the key supply cache, which would be a major factor in the unfolding tragedy. (SPRI)

the animals were 'much shaken' and warned that they could not stand more blizzards 'in their present state'.

But Scott was determined to put a brave face on events and continued to make light of Oates' well-known misgivings. He told his diary:

'The Soldier took a gloomy view of the situation, but he is not an optimist.'[2]

Scott ignored the reality of the situation, probably because by admitting any weakness on the part of the ponies, he would be accepting that he had made a bad mistake in sending Meares to buy the animals. Scott had made up his mind that the ponies were the best way of carrying his supplies over the Barrier and nothing, it seemed, would force him to change his mind.

Oates was more realistic and accepted the grim reality. In a hastily scribbled note to his mother, which was considerably more frank than his earlier missives, he declared:

'The surface of the barrier is very bad for travelling as the summer sun has melted the crust on the snow to a certain extent and the ponies break through almost to their knees. These poor ponies are having a perfectly wretched time, they have their summer coats on and this wind which is blowing now is bitterly cold for them, I don't know how they will get on atal (sic).'[3]

Oates had also spotted the inevitable problems of using many different forms of transport. The depot party was already using ponies and dogs, who travelled at different speeds in a long, strung-out cavalcade over the ice. To add to the procession, the Pole journey in the spring would see the men in harnesses man-hauling their sledges, possibly on skis, for hundreds of miles. There was also the vague possibility that the troublesome motor tractors would be revived in time for the main journey, increasing the modes of travel to four.

It required another important item of organisation for Scott to co-ordinate the different departures and arrival times of his fleet. Shortly before the party left Cape Evans, Oates dryly commented:

'It is trying to work three kinds of transport that knocks me. They can't do it in the army, so I am jolly sure Scott is not going to.'[4]

The muddling continued unabated. To his own amazement, Scott found that the ponies were more sure-footed and travelled better wearing snowshoes, the simple round bamboo devices which help spread the pressure of a horse's hoof-print on the

soft surface. It has the same effect as a human on ski. The weight of an unshod
horse's hoof-print is estimated at around 15 lbs per square inch, almost five times
that of a dog. Remarkably, they had brought only one set of the special shoes, which
had been developed in Norway and were known as *hestersko* or *hester-trugers*.

It was another case of Scott and – to some extent – Oates not learning the
lessons of recent history. Shackleton had taken ponies on the *Nimrod* expedition
only three years earlier and in his book, published a year before *Terra Nova* sailed,
he reported on 'poor beasts' sinking in the soft slushy snow of the Barrier. Even
a casual glance at his book, *The Heart of the Antarctic*, would have shown the
crucial importance of snowshoes for the animals. Observers later said that
Shackleton would have reached the South Pole in 1909 if he had taken *hester-
trugers* for his ponies.

The oversight this time was the fault of Oates. He had little experience of
travelling with horses over ice and snow. In the same way he failed to grasp the
value of skis, Oates also failed to comprehend the value of spreading the weight
of the animal's hoof-print on the ice. Instead Oates summarily dismissed the shoes
as ineffective. In his private log on the ponies, Oates had inserted a cryptic note:

> 'The ponies are unshod but have snow shoes which I believe will be
> an unmitigated nuisance to us – the snow shoes I mean.'[5]

Scott saw the light before Oates and promptly ordered Wilson and Meares to
race back to Cape Evans with their dogs to retrieve the other pony shoes. But luck
was against them and they returned empty-handed because the sea ice had now
disappeared altogether, shutting off the route between the hut and the Barrier. To
round off the hapless episode, the one solitary set of snowshoes was then
inadvertently left behind at camp on the fourth day out. Gran, giving a perfect
example of how humans can travel quickly over snow with skis, dashed back to
retrieve the shoes.

Temperatures sank further as the party penetrated deeper onto the Barrier and
the daily march became a gruesome torture for the woeful ponies. They were
particularly vulnerable to the cold and were getting thinner by the day, probably
because they were not eating enough to compensate for the hard work.

Scott described one poor beast as 'a miserable scarecrow'. At night, the animals
had to be stopped from supplementing their feed by eating their head ropes and
Wilson, a doctor, observed:

> 'They are dreadfully hungry, poor beasts. I think their compressed
> fodder isn't very feeding for them.'[6]

Oates knew at least some of the animals would not survive even the limited depot journey and he urged Scott to push the weakest ponies as far as possible before killing them and caching their carcasses as food for both dogs and men. The mawkish Scott was appalled at the prospect of slaughtering the animals and rejected the suggestion out of hand. Although he admitted it was 'pathetic' to watch the animals floundering in the soft snow, he could not see the logic of Oates' suggestion. He let his heart rule his head.

Scott first ignored the advice of his expert and then resorted to rebuking Oates, writing in his diary:

> 'The Soldier takes a gloomy view of everything, but I've come to see that this is a characteristic of him.
>
> The more I see of the matter, the more certain I am that we must save all the ponies to get better value out of them next year. It would have been ridiculous to have worked some out this year as the Soldier wished.'[7]

Scott went beyond simply questioning Oates' temperament. He also had major doubts about his well-established judgement on horses, which was altogether different. Scott, the beginner with animals, questioned the judgement of a man who had grown up with horses, had ten years military experience in the saddle and had managed his own personal stable of mounts. In an extraordinary diary entry, which was later excluded from the published version, Scott wrote:

> 'Oates is certainly a poor judge of the amount of work which different surfaces curtail. Oates does not show well as a judge of the animals' capacity for covering distance.'[8]

Oates, a far more realistic and unsentimental character, knew his proposal of pushing the animals to the limit and then slaughtering them would be far kinder to the distressed beasts. The alternative was to cut the depot journey short to ensure that the weakening horses were taken back to Cape Evans, although this would leave the Polar party exposed to badly placed caches of supplies.

What Oates was proposing was humanely putting the animals out of their misery at the end of their useful lives and ensuring that supply depots were built at the correct place. But Scott could not accept the suggestion at face value and refused to budge.

The clash between Scott and Oates over the ponies need never have taken place if Scott had been more forthcoming and explained his plans for the depot-laying journey to the key members of the expedition before they set out from Cape Evans. The issue of equipping the horses with snowshoes, for example, might have been resolved long before the party had marched onto the Barrier and not when it was too late to remedy the problem.

But it was not merely Oates who was excluded from the strategic planning. Scott kept everyone in the dark. The plans for the depot journey remained a closely guarded secret from the whole party until 30 January when the men were already out on the Barrier and there was little scope for modification or debate.

The weakness of Scott's management technique was soon recognised by other members of the depot-laying party. Debenham weighed up the prospects of beating Amundsen to the Pole and shrewdly observed:

> 'If the Owner (Scott) will consult the senior men I think it can be done but if he keeps them in the dark as they were on this depot trip things are likely to go wrong.'[9]

The worst fears about the animals were confirmed when two of the ponies, Blucher and Blossom, virtually ceased to function and a third, Jimmy Pigg, became very weak. Evans noticed that 'even their eyes were dull and lustreless' and Cherry-Garrard gloomily observed that 'all the care in the world' could do little for the beasts. He added:

> 'It must be confessed at once that some of these ponies were very poor material and it must be conceded that Oates who was in charge of them started with a very great handicap. From first to last, it was Oates' consummate management, seconded by the care and kindness of the ponies' leaders, which obtained results which often exceeded the most sanguine hopes.'[10]

The contrast with the dog teams could not have been more marked. Despite the conditions, the dogs had overcome their initial problems and now raced along. They travelled so well that each morning Meares and his animals had to sit around in the cold to ensure they all arrived in camp at roughly the same moment.

Scott never quite understood or trusted dog teams and continued to cling onto the mistaken belief that the ponies were better suited to ice travel. He did not believe that Amundsen's dog teams would survive the Antarctic winter. His mistrust stemmed from the *Discovery* expedition when he had failed to learn the skill of driving dogs and instead chose to distrust them. On one journey in 1902, Scott took over a team of dogs which had been working smoothly for another officer throughout the morning. By afternoon, the animals were in disarray and

Scott was moaning that '. . . the dogs have not pulled well today'. The patient training and understanding was totally foreign to him.

Scott had also developed an unreasonable dislike of his own dog expert, Meares, whom he regarded as lazy. In the same way that he questioned Oates' judgement on horses, Scott expressed similar doubts about Meares, though Meares, too, had been hired because of his expertise with animals. In one disdainful diary entry, he lumped Meares with the dogs saying ' . . they will never go the pace we look for'. On one occasion he scornfully dismissed the driver and the animals with the comment: 'Meares, I think, rather imagined himself racing to the Pole and back on a sledge.' The Norwegians, 400 miles away in the Bay of Whales, were preparing to do precisely that.

Oates had also begun the expedition with misgivings about the dogs. But he soon changed his mind after realising that they were far better suited to travelling across the ice than the painfully inadequate ponies. Oates, unlike Scott, was prepared to trust what he saw and was big enough to change his mind.

The depot-laying party's progress was slowed by blizzards and on 12 February, just two weeks after setting off and about halfway to their goal, Scott bowed to the inevitable and cut the three weaker ponies from the group. He decided to send them back to base with Evans, Forde and Keohane, ignoring the advice to slaughter the animals and deposit their carcasses as food for next year.

The three men were around 100 miles from Cape Evans and faced a difficult trip home with the pitiable animals. A blizzard struck shortly after separating from the main party and Forde's animal, Blucher, simply gave up the will to live. The pony, wracked by a combination of exposure and cold, lay down in the snow and refused to move. Forde, a rugged Irish seaman, was close to tears and had to watch Keohane end Blucher's misery by cutting the animal's throat. A little later, Keohane's own pony, the emaciated Blossom, also staggered to a halt, fell to the ground and died. Only the third, Jimmy Pigg, managed to get back to Safety Camp at the Barrier's edge.

The main party, with its reduced contingent of five ponies, was still aiming to reach 80° south, but it had also hit problems. Weary Willie, living up to his name, strayed behind the main group and was attacked by the plainly hungry dog teams who saw a free meal of fresh horseflesh in the doleful beast.

Temperatures on 15 February plunged to $-15°F$ ($-26°C$) and the unhappy ponies were close to cracking. Thin, worn out and hungry, they moved ever more slowly and stopped frequently in the soft snow which had been whipped up by bitter winds blowing from the Pole itself.

The crisis between Scott and Oates over the management of the animals was coming to a head and once again Scott angrily rejected Oates' suggestion of killing the weaker animals and leaving their carcasses. Scott said Oates' recommendation was 'ridiculous'.

What followed was a crucial exchange between the irrational, squeamish Scott and the practical, unemotional Oates. The pair confronted each other and Scott blurted out that he felt 'quite sick' over the animals' daily sufferings. The decisive exchange continued:

> *Scott*: 'I have had more than enough of this cruelty to animals and I am not going to defy my feelings for the sake of a few days' march.'
> *Oates*: 'Sir, I am afraid that you will come to regret not taking my advice.'
> *Scott*: 'Regret it or not, my dear Oates, I have taken my decision as a Christian gentleman.'[11]

A day later, on 17 February, Scott called a halt and established One Ton Depot at 79°28½' south, about 133 miles (155 miles statute) from Cape Evans and less than halfway across the Barrier. A 6-ft high cairn of snow was built and inside was stored 2,181 lbs (990 kgs) of food, fuel and other equipment. Scott said it was 'a pity' the party had not managed to reach the target of 80° but the depot would give the expedition a 'good leg up' for the next year's march.

The depot was about 32 miles (35 statute miles) farther north than planned or 32 miles further from the Pole. Fit, well-fed men in decent weather could cover the extra distance in three or four days. But a year later the returning Polar party would have been on the march for over four months in rapidly deteriorating autumnal weather and the 32 miles would represent the difference between life and death. Oates' outburst could not have been more prophetic.

Oates was feeling the cold and his nose showed worrying signs of frostbite as they built the cairn. Scott casually observed that 'some of our party will find spring journeys pretty trying'. Oates' nose, he wrote, was 'always on the point of being frostbitten'.[12]

Scott, perhaps stung by Oates' challenge to his authority, decided to split his forces and hurry back to base camp. He joined Meares, Wilson and Cherry-Garrard with the faster-moving dogs and left Oates, Bowers and Gran to plod their weary way home with the five worn-out ponies. It may have been a slight towards Oates, but after the rows and more solemn atmosphere of travelling with Scott, the men probably welcomed the more relaxed informal environment of their party.

The journey also enabled Oates to settle an important difference with Gran. Much to Gran's puzzlement, the pair had never quite seen eye to eye since leaving

England. Oates once told his mother that 'I can't stand this Norwegian chap' and
Gran remembered:

> 'Oates was a completely closed book to me until I shared camp life
> with him. . . I (had) gained the impression that I did not find grace in
> his eyes.'[13]

It was nothing personal. Oates had developed an intense dislike of virtually all
foreigners which bordered on xenophobia. Oates' upbringing had given him the
superior English attitude towards other cultures and his army life, itself largely
involved in subduing native populations in every corner of the Empire, had
intensified his misgivings and lack of respect for others. Even the Australians in
the expedition were taunted and occasionally felt uneasy in Oates' company.

It was impossible to disguise Oates' unpleasant aversion in the close confines
of a small tent. Many years later Gran recalled a telling conversation:

> 'On the return journey from One Ton Depot, Oates told me straight
> out what he had against me was not personal; it was just that I was a
> foreigner. With all his heart he hated foreigners, because all foreigners
> hated England. The rest of the world led by Germany were just waiting
> to attack his Motherland and destroy it if they could.
>
> I was just about to reply when Bowers quickly intervened: "Could
> be something in what you say, Oates but all the same I wager what you
> will that Gran would be with us if England is forced into war through
> no fault of her own."
>
> "Would you?" asked Oates. "Of course," I replied and the next
> instant he grasped my hand.
>
> From this moment, the closed book opened and Oates and I became
> the best of friends.'[14]

The relationship may also have been cemented by the growing doubts which
they shared about the competence of the expedition. As they prepared to return
home from One Ton Depot, Gran recorded a cryptic note in his diary:

> 'I am rather disappointed and foresee difficulties with the complicated
> transport arrangements. Of one thing I am certain, that we shall need
> luck if we are to reach the Pole next year.'[15]

Oates added his own distinctively sardonic touch to proceedings by betting
Gran a biscuit that Blucher, Forde's sickly pony which had been forced to return
to base camp, would be dead by 19 February. Unknown to Oates or Gran, Blucher

144

was already dead. Oates followed this minor triumph by placing a similar wager on the demise of Jimmy Pigg, which proved to be misplaced pessimism.

The three men and five ponies finally reached Safety Camp on 25 February where a great shock awaited them. Amundsen's expedition had been discovered camped at the Bay of Whales, about 400 miles further east from McMurdo Sound. The astonishing discovery, which had been made by Campbell in the *Terra Nova*, answered all lingering questions about Amundsen's intentions. He was preparing to race Scott to the Pole.

The *Terra Nova* had inadvertently stumbled on Amundsen's ship, *Fram*, while searching for a place to land the six-man party under Campbell, which intended to explore the nearby King Edward VII Land. Campbell, a Norwegian speaker, strode across the ice and politely opened up a diplomatic channel between the two expeditions.

Campbell and two colleagues were invited for breakfast on the *Fram* and reciprocated by inviting Amundsen and two Norwegians to *Terra Nova* for lunch. Both meetings were stiffly formal, uncomfortable affairs with each side gently probing for snippets of information about the other's plans.

Amundsen was concerned about Scott's motor tractors and the English were impressed with the Norwegian dog teams. However, they learned little about each other and 30 minutes after lunch, *Terra Nova* steamed away from the Bay of Whales with the electrifying news about their discovery. Amundsen later discovered that some of the *Fram*'s party had caught irritating head colds.

Campbell returned to McMurdo Sound with a note informing Scott about Amundsen's presence and dropped off the two ponies, Hackenschmidt and Jehu, who were now surplus to requirements. Scott was deeply shocked by Campbell's letter and even the scholarly Cherry-Garrard was in pugilistic mood, writing:

> 'For an hour or so we were furiously angry and were possessed with an insane sense that we must go to the Bay of Whales and have it out with Amundsen and his men in some undefined fashion or other.'[16]

Oates took a different approach, not for the first time. He had a professional respect for Amundsen and wrote:

> 'If it comes to a race, Amundsen will have a great chance of getting there as he is a man who has been at this kind of game all his life and he has a hard crowd behind him while we are very young.'[17]

Gran was more aware than anyone of the capabilities of his countrymen and was in no doubt about the outcome of the race to the Pole. He recorded in his diary:

'I believe, from what I have seen, that Amundsen's chances are better than ours. First he is one degree (of latitude) further south than we are and, secondly, his speed is far superior to ours, since our horses are not first class. If we reach the Pole, then Amundsen will reach the Pole and weeks earlier. Our prospects are thus not exactly promising. The only thing that can save Scott is if an accident happens to Amundsen.'[18]

The threat of Amundsen was not the last blow to strike the unhappy depot-laying party. Towards the end of February, the rump of the group had assembled again at Safety Camp where Crean and a fit-again Atkinson were also waiting. With the colder autumn season closing in, it was decided to travel the short distance to Hut Point, the site of the *Discovery* hut a few miles away, and wait for the sea ice to freeze over before completing the return to Cape Evans for over-wintering.

Meares and Wilson galloped off with the dogs and Scott, Oates, Crean, Bowers and Cherry-Garrard followed at a more leisurely pace with the remaining five ponies. Soon after starting, Weary Willie finally succumbed and collapsed on the ice. Instead of ending the doomed animal's suffering with a bullet in the head, Scott irrationally built a protective wall of snow-blocks and decided that he, Oates and Gran would remain behind to nurse the dying pony on its deathbed.

Bowers, Crean and Cherry-Garrard were told to push on for Hut Point with the four other survivors. Weary Willie died shortly after and Gran gloomily recorded:

'Our party is split up and we seem like a defeated army – dispirited and inconsolable.'[19]

Bowers, Crean and Cherry-Garrard soon ran into trouble as they climbed down off the Barrier onto the sea ice between Cape Armitage and nearby Hut Point. Bowers, nominally in charge, decided to rest the tired ponies by making camp on the ice. Bowers was enormously enthusiastic and capable, but a novice in Antarctica, and he badly misjudged the situation by setting up camp on sea ice. After barely two hours rest, the men awoke to find the ice all around had broken up and they were drifting offshore like flotsam in a jumbled sea of icefloes. One pony, Guts, had completely disappeared in the black, freezing water.

Their own floe began to break up and the alarmed men were surrounded by a threatening host of killer whales. Whales were known to attack in groups, often overturning ice floes to tip their prey into the water. Cherry-Garrard recalled that it was a 'quite hopeless situation'. Initially, the men tried leaping from floe to floe in a bid to climb back up onto the Barrier but it was impossible to persuade the ponies to make the same jump across patches of open water.

*On duty. Oates threw
himself into the task of
looking after the woeful
ponies. Ponting's
photograph captures his
firm resolve. (SPRI)*

After six hours of aimless drifting, Crean, the only one with knowledge of the ice, effectively took charge. He bravely volunteered to go for help, jumping from one floe to another and then climbing up the face of the Barrier itself. Despite the immense risk to himself, he scrambled up the Barrier face and, exhausted by his efforts, staggered towards Safety Camp where he met Gran.

Oates, Scott and Crean hurried back to the Barrier edge and managed to haul Bowers and Cherry-Garrard off the floe. Oates tried to dig out a slope to help pull the ponies up onto the Barrier but the ice began to break up and the rescue had to be abandoned. Reluctantly, the men withdrew from the edge and made camp with the ponies still drifting in the icy turmoil, surrounded by predatory whales. Cherry-Garrard heard Scott say: 'This is the end of the Pole.'

A fresh attempt to rescue the stricken ponies was made the following morning. Although they managed to reach the animals on the floe, getting them up onto the Barrier was almost impossible. Oates and Bowers tried to pull Punch over a gap between the ice-floes but the terrified animal struggled and plunged into the icy waters. It was impossible to drag the heavy floundering animal out of the water and Oates was forced to kill the beast in bloody fashion with an ice-pick to the head.

Oates and Bowers somehow managed to pull and cajole Nobby towards safety, finally dragging the reluctant animal up a slope and out of danger. But they had no such luck with Uncle Bill, whose hind legs slipped into the freezing water as the whales circled menacingly. Oates and Bowers dragged him back onto the ice but the pathetic creature lay deathly still and too terrified to move. While Oates and Bowers did not want to abandon the animal to the killer whales, it was clear that the beast was finished. Oates, still splashed with blood from the slaughter of Punch, remarked: 'I shall be sick if I have to kill another horse like that.'[20] Bowers, at Oates' clinical instructions, duly put the animal down with a hefty blow from the ice-pick.

It was the last mournful act of the disastrous depot-laying party. The expedition had lost six of their eight ponies, struggled to comprehend the importance and efficiency of dogs and had compromised the entire mission by not placing the vital supply depot far enough to the south.

The sorry episode had also thrown Scott's complicated transportation plans into total disarray. It meant that, as Markham wished, the expedition would have to resort to the grim ordeal of man-hauling sledges for much of the 1,800 miles (2,890 kms) to the Pole and back.

Another critical point was that, because of the deficiencies of the ponies, Scott now intended to start for the Pole later than originally planned. He had seen what damage the cold weather was capable of inflicting on the ponies and was determined not to risk starting too early in the Antarctic spring when temperatures would be lower. The delayed start, however, would also mean a later return when autumnal temperatures on the Barrier would plunge to dangerously low levels, putting the returning Polar party at serious risk.

After considering the hapless depot-laying journey, Scott told his diary:

'It makes a late start necessary next year.'[21]

Scott's woes were in stark contrast to the sense of well-being 400 miles along the coast at Framheim in the Bay of Whales. The Norwegians, too, had been out on the Barrier laying depots for the spring attack on the Pole but they had emerged largely unscathed.

Amundsen, with almost 120 dogs to call upon, took his sledges and deposited a total of 3 tons (3,050 kgs) of supplies at depots as far south as 82°, at least 150 geographic miles further south than Scott's best-placed depot. While Scott's men struggled to cover more than twelve miles a day, Amundsen's eager and disciplined dogs propelled the Norwegians along at remarkable speeds. The sledges managed up to 25 miles a day with heavy loads and when free of their burden on the journey home, the dogs accelerated to an astonishing 62 miles (99 kms) in one record-breaking day.

After their two depot-laying forays, the Norwegians were better equipped, capable of faster travelling, had stationed their depots nearer the Pole than the British and would be able to start earlier, which meant they would probably avoid the vicious autumnal weather on the return journey.

Even before the race had begun, there was one clear winner.

17

Friends and enemies

The dejected depot party returned to Hut Point in early March and waited for the sea ice to freeze over before making the short trip back to winter base at Cape Evans. The full consequences of not establishing One Ton Depot half a degree further south were far from apparent, although the mood was gloomy as the men pondered the lost ponies and for many, their first struggles travelling over the Barrier. It had been a sobering experience.

It was a frustrating spell in the cramped, poorly equipped little hut and made worse soon after when the men there were joined by Griffith Taylor, Debenham, Wright and Taff Evans, who came in from a trip to the western mountains. Cooking had to be done on an improvised stove using seal blubber which smeared the hut and covered the inhabitants in a greasy black film.

After a month of kicking their heels, Scott's patience ran out and he decided to make a dash for home across the barely frozen ice, encouraged by the steady drop in temperatures as winter advanced. Fortunately, their luck held and the party reached Cape Evans where they discovered that another pony, the vicious Hackenschmidt, had died.

Oates remained behind with a party of seven under Wilson to look after the dogs and ponies. It was a more pleasant interlude in the spacious conditions, though temperatures dipped below −20°F (−29°C). Scott returned on 18 April with a party of eight to supervise the return to Cape Evans, leaving behind the dogs and ponies with Meares and five others who were ordered to travel only when the sea ice had become safely frozen solid.

Oates left his ponies behind and joined Scott on what was supposed to be a routine return journey of little more than fourteen miles. However, conditions in the late autumn were deteriorating fast and it took two days of very difficult

travelling to cover the short distance. When they arrived on 21 April most were
nursing frostbite, another painful reminder of late autumn travel on the ice.

Oates had been away from Cape Evans for nearly three months and only three
days after his return, the sun disappeared for four months. The bleak Antarctic
winter, which on earlier expeditions had driven men to insanity, had begun.

Scott, wisely, ensured the men were kept busy during the winter. The scientists
kept up a steady schedule of biological, meteorological and other work, while
others were deployed preparing supplies and equipment for the spring attack on
the Pole. After dinner the men passed the time reading, playing assorted games
and chatting, often to the welcome background of the gramophone.

The men were also encouraged to exercise as much as possible and there were
regular games of football in the twilight of the late autumn days. Oates captained
one of the sides and stood out as one of the best players alongside Atkinson and
the Petty Officers, Crean and Evans. One of the first games was played in a
howling 30 mph gale and temperatures down to –10°F (–23°C). Most players
came off with touches of frostbite and Gran remembered that the biting frozen air
'took our breath away'.

Away from recreation, Oates had his own concerns. Soon after returning to
Cape Evans, he inspected his ponies and realised the animals had deteriorated
even further. Cherry-Garrard observed that some were 'scarecrows' and two or
three of the others were of 'more than doubtful quality'. The two ponies still at
Hut Point – Jimmy Pigg and Nobby – also faced another harrowing journey
along the frozen shoreline to Cape Evans in darkness and sub-zero
temperatures.

The ponies had suffered badly from the cold and it was brutally clear from their
skeletal frames that, particularly on the march, they did not get enough
nourishment. Despite ample supplies of compressed fodder – green cut and
pressed wheat – the ponies were always hungry. Oates addressed the problem
during the winter by supplementing their feed with oilcake and oats, although
strictly speaking this had been reserved for the main Polar journey in the spring.

Exercise was also important for the animals in spite of the darkness. Under
Oates' careful scrutiny, Scott assigned the men chosen to go on the Polar journey
to give a specific pony daily exercise.

The animals were usually taken out after breakfast, weather permitting,
although even this simple routine was fraught with danger. The animals
frequently rebelled against the freezing temperatures and kicked out violently
against the nearest moving object. It needed enormous depths of patience from
the men – officers, seamen and scientists alike – to control the mutinous beasts.

Almost inevitably though, bonds soon developed between the handlers and the animals and, in many cases, the men became very attached to their chosen pony, fondly caring and tending to their animal as though it were a child. Crean, a devoted animal lover, was mocked by his colleagues because of his attachments and even a hardy little character like Bowers developed great affection for his pony. The surrogate friendships were understandable and it was no surprise when even the toughest sailors mourned the inevitable death of their chosen animal.

The animals rarely returned the affection, frequently biting and kicking the nearest person. One unkind soul speculated that the recently deceased Hackenschmidt had died of 'cussedness' and a wary Cherry-Garrard came to the conclusion that Christopher was a 'man-killer'.

Life inside the hut was surprisingly congenial, with the temperature usually kept around the 52°F (11°C) mark. The 25 men were packed together, although the sleeping accommodation was organised to afford a modicum of privacy. In true naval tradition, the officers were separated from the ordinary seamen by a makeshift wall of provision boxes and the two groups even ate their meals separately. The sixteen officers and scientists occupied about two-thirds of the space and found room for two small laboratories and a 6 ft × 8 ft darkroom, complete with sink, for Ponting to develop his photographs.

Oates was in a compact five-man unit in the centre of the hut, flanked by the bunks of his soulmates Atkinson and Meares. It was a meagre setting which included Bowers and Cherry-Garrard. Oates dismissed the extravagance of curtains as 'effeminate luxury' and poured scorn on the scientists opposite for occupying a 'ladies boudoir'. To everyone, the sparse accommodation zone was known as The Tenements.

It was an inelegant wooden structure, lightly decorated with various items of horse tackle, lines of rope, drying socks and an assortment of boots, clothing and a desultory collection of other personal items like pipes, books and a spoon. The enterprising Oates had raided the stables, taking some planks from the dead ponies' stalls to build his own precarious-looking bunk. It was perched 5 ft off the floor on shaky legs at a slightly awkward angle and only held steady by a single piece of timber that had been unceremoniously nailed to Bowers' bunk.

Gran said it resembled 'five horse-stalls'. Adequately equipped, but without frills and luxuries, it was the epitome of a soldier in the field. Over his bed, Oates had pinned a small portrait of his own favourite soldier, Napoleon.

The atmosphere was basically cordial, the men generally rubbing along together even in the confined space of the crowded hut where they saw the same faces day in and day out. Although there were many different and some very strong personalities inside the hut, they managed to avoid any serious unpleasantness and individuals normally reserved their criticisms of each other for the intimacies of their diaries and journals. Each man somehow found ways of carving out a little privacy.

Oates was accustomed to living in close quarters with men and personal tensions in the field. But he was pleasantly surprised by the generally friendly atmosphere and observed:

'We got on very well together and there was none of the quarrelling which usually accompanies a winter where a number of men are confined together in a dark hut.'[1]

The Tenements. The unpretentious home of Oates and his closest friends in the hut at Cape Evans, 1911. (Left to right) Cherry-Garrard, Bowers (standing), Oates (centre), Meares and Atkinson (bottom right). (SPRI)

It was also possible to let off steam in noisy and heated arguments over all manner of issues. They indulged in exaggerated boyish ribaldry of each other, which reminded so many of the officers and scientists of their public school roots. Most were given eccentric nicknames, such 'Jane' Atkinson, 'Mother' Meares and 'Ponko' Ponting. Almost everyone stuck to Oates' established names of 'Titus' or 'Soldier,' except Bowers, who lampooned him as 'Farmer Hayseed'.

Oates tolerated Bowers' irreverence because they shared a similar professional service background and it was typical banter of the mess. However, they also shared another more private characteristic – their mothers were the most dominating influences in their lives. Bowers was raised by his doting mother after his seafaring father, Alexander, had died when he was only four and there was still only one woman in the life of Laurie Oates.

The residents of the Tenements, usually led by Oates, exchanged frequent volleys of verbal abuse with the scientific contingent opposite, which comprised Gran, the Canadian Wright and two Australians, Debenham and Griffith Taylor. It was basically good-natured stuff, but proceedings were given an extra edge by Oates' xenophobic tendencies.

Aside from the scientific and meteorological work, the days were also broken up by regular semi-academic lectures designed to inform, educate and relieve the boredom. The subjects ranged from Wilson on penguins to Ponting's lantern slide show of photographs taken on his visits to far off corners of the world. Others touched on meteorological instruments, volcanoes, mineralogy and tips on sketching.

But the lectures did not appeal to the likes of Oates and Meares. The talks, Meares confessed, were 'dreadfully boring' and the pair often escaped to the privacy of the stables for a chat. Oates, predictably, chose his favourite topic of horses – under the official sounding title of The Management of Horses – for his lecture in mid-May. It was full of basic common sense and proved so popular he was called back to give another talk on the same subject in August.

Although there was a boisterous feeling of the university debating society about the gathering, Oates managed to get across the importance of the horses to the expedition and the serious message about the value of proper feeding. The ponies, he explained, had to be fed 'soft' in the winter and 'hard' in the spring and because animals were used to grazing in meadows for twenty hours a day, they would be fed three times each day.

Oates, despite his normal reserve, was a big hit with the group, who were probably surprised that the normally quiet, withdrawn character could speak so fluently. Oates found extra reservoirs of confidence when it came to discussing horses and unlike all the other speakers, he dispensed with protocol and made his audience roar with laughter by rounding off proceedings with a throwaway joke. Oates wrapped up one talk by recalling the story of how an innocent young woman had arrived late for a dinner party because of problems with the horse-drawn cab. He finished:

> "'Ah, perhaps he was a jibber,' suggested her hostess.
> "Oh no," smiled the damsel, "he was a bugger, I heard the cabby say so several times.'"[2]

The most serious discussion took place on 8 May 1911 when Scott outlined his plans for the assault on the Pole in the coming season. The men listened in silence as he announced that the expedition's timetable and route would be based almost entirely on Shackleton's failed attempt to reach the Pole in 1908–09.

The journey to the South Pole and back, the longest Polar trek ever undertaken, was around 1,800 statute miles (almost 1,600 geographical miles or 2,800 km) and would be travelled in three clear stages. The first 400 miles (640 km) would take the men and ponies across the flat ice Barrier to the foot of the Transantarctic Mountains. They would then climb the formidable Beardmore Glacier, which stretches for 120 miles (190 km) and rises 10,000 ft (3,000 m) to the Polar Plateau. It was then about 350 miles (560 km) to the Pole itself.

Scott had lost all faith in the dogs and the motor tractors had been a dismal disappointment, which left the ponies as the principal means of carrying supplies on the first stage of the long journey to the foot of the Beardmore Glacier, where they would be shot. After that the men, in teams of threes or fours, would drag their own sledges. The men selected to reach the South Pole with Scott would be forced to man-haul their sledges for at least 1,400 miles (2,240 km) over the worst terrain in the world in sub-zero temperatures.

Scott estimated that the trip would last for 144 days, including twelve weeks on the intimidating Polar Plateau where the combination of high altitude – the Plateau is almost two miles above sea level – and low temperatures would test their endurance to the very limit. Scott knew this was the riskiest part of the whole enterprise and admitted:

> 'I don't know whether it is possible for men to last out that time, I almost doubt it.'[3]

The start of the journey was to be delayed by about a month until late October or early November to protect the feeble ponies against the biting temperatures of the late Antarctic spring. It was a calculated gamble because the Polar party would be struggling back over the Barrier towards the end of March when weather conditions deteriorate fast.

The later return also meant the men on the Polar trip would probably miss *Terra Nova*, which had only a small window in the Antarctic summer to get in and out of McMurdo Sound before the autumnal ice trapped the ship. Those chosen for the prestigious final march to the Pole would face a second winter at Cape Evans for their troubles.

Scott had initially suggested that the party could easily travel at an average of 10 miles (16 km) a day and had planned to reach the Pole by about 22 December. But with the start delayed for about a month, the date for the return to Cape Evans was now set for 27 March, exactly ten days after Oates' thirty-second birthday.

It was clear there would be little margin between success and failure. Simpson, the meteorologist, warned that a few accidents or a spell of bad weather would 'not only bring failure but very likely disaster'. Gran wondered whether Scott was being complacent in overlooking the value of the dogs.

In contrast, the eager but occasionally naïve Bowers saw the monumental man-hauling task as something of a test of national manhood. Bowers revelled in heroism for heroism's sake, typifying the national fascination with making a virtue out of doing things the hard way. He pronounced himself 'delighted' at Scott's plans and suggested that it would be a 'fine thing to do that plateau with man-haulage in these days of the supposed decadence of the British race'.

Wilson, who was to be a key figure in the march to the Pole, chose to skip over the daunting details and instead sought to put the best face on things, writing:

> 'Things always turn out for the best and generally in a different way to what one expects.'[4]

Oates' reservations were more profound and centred on the frailty of the ponies and his lack of confidence in Scott's management. Oates, the realist, saw the flaws even before setting out. Nothing had happened during the winter sojourn to change his mind about either the fitness of the animals or his respect for Scott. According to Meares, Oates was 'disgusted' at Scott's leadership.[5]

Meares shared these reservations, particularly over Scott's poor management of the transport arrangements. Meares and Oates spent hours together during the long winter of 1911, usually playing chess or huddled over the seal blubber stove in the stables away from the clutter and claustrophobia of the crowded main hut. It was also a deliberate move to distance themselves from Scott.

Ponting took a memorable photograph of the pair on 20 May, with Meares contentedly sucking on his pipe and Oates, wearing the crude corduroy balaclava he had made for himself, lazily poking the fire. As he pointed his camera, Ponting recalled that Meares was telling Oates that Scott should buy a 'shilling book about transport'. It was a remark overheard by Scott.

Oates and Meares were naturally drawn to each other, both outsiders in a small group outnumbered by starched naval officers and earnest scientists. Both were unfulfilled, restless characters who struggled to find a suitable role in life and were coming to realise that Polar exploration was not the answer.

Meares had taken to the road at the age of only nineteen and always seemed to be on the move somewhere. He had travelled extensively in China, Siberia and Russia and had developed a distinct flair for languages. He was fluent in Russian, French, German, Spanish and Italian and had a good knowledge of Chinese and Hindustani.

Meares, whose father was a major in the Royal Scots Fusiliers, served for two years as a trooper and sergeant with the Scottish Horse regiment during the Boer War. He later gravitated towards Russia and Siberia, performing a more shadowy role as an 'observer' in the Russo-Japanese war of 1904–05. Observer was frequently a pseudonym for spy and it was a role Meares would return to in later life. On his service record, Meares' civilian occupation is listed as 'None'.

Oates found the inveterate wanderer an interesting character because of his rich and varied experiences and Meares was attracted by the cool assurance of the cavalry officer. Oates spent hours with Meares helping to make dog food from seal meat, chatting quietly about their Boer War experiences, military affairs or the shared interest in animals. They were comfortable together since neither had anything to prove to the other.[6]

Scott always struggled to come to terms with Meares, remarking that he 'has no happiness but in the wild places of the earth'. In an entry erased from the published version of his diaries, Scott also wrote:

> 'Meares is a nice fellow but he hates exercise and doesn't inspire the confidence to see things through'.[7]

Oates conceded that there was 'no love lost' between Meares and Scott. That, too, probably drew him closer to Meares.

The pair were invariably joined by Atkinson, the naval surgeon who doubled up as parasitologist. Together they formed a little clique, though Atkinson, widely known as Atch, struck up a particularly close friendship with Oates. At times they seemed inseparable.

Atkinson, a neat and tidy man, had qualified as a doctor only four years before *Terra Nova* left London and had spent much of his time at a military hospital drearily vaccinating sailors. But his real passion was parasites and research into diseases and he spent hours surrounded by test tubes at his tiny table-top laboratory in a corner of the Cape Evans hut. In later life he won prizes for his contribution to health in the navy.

Atkinson, like Oates, was a decent boxer, who won trophies as a student. The quiet exterior obscured a determined and courageous character who would be awarded the DSO and Albert Medal for outstanding bravery during the First World War.[8] Atkinson was another perfectly happy with his own company and even when together, he and Oates were known for their long silences. Observers said it was difficult to imagine two more naturally silent men and even Oates commented on Atkinson's reserve, finding him 'an extraordinarily quiet man'. Debenham recorded:

Oates (right) spent hours during the Antarctic winter at the blubber stove with his friend, Cecil Meares. Both men had grown to dislike Scott and preferred the privacy of the stables. At the moment Ponting photographed the pair on 20 May 1911 Meares was advising Scott to 'buy a shilling book on transport'. (SPRI)

'Oates and Atkinson great friends – both taciturn and reserved and of few words.'[9]

It was said that the hut at Cape Evans contained enough characters to suit all tastes. Those who wished to talk found talkers and there were listeners for those who wanted someone to listen. For quiet there was Oates.

Atkinson was also critical of Scott. He was privately appalled at Scott's erratic behaviour and the way in which one minute he swore at subordinates such as Teddy Evans and moments later became friendly. Both Atkinson and Oates expected higher standards and consistency from superior officers.

Oates and Atkinson were also united by their innate conservatism. Oates, as a member of the landed gentry, and Atkinson, with his minor public school background, were conservatives who clashed with what they regarded as radical colonials like Griffith Taylor and Debenham. Taylor, whose family emigrated to Australia when he was young, had a biting wit and frequently baited his rivals with fierce arguments on topical issues of the day, such as women's suffrage. He sported a goatee beard and was invariably christened Keir Hardie, the Labour leader he closely resembled.

The arguments were frequently heated, lasting well into the night and given an extra dimension by Oates' faint suspicion of the university-educated cluster within the hut. Four of the sixteen members of the Cape Evans wardroom – Wilson, Griffith Taylor, Nelson and Wright – had been to Cambridge, Cherry-Garrard had graduated from Oxford, Simpson from Manchester and Debenham from Sydney University.

Oates occasionally appeared ill at ease in the intellectually-charged atmosphere, which almost certainly arose from personal bitterness and embarrassment at his own school failings and in particular, the repeated inability to pass the entrance exams to university. Oates had dearly wanted to go to university. He did not lack confidence in his own abilities and Debenham recalled, for example, that Oates was by far the best student of history at Cape Evans. But, surrounded by highbrows in the close confines of the hut, the constant reminder that education was his Achilles Heel seemed all the more painful.

One incident illustrated his unease. Oates liked a drink and was irritated that the 'medical comforts' – brandy – was held in the firm grip of the doctors and scientists. After failing to get his hands on the bottle, Oates demanded that the expedition should be split into 'gentlemen' and 'scientists'. Although offered in jest, there was an element of wishful thinking behind the remark.

Oates was universally popular at Cape Evans, even if some of the later recollections were undoubtedly coloured by the ultimate tragedy of the expedition.

The only person on the expedition known to speak badly of Oates was Scott, but these thoughts were later excised from the published version of his diaries.

His lack of pretension and dislike of custom endeared him to all. There was precious little evidence of his aristocratic background and Oates was a man without a shred of vanity. His colleagues were also impressed by his even temper, unhurried straightforward manner and laconic wit. Oates did not have much to say but when he spoke it was generally worth hearing.

Oates was never rushed and seemed to give careful consideration to even the

A man apart. Oates (standing, left) watches the birthday celebrations for Scott on 6 June 1911 with a lofty detachment. (SPRI)

most mundane of questions. Wilson said one day: 'The way thoughts flash through your mind, Titus, reminds me of snails climbing up a cabbage stalk.' Even his rivals from the university assembly hall warmed to him. Debenham said Oates was 'slow of speech but always effective when speech came'. He rarely, if ever, used superlatives. Ponting offered a more telling verdict:

'Oates had a personality that could be felt.'[10]

Oates never appeared flustered, even when subjected to witless public school pranks or excessive baiting from what he saw as the upstart colonials. Griffith Taylor's argumentative style rubbed some people up the wrong way but Oates remained imperturbable to the incessant hectoring.

Debenham, one of the scientists who took time to make up his mind about Oates, said he possessed a 'temper such as I have never met'. Debenham said it was 'impossible to make him even testy' and added:

'He is not reserved in the ordinary sense and though he loathes society, I fancy that when he does mix in it he is quite a brilliant member. His talk, though slow and measured, is brimful of wit and straight as they make them.'[11]

Oates had also become a specialist in hiding his true feelings, the enduring English trait which regards displaying emotions as somehow weak. Oates had taken inscrutability to new heights and Debenham observed:

'He was thoroughly English in going to great lengths to hide his feelings, even from his family apparently.'[12]

Apart from Atkinson and Meares, Oates enjoyed the company of the ordinary seamen as much as the scientists and officers. Even though there was a long history of antagonism between different branches of the service, Oates also overcame the inter-service rivalry with the same ease he bridged the social gap.

The men, in turn, invariably found it easier to talk to Oates than they did to their immediate officers like Scott or Teddy Evans. Oates was more approachable than the typical officer, particularly as he saw little need for rank and formality in a crowded hut cut off by thousands of miles from civilisation.

Taff Evans came near to having a fight with another sailor on the quayside in New Zealand because the bluejacket had mocked Oates' scruffiness. Patsy Keohane, the experienced Petty Officer from Cork, was impressed with the cavalry captain and observed that Oates was 'not much talk, but chock full of grit'. Teddy Evans, recalled:

'Oates was more popular with the seamen than any other officer. He understood these men perfectly.'[13]

Friends and enemies

Oates also found time for the Russian groom, Anton, who spoke hardly any English and suffered from melancholic bouts of homesickness and concern for his one-legged girlfriend at home. He was a superstitious, nervous character who worked tirelessly with Oates in the stables but was rarely comfortable in the Cape Evans environment.

Although the two were drawn from totally different worlds, Anton and Oates developed a quiet respect for each other. Oates described the Russian as 'excellent' and Gran noticed that Anton came to worship Oates. He recalled that in reply to most questions, Anton would simply explain: 'Captain Oates good to horses, good to Anton.'[14]

Oates was an imposing figure at Cape Evans, taller, broader and heavier than most of the men in the wardroom, even if his face bore the unappealing scars of the smallpox contracted in India. Atkinson dutifully measured and weighed the party at regular intervals and Oates came in at 12 st 4½ lbs (78 kg) which was only 3 lbs (1.3 kg) heavier than his weight at eighteen years of age. Only the taller Gran weighed more. Oates stood slightly over 5 ft 9 ins (1.75 m), almost 2 ins (5 cm) less than the measurements taken in teenage years, which reflected the war wound that made one leg shorter than the other. His chest measurement of 40 in (101 cm) was among the largest of the entire party.[15]

Oates also stood out at Cape Evans because of his idiosyncratic dress sense. He made an art form of dressing down, preferring well-worn jumpers, tattered trousers and hob-nailed boots in what was clearly a rebuke to style and petty convention. It was a scruffiness that he had carried over from his youth. His sister Violet recalled one occasion when the young squire had gone shopping at Gestingthorpe with his shoes tied up with wire.

He looked more like a stableman than the owner of stables and Debenham, who smiled at his 'slovenly dress', remembered:

> 'Oates hated swank – so much so that he erred on the other side almost perversely and was rough and ready to the last degree.'[16]

Winter routine was interrupted in some style on 22 June – midwinter's day – when Polar explorers traditionally enjoyed a surrogate Christmas. It was a good excuse for a mighty feast, which included roast beef and Yorkshire pudding, flaming plum pudding and endless glasses of Heisdeck 1904 champagne.

Bowers made a Christmas tree from a ski-stick and penguin feathers and everyone was given a little present. Oates received a sponge, a whistle and the singularly appropriate gift of a pop-gun. Drink flowed well into the night, songs were sung and a merry Oates rose from the table to dance the Lancers' quadrille with little Anton. Later he found himself in the role of peacemaker when a drunken Keohane caused a minor stir with inflammatory remarks about Irish nationalism, which were not well received in the overwhelmingly English setting.

Midwinter's day also marked the turning point in the Antarctic winter and the realisation that, with the light soon to return, the expedition would be able to get down to its main purpose. However, there were several alarming intrusions which were a constant reminder that, regardless of the cosy comforts of Cape Evans, the Antarctic remained a formidably hostile and threatening environment.

Preparations for the Pole were first interrupted by an eccentric spot of bird-nesting. Wilson, exercising his understated but powerful influence over Scott, wanted to obtain the egg of the Emperor penguin from the rookery at Cape Crozier during the incubation period which occurs at the depths of the ink-black Antarctic winter.

Scott reluctantly approved the extraordinary venture and agreed to send Bowers and Cherry-Garrard along with Wilson into the Polar night. It was another bizarre decision. Scott was exposing three of his men to the most extreme hazards at the worst point in the hostile winter. Scott tried to justify the risky exercise by arguing that the men would be able to test their food and equipment in the most rigorous environment but, in reality, few practical lessons were ever absorbed.

Although Cape Crozier was no more than 70 miles (112 km) across the other side of Ross Island, the outward journey took nineteen harrowing days. The three men, dragging 750 lb (340 kg) of supplies and equipment, stumbled like blind men across the appalling terrain in pitch blackness while winds screeched to gale force and temperatures plummeted. The thermometer frequently plunged to $-50°F$ ($-45°C$) and on one horrendous night sank to $-77½°F$ ($-61°C$) or $109½°$ of frost. Cherry-Garrard, whose great work, *The Worst Journey in the World,* was named after the Crozier ordeal, said that he saw death as a friend. Remarkably, the men survived the terrible 36-day nightmare, returning with a hard-won haul of three penguin eggs. Unfortunately, the eggs proved of little scientific value.

It was undeniably an astonishing act of endurance and fortitude but, in truth, the journey should never have been undertaken. While Scott did not wish to upset Wilson, he should at least have postponed the hazardous venture until the following season when the Polar journey had been completed.

The single-minded Amundsen would never have permitted such a foolhardy venture to jeopardise his attempt on the Pole. But the *Terra Nova* expedition was not conceived with the same single purpose of the Norwegian venture and the horrors of the 'worst journey in the world' reflected the underlying conflict between science and exploration on Scott's campaign.

Another near disaster struck Scott while the Crozier party were out chasing penguin eggs. Atkinson, Gran and Griffith Taylor went out in early July on a routine mission to take temperatures a few hundred yards away from the hut. In the blackness and swirling wind, Gran and Griffith Taylor took half an hour to move 200 or 300 yards and were relieved to get back to safety.

But in winds roaring to 60 mph (100 kph) Atkinson quickly became disorientated in the darkness and swirling drift. Search parties were dispatched and Atkinson was found by Meares and Debenham after a terrifying six-hour brush with death. He had suffered a very bad dose of frostbite which left his right hand swollen sausage-like with painful blisters. Scott, fully aware that he had come close to losing one of only two doctors in the party, warned 'we must have no more of these very unnecessary escapades'.

Days later a fresh alarm struck the party when Bones, one of the more reliable ponies, suddenly stopped eating and was seized with spasms of stomach pain. Oates gave him two opium pills but there were fears that he would die. His handler, Crean, kindly sat through the night with Oates to help nurse the pony towards recovery.

His problem was a small ball of half-digested hay covered with mucus and tape-worms. To the relief of the entire party, Bones duly recovered, although it was also discovered that other ponies were suffering from worms. Years later it was suggested that the animal was probably suffering from anthrax, an infection which may have had implications for the Polar party itself.[17]

Scott took the opportunity to settle the dispute with Oates about the use of snowshoes on the ponies. The ponies, he said, would have two different types of shoe – a grating or racquet style for soft snow and a stiff bag over the hoof for hard ice. Scott said the discussion had 'cleared the air a good deal' and Oates had to accept defeat.

Oates was now fully engaged in the task of preparing the ponies for the trek across the Barrier. He increased the animals' feed, stepped up their exercise and gave the chosen handlers suitable advice on how to cope with their unpredictable and occasionally vicious behaviour.

Oates had chosen to lead the particularly truculent beast, Christopher, who kicked and bit everyone who approached. Sometimes it needed four men to get

Christopher into a sledging harness and Oates dryly observed that a person needed the 'temper of an archangel to get on with a swine like him'.

Oates also knew that the sledging season would provide a searching test of his patience. His relationship with Scott had not improved through the winter and the frank-speaking Oates was aware of the risk of a spectacular bust-up while on the march. He wondered whether he could tolerate many months of tortuous hard work face to face with a man he loathed.

One consolation for Oates was he did not expect to be a member of the final team chosen for the Pole. He believed that his work would be finished when the ponies had carried their supplies 400 miles (640 km) to the foot of the Beardmore Glacier. He told Teddy Evans that his ambition was to get the ponies to the Beardmore and perhaps assist the man-haulers to climb the 120 miles up the Glacier to the Polar Plateau, the most arduous phase of the trip. Evans remembered that he saw little prospect of going to the Pole and added:

Preparing the ponies. Oates in the stables shortly before starting on the march to the South Pole. (SPRI)

Oates struck a slightly more positive note about his chances in a letter to his mother shortly before the expedition departed for the south. As usual, he sought to reassure her about the nature of the venture but could not conceal his feelings about Scott. He wrote:

> '. . . I think I have a fairish chance (of inclusion in the final Polar party), that is if Scott and I do not fall out as it will be a pretty tough having four months of him, he fusses dreadfully. . .'19

Scott had kept his opinions on the make-up of the Polar party close to his chest. In mid-September he sketched in a few more details about the coming trek, reemphasising that a successful mission turned on the ability of the ponies and endurance of the man-hauling teams. He had not changed his mind about the dogs or the tractors, which would be used only in a supporting role. But he did disclose that the main southern party would consist of three four-man teams of man-haulers. And only four of the twelve men would go to the Pole.

Initially, the party would total sixteen men. The pony handlers, led by Scott, would be: Wilson, Bowers, Cherry-Garrard, Atkinson, Wright, Crean, Taff Evans, Keohane and Oates. The motor tractors would travel as far as possible under Teddy Evans, who would take Lashly, Day and Hooper. The dog teams would consist of Meares and Dimitri. The total would be pared down to twelve after Day, Hooper and the dog teams turned back to Cape Evans.

The general assumption was the final four-man party for the march to the Pole would include two navigators, one doctor and a seaman. Scott, as leader, was a certain starter and Wilson, the only person close to him, fitted the bill as doctor and mentor. Teddy Evans, an accomplished navigator, probably felt that as the expedition's second-in-command he would be included. But Scott had grown to distrust Evans and regretted making him number two. Before setting out, Scott had written that Evans was 'not a rock to be built upon . . . I cannot consider him fit for a superior position'.

The dark horse for a place in the final party was Bowers, who had made a deep impression on everyone with his enthusiasm and organisational ability. He could also navigate. It was generally agreed that if Scott took an ordinary seaman, the choice would be Welshman, Taff Evans.

In this team there was no place for a limping cavalry captain.

Remarkably Scott did not appear to finalise the Polar party or discuss the suitability of individuals before they set out. Even Wilson was not party to the secret. All anyone knew was that the final team would be picked on the basis of condition and fitness nearer to the Pole.

A wiser, less furtive leader would have taken advice about the strengths and weaknesses of the men from intelligent people like Wilson, weeding out the less able and drawing up a short list of the most capable. It would also enable him to ensure that the quartet chosen for the final assault on the Pole was protected from the hardest work in the initial leg of the journey and kept fresher for the crucial later stages. In these circumstances, Oates' contribution would have ended when the ponies were shot at the foot of the Beardmore.

What is particularly strange about Scott's secretiveness is that he regularly studied the personalities and characters around him. His diaries are full of frank judgements and dry comments about individuals, which shows that while he frequently thought deeply about his personnel, he could not express himself. Instead he chose to lock away his thoughts in the darker recesses of his mind or confine them to the privacy of his journals.

As the party prepared to embark on the Polar journey, he wrote: 'There does not seem to be a single weak spot in the twelve good men and true who are chosen for the Southern advance.' It was a sentence later deleted from the published version of his diaries.

At Gestingthorpe, Caroline Oates received a letter from Lt-Col Fryer, the Inniskilling's commanding officer at Mhow, who had battled to prevent Oates joining the expedition. Fryer set his anger aside and wrote: 'I hope he will return safe and well.'

18

'. . .there is no cause for anxiety. . .'

Half a world away, Caroline Oates found that her conscience had been pricked. Unknown to her son and most people in the hut at Cape Evans, the expedition was facing bankruptcy.

Kathleen Scott was warned in September 1911 that the money would run out at the end of October, precisely the moment when the expedition was destined to begin its epic journey. More money was needed but Kathleen was reluctant to involve her son, Peter, in the fund-raising activities. One journalist offered to help raise £4,000 by arranging for the *Daily Mirror* to publish pictures showing Peter writing a begging letter. But Kathleen Scott rejected the offer, declaring that she did not want the two-year old child 'bandied about in the halfpenny press'.

But Caroline Oates responded to the crisis. She had not given any money to Scott during the first public appeal for funds in 1910 but in a typically generous gesture she now donated £200 to the struggling expedition,[1] the equivalent of over £9,000 today. She believed she was helping, although her generosity would come to haunt her in later years.

Scott revealed the scale of the financial problems when he called the entire Cape Evans party together on the eve of departure to ask if anyone could afford to waive their salary for the second year in the south. Some agreed, while others like Griffith Taylor and Ponting, were already committed to leaving when the *Terra Nova* returned in January.

Money was not an issue for Oates, who had already agreed not to draw a salary. More important, he was still undecided whether to remain with the expedition. Scott wanted him to stay for a second year, particularly with fresh horses coming down with *Terra Nova*. The decision-making process was further complicated by Oates' mood on the brink of embarking to the Pole.

The tedium of the long dark Antarctic winter had weighed heavily on him and the responsibilities of the abject ponies caused further anxiety. As the expedition prepared to set off southwards, Oates was suffering from a touch of depression.

The despondency was deep enough for Oates to resign from the expedition. He had reached rock bottom with Scott and threatened to withdraw from the venture on the very eve of the party's departure to the south.

Oates told friends at Cape Evans that he was pulling out of the Polar party and would return home on the *Terra Nova*. He was so determined to resign that he sat down at one point to write a cheque to Scott to cover the expenses incurred by the expedition on his behalf. It needed the combined diplomatic skills of Wilson, Meares and Teddy Evans to persuade him to stick with the endeavour. Evans later confirmed that Oates 'very decidedly' wanted to resign before the party set out.[2] In the event the trio persuaded him to withdraw his resignation.

But there was no disguising the blackness of his mood. He complained 'life here is so monotonous' and was so depressed that he neglected to write a farewell letter to his mother. Oates had always maintained a regular flow of correspondence with her throughout his long periods away from home, at school or in the army and it was highly unusual for him to stop writing. But the *ennui* of Antarctica had interrupted his routine.

It needed a last-minute intervention by a considerate Debenham to coax him to compose a parting note to his mother. Without that timely contribution, Oates would have marched away from Cape Evans without a last note for *Terra Nova* to carry back to Gestingthorpe. Debenham, who had grown increasingly fond of Oates in the winter months, grabbed him by the shoulders, forcibly sat him down at the table and bullied him to write a few lines home. Debenham charitably blamed Oates' 'incurable reticence' for not writing.[3]

In the long, rambling, occasionally contradictory dispatch, written over five days before leaving for the south, Oates displayed mixed and conflicting emotions. His depression and loathing of Scott were apparent but there was also an underlying ambition to be among the first men to set foot at the South Pole.

He began by telling his mother that he would be home soon after she received his letter. He added:

> 'Scott wants me to stay on here another year but I shall clear out if I get back in time for the ship which I hope to goodness will be the case. It will only be a small party to remain next year. Scott pretends at present he is going to stay but I bet myself a fiver he clears out, that is if he gets to the Pole. If he does not and some decent transport animals

come down in the ship, I have promised him I will stay to help him have another try but between you and me I think if he fails this time he will have had a pretty good stomach full.'[4]

A little later in the same letter, he had 'half a mind' to see Scott and demand to leave. But then added that it would be a pity to spoil his chances of being in the final party because the army and the regiment would be pleased if he reached the Pole. On another page he moaned:

'You will not catch me on another Antarctic winter if I can help it.'[5]

The centre of his unhappiness was, of course, Scott, who he felt simply failed to comprehend the acute difficulties with the ponies and would not listen to sound advice. The exasperation spilled over into animosity shortly afterwards when Scott had a blazing row with Oates' pal Meares. He wrote:

'Myself, I dislike Scott intensely and would chuck the whole thing if it were not that we are a British expedition and must beat these Norwegians. Scott has always been very civil to me and I have the reputation of getting on well with him. But the fact of the matter is that he is not straight, it is himself first, the rest nowhere. . .'[6]

A little later in the same letter he changed his mind again, warning his mother:

'. . . please remember that when a man is having a hard time, he says hard things about other people which he would regret afterwards.'[7]

Scott, too, had not given up hope that Oates would stay a second year with the expedition. He wrote to Caroline Oates warning 'there is a possibility that your son may not return to England this year'. This indicated that, at the point of departure from Cape Evans, Oates had still not made up his mind about his future and had not informed Scott about his reluctance to spend a second year in the south.

Scott was evidently unaware of Oates' intense dislike and paid a genuinely warm tribute to him in a letter to Mrs Oates. He said her son had 'rendered very great service' to the expedition and that the officers and scientists would not have known what to do without him.

Scott clearly liked and respected Oates but found it excruciatingly difficult to express himself. Any warmth and true feeling seemed to emerge clearest in his writing. He told Mrs Oates:

'To this really great service his welcome personality is a great addition. He has been and remains one of the most popular and cheery members of our small community. Also in spite of the troubles and responsibilities of his fractious animals, I think he has enjoyed himself very much. Meanwhile, it is a pleasure to tell you how well he is and how popular with the exceedingly diverse set of men with whom he is living.'[8]

The simmering discontent with Scott always came to a head on the subject of the ponies. While Oates had purposefully understated his reservations in previous letters to his mother, his last note from Cape Evans pulled no punches. He revealed:

'From what I see, I think it would not be difficult to get to the Pole provided you have proper transport, but with the rubbish we have it will be jolly difficult and means a lot of hard work.

. . . they (the ponies) are without exception the greatest lot of crocks I have ever seen that were seriously meant for use, four are lame now and another only wants a day's hard work to be lame too.'[9]

Few in the party doubted Oates' judgement, even if Scott publicly refused to accept his verdict. Even Wilson, who always sought to put the best gloss on even the most dire circumstances, was realistic about the animals. As he prepared to leave, he commented:

'We really have very few decent horses among the whole lot and several of them are as old as the hills and have passed a life of ill-treatment, hard work and poor food. Laminitis is one of their troubles and general debility seems another.'[10]

Despite the pervading sense of gloom, Oates clung to the prospect of getting to the Pole, which meant delaying his homecoming by a year. Anxious not to worry his mother, he concluded his final letter from Cape Evans with the poignant remarks:

'If you happen to get this without hearing of the return of the Polar party and I happen to be in the party, there is no cause for anxiety as the only dangerous part of the journey is the ascent of the (Beardmore) glacier and you will have heard if we get up that safely. The coming back is not nearly so bad.

If anything should happen to me on this trip, which I don't think likely, ask for my note book. I have written instructions on the fly leaf that it is to be sent to you.'[11]

19

To the last place on earth

Oates said he expected a 'bit of circus' when the expedition finally set off for the South Pole, the last great land journey to be completed by man. He was not far wrong.

The plan was for the slow-moving motor tractors to start first, a week ahead of the main party with the aim of transporting some heavy loads as far south as possible. The main party of twelve would follow leading the ponies and the swifter-moving dog teams under Meares would supplement the two by ferrying supplies back and forth along the route.

When the machines and animals finally succumbed, the men would resort to dragging their own sledges. It was a round trip of 1,800 miles (2,800 km) and the bulk of it would be achieved in the man-hauling harness.

Scott's assault on the South Pole began in low-key, almost apologetic fashion. On 24 October, the two motor tractors spluttered into life and trundled slowly away from Cape Evans, each dragging about 1½ tons (1,500 kg) of supplies and equipment at a walking pace. It took three hours to travel the first three miles from the hut and even on good surfaces the motors rarely crept above 3 mph.

In charge was Teddy Evans, nominally second-in-command of the entire venture but now sidelined to a subsidiary role with the tractors that Scott had already written off as virtually worthless. Evans, with Lashly, Day and Hooper on board, was ordered to get the tractors to One Ton Depot and if possible push them about 60 miles further south to 80½°.

The motors stuttered and strained over the soft snow, frequently breaking down and driving the mechanics, Day and Lashly, to distraction. Working with cold metal in temperatures down to −25°F (−32°C) was excruciating, but their efforts were in vain.

The first machine came to a standstill on 30 October when the big-end bearing broke and on 1 November the second ground to a halt about one mile beyond Corner Camp. The experiment with the motor tractors had been a miserable failure. In seven frustrating days, the vehicles had travelled just 51 miles (82 kms) and the burden of the expedition fell on the ponies and men much sooner than expected.

It was a symbolic moment as the four men abandoned the mechanical vehicle and yoked themselves in the man-hauling harness. Their sledge weighed almost 800 lb (360 kg) and Lashly glumly wrote:

'Now comes the man-hauling part of the show.'[1]

On the same day as the tractors were abandoned, the caravan of ponies began the great trek from Cape Evans to the foot of the Beardmore Glacier 400 miles

South. The Southern Party poses for Ponting shortly before embarking on the ill-fated march to the South Pole. Oates (back row, sixth from left) looks grimly determined. Also pictured: (Back row, left to right standing) Griffith Taylor, Cherry-Garrard, Day, Nelson, Evans, Oates, Atkinson, Scott, Wright, Keohane, Gran, Lashly, Hooper, Forde, Anton, Dimitri; (Sitting, left to right) Bowers, Meares, Debenham, Wilson, Simpson, Taff Evans, Crean. (SPRI)

(640 km) to the south. The ponies were strung out in a long cavalcade on the way to their first port of call, the old *Discovery* hut fourteen miles away at Hut Point.

Oates was leading the demonic Christopher, who kicked and raged against being harnessed to a sledge. It required all his skill and patience to control the violent animal and Scott said the 'greatest consideration is to safeguard Oates' from Christopher. Griffith Taylor, not a member of the southern party, watched the grim battle between man and beast and recalled:

> 'Dear old Titus – that was my last memory of him. Imperturbable as ever; never hasty, never angry, but soothing that vicious animal; and determined to get the best out of the most unpromising material in his endeavour to do his simple duty.'[2]

Scott was optimistic and in one of the last entries before the convoy set out, he wrote in his diary:

> 'The future is in the lap of the gods; I can think of nothing left undone to deserve success.'[3]

Almost immediately the words were thrown back in his face. After reaching Hut Point, Scott suddenly discovered that he had forgotten the Union Jack, given to him by Queen Alexandra, the Queen Mother, to place at the Pole. He quickly summoned the flag from Cape Evans and Gran, by far the most proficient skier, was dragooned into making the trip. 'By an irony of fate,' Gran said, 'a Norwegian carried the British flag on the first few miles towards the South Pole.'[4]

Across the snow plain, the Norwegians under Amundsen had reached 82°S and were already some 200 miles (320 km) nearer the Pole. Amundsen's five-man party struck out from Framheim two weeks earlier on 19 October, the teams of 52 dogs skipping over the surface with comparative ease. On occasions the men were afforded the luxury of sitting on their sledges as the dogs raced along. The first four marches alone carried the Norwegians 99 miles (160 km) closer to the Pole and the race for the last unconquered spot on the globe was effectively over before Scott's cavalcade left base camp.

Scott's fleet set off from Hut Point on 2 November, with Ponting dutifully recording the scene for posterity and a few lusty cheers from the handful of men left behind echoing across the snowy wastes. Ponting was close to tears.

The weakest ponies, led by Atkinson and Keohane, went first trudging slowly southwards, followed by the steady plodders under Scott and the fliers bringing up the rear with Bowers, Crean, Taff Evans and Oates.

The plan was to march at night in lower temperatures when the surfaces would be harder, averaging 11¼ miles (18 km) a day from Hut Point to One Ton Depot and then at 15 miles (24 km) a day to the bottom of the Beardmore. The ponies would then be shot and Oates' duties would be finished.

The procession moved fairly well in the early days, although it was soon evident there would be difficulties with the different parts of the convoy travelling at varying speeds. Scott had to juggle the starting and arrival times of three sets of ponies and the faster-moving dog teams of Meares and Dimitri. The process added another administrative burden to proceedings and once again Meares had to sit around for hours to make sure that he reached the next camp at roughly the same time as the slower train of ponies.

The first setback came on 7 November when a blizzard struck. While the men were confined to their tents and the ponies sheltered behind a hastily-built snow-wall, Meares and the dogs raced into camp seemingly undisturbed by the atrocious weather. It was another uncomfortable reminder that dogs were far better suited to the ice than the ponies or motors.

Oates and Meares understood and saw evident dangers ahead for the party. Oates confided to his diary:

> 'We both damned the motors. 3 motors at £1,000 each, 19 ponies at £5 each. 32 dogs at 30/- each. If Scott fails to get to the Pole he jolly well deserves it.'[5]

Scott was unaware of the scornful judgement and told Oates he was 'very pleased' with the way the ponies were going. Oates, perhaps feeling some guilt at the unrelenting criticism of his leader, said that Scott was 'kind enough to say that he owed me a lot for the trouble I have taken'.

Oates, too, had been pleasantly surprised at the ponies on the initial stages of the journey. Some had performed better than expected, helped by the harder surfaces. But he knew it was only a matter of time before they disintegrated. The ponies, he said, were 'wretched old cripples' and added:

> 'I only hope it will be kept up.'[6]

It was well-placed caution. A few days later the surface deteriorated badly, leaving the ponies floundering in soft, fresh snow. Scott said a worse set of conditions for the ponies could scarcely be imagined and he halted the day's march after 9⅜ miles (15 km). Soon after the dogs scampered into camp having covered 20 miles (32 km) in the same conditions.

The withering cold, hard work and soft ground took a heavy toll and the weaker ponies, notably Chinaman and Jehu, were in decline only a matter of days after leaving Hut Point. A further worry was the realisation that the supplies of forage would not be sufficient to get all the ponies to the Beardmore, which meant slaughtering the weaker animals as they began to fail. This suited Oates, but concerned the sentimental Scott.

Scott's diary, written at the end of each day's march, showed his mounting concern about the capabilities of the ponies. On 13 November, he wrote:

> 'I am anxious about these beasts – very anxious, they are not the ponies they ought to have been and if they pull through well, all the thanks will be due to Oates.'[7]

The men and animals were given a welcome rest after reaching One Ton Depot. Oates believed that, with luck, some of the ponies would get through to the Glacier, although he noticed that they were all starting to lose condition. Scott retained his outward confidence and reached the remarkable conclusion that some animals were in better shape than when they started out. There was 'no need to be alarmed,' he wrote.

Scott frequently contradicted himself, even in his own diary, where he veered from optimism to deep pessimism about the state of the ponies on which he had pinned so much. However, his public comments about the animals almost certainly concealed his own reservations.

A glimpse of his true feelings was conveyed in a private letter written to his wife, Kathleen, while sitting in his tent on the Barrier just three weeks into the march. He admitted that the animals were '. . . not well selected. I knew this in New Zealand, though I didn't tell you'. He described Oates as a 'treasure' for making the most of a bad lot but could not bring himself to admit that Oates' damning judgement was 100 per cent correct.

Oates preferred not to prevaricate and after little more than two weeks on the Barrier, he told Scott bluntly that Chinaman and Jehu were near the end of their tether. It was an uncomfortable realisation and Oates recorded:

> 'Scott realises now what awful cripples the ponies are and carries a face like a tired old sea boat in consequence.'[8]

To ease the strain, the ponies' loads were lightened at One Ton, though even the weakest were still dragging over 400 lb (180 kg) on their sledges. But the exertion began to tell on the men themselves and Scott clashed with Bowers over the loads, which Oates interpreted as a sign of Scott coming to terms with the reality of the situation. Oates, too, had a run-in over some unreported difference of opinion, which served only to harden his contempt. He wrote:

'Had words with Scott when he arrived. He is a very difficult man to get on with.'[9]

Oates had an altogether different problem. His pony, Christopher, was a nightmare to control and even the immensely patient Oates was tested to the limit. Getting the pony into a harness was a daily battle which invited bites and kicks and once started, Christopher refused to stop until the day's march had been completed. It meant that Oates frequently sacrificed his midday rest, which was seen as only mildly inconvenient at the time, although it would ultimately have an effect on his strength and endurance when he needed them most.

Spirits were raised on 21 November when the men caught up with the motor party under Teddy Evans, who had cached a large stock of supplies under an imposing 15-ft cairn of snow. They called it Mount Hooper after the youngest member of the tractor team.

However, the main surprise was that Evans' team looked weary and complained of hunger. Day was positively emaciated. The four men had been man-hauling for barely three weeks and the warning signs were stark. Those selected for the final dash to the Pole still faced the daunting prospect of man-hauling another 1,600 miles (2,500 kms) on the round trip back to Cape Evans.

The aim was to establish food and fuel depots roughly every 65 miles, marked by large black flags flying from bamboos to attract the travelling parties on the white landscape. Each depot contained a week's ration for a four-man party which was deemed sufficient to carry them forward to the next depot. The gap between fresh supplies was acceptable for fit, well-fed men in ideal conditions on the outward journey. But 65 miles was cutting things fine on the return journey when the inevitably tired men would be travelling more slowly in worsening weather.

Oates had no doubts about the appropriate action if the safety of the party was jeopardised by any one member incapacitated by serious injuries like a broken leg. The man, he insisted, should be sacrificed to save the others. Oates had discussed the predicament with other members of the expedition, particularly Meares. The delicate issue had been debated at length during their long hours together in the stables and Meares recalled:

'Before there was any thought of his going with the Polar Party, he repeatedly brought up the question, "What should a member of the Polar Party do if he felt that, through illness, he was a hindrance of the party?" And he always said that he should sacrifice himself for the good of the others.'[10]

Ponting also recalled the discussion and in his book, *The Great White South*, he wrote:

> 'I recall very clearly a memorable conversation that Oates had with Nelson and me one evening in my dark-room, during the winter of 1911. The point was raised as to what a man should do if he were to break down on the Polar journey, thereby becoming a burden to others. Oates unhesitatingly and emphatically expressed the opinion that there was only one possible course – self-sacrifice. He thought that a pistol should be carried and that, "If anyone breaks down he should have the privilege of using it." We both agreed with this.'[11]

Oates took the same practical, unemotional attitude towards most humans as he did towards horses. He told Ponting that a weakened member should 'emphatically not be a burden to the others'. His own code of conduct, nurtured at public school and stimulated in the army, preached self-sacrifice. He had practised it most honourably in the engagement at Aberdeen and emerged with one leg shorter than the other. Oates was a man of considerable courage and the notion of self-sacrifice was inextricably bound up with duty. It held no fear for him.

Wilson, the moral guardian of the party, could not accept either suicide or the prospect of leaving any member of the team behind. He was someone prepared to accept whatever the fates dealt him. Wilson saw God's hand in most things and accepted that God knew best. A passage in a theological book he carried on the march contained the quotation: 'Suffering is the badge that Christ hath put upon his followers.' In the margin alongside, Wilson had scribbled: 'May God grant this true.'[12]

Wilson's wife, Oriana, made a surprising confession to Caroline Oates when they later met. 'In all her husband's letters from the base, he wrote to her as though he would not return and told her all he wanted to do in case he did not come back,' Mrs Oates remembered.[13]

It was Wilson who imbued in Scott the belief that the entire party might be sacrificed to save one fallen comrade. Wilson's conviction was spelt out in response to questions from Griffith Taylor, which included the revealing exchange:

> 'Griffith Taylor tells how he had put to Wilson the question, what should be done if one of the exploring party broke a leg? "Pitch camp," said Wilson, "kill plenty of seals and wait till you are relieved or till the

leg has healed enough to march." The possibility of abandoning a comrade was definitely ruled out; the implications of that advice were plain; and they held firm even in the wastes where no source of food was available.'[14]

Significantly, Wilson had changed his mind about self-sacrifice. Shortly after coming back from *Discovery* in 1904, a journalist asked what would happen on an expedition if one of the party was too ill to continue. Wilson replied:

'There is a code of honour among Arctic (*sic*) explorers. A man who is very ill knows perfectly well that he may cause grave risks to all his comrades and if the immediate risk of delay are indeed grave and he feels very feeble he walks out.'[15]

Such thoughts were far from their minds as the explorers moved slowly southwards. The entire party was now united for the first time, having travelled about 200 miles (320 km) from Cape Evans in three weeks. By contrast, Amundsen was well over half way to the Pole, carried south over virgin territory by his eager teams of dogs.

The ponies laboured badly in the snow, frequently sinking up to their hocks in the soft mushy conditions. Although their handlers displayed remarkable patience and frequently cared for the animals by giving them extra biscuits from their own ration at the end of a day's march, it was clear that the ponies were going downhill. Alongside, Meares and his hungry dogs hovered like four-legged vultures, waiting for the doomed animals to die and gorge themselves on an invigorating meal of fresh meat.

Oates put the first pony, Jehu, out of its misery on 24 November with a single shot to the head. It was about 15 miles (24 km) beyond where Shackleton killed his first horse three years earlier, which was taken as a minor triumph. Although he was used to seeing animals die, Oates derived no pleasure from the necessary deed. He admitted:

'It is a brutal thing killing these poor ponies. The sad part is that Jehu had plenty of march left in him but the dogs have to have food and forage is becoming short.'[16]

Both the dogs and men tucked into Jehu's flesh and felt revived by the fresh meat. The cuts were a brief and welcome variation for the men who had been eating an uninterrupted diet of sledging rations – dried meat pemmican mixed with water and biscuit to make what they called 'hoosh'. While 'hoosh' was immediately warming and filling, it was insufficient for the heavy labour of man-hauling. Even at this early stage in the expedition, the men were undernourished and on the way to being deficient in vital vitamins.

The loss of the first pony brought an immediate reorganisation, with Day and Hooper sent back to Hut Point with a pair of the weaker dogs and Atkinson, Jehu's handler, climbing into a man-hauling harness. On 28 November, Wright's pony Chinaman, was shot and the Canadian physicist joined the man-haulers.

For the first time, the party was now split into three four-man teams and the pattern for the expedition had been set. Scott took Wilson, Cherry-Garrard and Lashly, the second team contained Oates, Bowers, Taff Evans and Crean and the final group comprised the man-haulers, Teddy Evans, Atkinson, Wright and Keohane. Meares and Dimitri ran alongside with the dogs.

They were about 90 miles (145 km) from the Beardmore Glacier and spirits were revived by the added horseflesh and the sudden appearance of mountains on the distant horizon, which signalled an end to the boring and featureless Barrier stage of their journey. Even Oates was more cheerful, although he retained his strong sense of realism. On the 29 November, he wrote:

> 'I think we shall get to the Pole now but I think there is a very good chance of the Norskies getting there before us.'[17]

Oates was correct. By 29 November, Amundsen had crossed the Barrier and climbed the previously unexplored Axel Heiberg Glacier onto the Polar Plateau, about 200 miles (320 km) from the South Pole. With merciless efficiency, Amundsen was butchering his dogs to feed the survivors, thus reducing the weight of food he had to carry.

Oates shot the fiendish Christopher on the first day of December, although even in death the animal was troublesome. Just as Oates fired the gun, the animal moved and charged off with the bullet lodged in the side of his head, smashing into the camp and threatening to attack the nearest person. He was finally caught and put down with few regrets. Some of Christopher's remains were stored at the Southern Barrier Depot, the last supply cache before the Beardmore.

With the forage now beginning to dwindle, the ponies were shot with greater regularity, starting with Victor and Michael. Each pony was likely to provide at least four days food for the dogs and a welcome variation to the men's repetitive pemmican diet. It was, nonetheless, a sordid business for the men and a sorrowful moment for those who had developed a close attachment to their animals. Bowers cut off Victor's hooves and stored them in the snow, hoping to retrieve them on the way back to Cape Evans.

The weather began to deteriorate shortly before reaching the end of the Barrier, a full gale whipping up the drift and at one point blowing down the snow-walls which Oates had built to protect the ponies. On 5 December a blizzard halted the march in its tracks. It was impossible to see a few yards ahead in the swirling white-out. To their utter frustration, the men were confined to their tents for four days.

It was a gloomy time, particularly as the men had been forced to break into the rations set aside for the demanding Glacier stage of the journey. Bowers remained blissfully optimistic about the decision and said that delay would mean nothing worse than 'a little short commons' on the return journey. It was a 'trifling matter', he suggested.

The grim reality was that the men were eating food supplies which were meant to sustain them through the long return journey to Cape Evans. At that point, the party had covered under 400 miles (640 km) of a round trip of 1,800 miles (2,800 km) and would have to endure the remaining 1,400 miles (2,200 km) – over 75 per cent of the journey – dragging their sledges on reduced rations.

It was inevitable that the returning Polar party would be very tired after months of foot-slogging and, with hindsight, the march to the Pole should have been abandoned even before they began the dreadful climb up the Beardmore Glacier.

The blizzard was particularly hard on Oates, who struggled outside the tent through waist-high snowdrifts to tend the pitiable, freezing animals. On some occasions he added to his own discomfort by remaining outside with the ponies, crouched behind the snow wall in search of shelter from the howling winds.

It was a vigil which cost him badly-needed rest and frequent soakings. Evans remembered:

> 'The cutting wind whirling the sleet round the ponies gave them a very sorry time. But whenever one peeped out of the tent door there was Oates, wet to the skin, trying to keep life in his charges.'[18]

Temperatures of 33°F (½°C) were comparatively high in the Antarctic summer, although the downside was the area in and around the tents was a pool of slush about 18 inches (45 cm) deep which left everyone sopping wet. When the weather duly lifted on 9 December, they found it almost impossible to travel, with men and animals sinking deep into the layers of soft snow.

Every step was slow, tortuous labour and Wilson recalled that the animals could move only five or six yards at a time on the soft surface. Cherry-Garrard wrote:

> 'The horses could hardly move, sank up to their bellies and finally lay down. They had to be driven, lashed on. It was a grim business.'[19]

The forlorn procession took eleven hours to struggle only eight miles, the men and animals united in a supreme effort, desperately trying to avoid the dangers of hidden crevasses which could swallow a horse and sledge at the blink of an eye. The labouring man-hauling team under Evans was also finding the going very tough, toiling for fifteen hours in the appalling conditions and arriving at camp 'dead cooked'.

The exhausted party finally camped near the foot of the Beardmore, where the mountains and the Barrier come together in a confusion of broken ice and waves of pressure. It was the last resting place for the remaining five ponies, including Jimmy Pigg and Nobby, the only survivors of the depot-laying journey nine months earlier. Oates delivered the *coup de grace* with clinical efficiency and the depot was named Shambles Camp. Many were upset at losing the animals and Wright said it was a 'black day'.

Oates had fulfilled the remarkable task of coaxing the unsuited animals 400 miles across the Barrier. He had exceeded all expectations. Wilson strode up to Oates and said: 'Well! I congratulate you, Titus.' Scott, who was standing alongside, said: 'And *I* thank you, Titus.'[20]

Many of the men were thoroughly grateful that the ordeal of man-handling the ponies was at an end and positively relished the prospect of dragging their heavy sledges up the Glacier. Some saw something gallant and pure about the unremitting hard slog and Wilson blithely wrote:

'Thank God the horses are now all done with and we begin the heavier work ourselves.'[21]

Standing at the foot of the Beardmore, the men gazed up at the long chain of mountains poking out from either side of the frozen river of ice, which leads conveniently up to the Polar Plateau 120 miles (190 km) away. It was a fascinating, daunting sight of awesome beauty.

The Beardmore is the gateway to the Pole, the *Via Dolorosa* for British explorers. It represented a formidable challenge, especially for men climbing uphill and dragging 200 lb (90 kg) per head across the broken, crevasse-lined terrain. The glacier was discovered by Shackleton in 1908–09 and named after the Glasgow industrialist, William Beardmore, who had helped bank-roll the *Nimrod* expedition. It is about 14 miles wide (23 km) and rises almost 10,000 ft (3,000 m) to the plateau. Years later it was found to move relentlessly towards the Ice Barrier at over 3 ft (1 m) a day.

Oates felt quietly optimistic about the ascent because he was now in the strongest team, which was completed by Scott, Wilson and Taff Evans. The other four, who were also progressing very well, comprised Bowers, Cherry-Garrard, Crean and Keohane. The weakest group – Atkinson, Teddy Evans, Wright and Lashly – was showing distinct signs of weariness and causing the most worry. Teddy Evans and Lashly had already been man-hauling for over 350 miles and Atkinson and Wright were the first of the pony handlers to lose their animals two-thirds of the way across the Barrier.

Atkinson warned fellow doctor, Wilson, that Lashly and Wright were 'knocking up' with the heavy work and Scott noticed that Evans could not keep up the pace. He added:

'It is a very serious business if the men are going to crock up.'[22]

The other agenda was that Scott had finally decided that Teddy Evans would not be included in the party for the drive to the Pole. Scott's diary at this stage makes it clear that his official deputy had no place in the final group and he rearranged the make-up of the two other groups. But from the moment he left Shambles Camp, the personnel in Scott's tent remained undisturbed – Scott, Wilson, Taff Evans and Oates.

The dog teams under Meares and Dimitri were taken the first few miles onto the Beardmore, where the Lower Glacier Depot was established, but their valuable contribution to the project was over. On 11 December Meares and the Russian turned for home, carrying good wishes and a surprisingly gloomy letter from Scott to his wife which warned that 'things are not so rosy as they might be . . .'

Shortly before the friends parted, Oates strolled across and sat on Meares' sledge, chatting amiably together. The two outsiders then shook hands and said goodbye.

Meares had come much further than anticipated. Scott had intended to send him back to Cape Evans before the party reached the Beardmore, somewhere between the Mid Barrier and South Barrier depots at around 81°. But at the last moment, he added to the general confusion by taking him a further 100 miles (160 km) south and then changing his instructions for using the dog teams to assist with the return journey of the Polar party.

Meares was utterly fed up with Scott and toying with the idea of rushing back to Cape Evans to catch *Terra Nova* before the man-hauling Polar teams arrived back. The idea of returning to base in time to board the ship also appealed to Oates, who despite earlier indications, had made up his mind to return to the Inniskillings. Cherry-Garrard, among the last to speak to him, wrote that Oates 'meant to return' to the army. But Oates did not tell Scott.

Meares' new instructions were vague. Scott said the dogs should be taken south only to help speed the men back to Cape Evans to catch *Terra Nova*. There was no hint of urgency in the orders.

Scott's instructions were explicit in one crucial detail, which was that the dogs were not to be risked by coming too far south because they would be needed for other field duties. Cherry-Garrard set the record straight some years later when he wrote:

> 'It is necessary to emphasise the fact that the dog teams were intended to hasten the return of the Polar party, but that they were never meant to form a relief journey.'[23]

It is clear that the failure of Scott's party to appreciate the strengths of the dogs was a major contributory factor to the looming tragedy. Scott himself frequently remarked at how well the dogs travelled in difficult conditions and even determined man-haulers like Bowers paid grudging respect to the animals. In his diary, Bowers wrote a prophetic entry:

> 'The dogs are doing splendidly; when one sees how well our two teams have done, I must say that Amundsen's chance of having forestalled us with 120 dogs looks good.'[24]

As Meares turned northwards, Cherry-Garrard also recognised the obvious and observed:

> 'It began to look as if Amundsen had chosen the right form of transport.'[25]

Wilson was so impressed with the fitness of the animals that he prophesised Meares would have a 'very easy journey' back to base. In fact, Meares suffered badly on the 400-mile trip back to Hut Point.

Meares had travelled well over 100 miles further south than originally intended and he and Dimitri had to eke out their meagre rations, skipping one meal a day to avoid plundering Scott's food depots. Meares eventually made it back to Hut Point on 4 January. But it was a close shave and Meares and Dimitri would probably not have survived a prolonged bout of hostile weather on the Barrier.

Nevertheless, Meares confirmed the strength of the dogs by travelling far quicker than on the outward leg. On one day he made over 25 miles (38 km). But on arrival at Hut Point he learned from the *Terra Nova* that his father had died and he immediately elected to return home with the ship.

Shortly after Meares turned for home, the race for the Pole drew to a close. At 3 pm on 14 December 1911 Amundsen and his dogs reached the South Pole.

Scott was still about 400 miles behind, heaving and struggling up the Beardmore. It was a remarkable triumph of planning and execution and in a fine egalitarian gesture, Amundsen insisted that the five men – Olav Bjaaland, Helmer Hanssen, Sverre Hassel, Oscar Wisting and himself – should celebrate their achievement by planting the Norwegian flag together. He recalled:

> 'This was the only way in which I could show my gratitude to my comrades in this desolate spot. Five weatherbeaten, frostbitten fists they were that grasped that pole, raising the waving flag in the air, and planted it as the first at the geographical South Pole.'[26]

Amundsen stayed at the Pole for three days, completing his observations and leaving a few superfluous items like spare mitts and a sextant inside a spare tent. Inside also were the names of the five men and above flew the Norwegian flag and a pennant from *Fram*.[27]

The triumphant celebration at the Pole contrasted starkly with the suffering of Scott's party. The steep climb up the Beardmore was a debilitating ordeal, with the soft snow making the going very heavy. Most men were struck by painful attacks of snowblindness caused by the glare from the glistening white surface. But nothing compared with the intense strain of dragging the equivalent of nearly 190 lb (85 kg) per man uphill across soft, sticky snow with the ever-present threat that they might crash through the ice down an unseen crevasse.

The indefatigable Bowers said it was 'the most back-breaking work I have ever come up against' and Wilson, it was 'killing work'. On 13 December the men dragged the sledges uphill for nine and a half hours and managed to cover little more than 3 miles (5 km).

Bowers wrote a memorable account sitting exhausted in the tent one night which graphically illustrated the daily torture of man-hauling heavy loads up the Beardmore for hour after hour. He wrote:

> 'It was all we could do to keep the sledge moving for short spells of a few hundred yards, the whole concern sinking so deeply into the soft snow as to form a snow-plough. The starting was worse than pulling as it required from ten to fifteen jerks on the harness to move the sledge at all. I have never pulled so hard, or so nearly crushed my inside into my backbone by the everlasting jerking with all my strength on the canvas band round my unfortunate tummy.'[28]

This was the crucial stage of the journey, both the exhausting climb up the glacier and the moment fast approaching when Scott would make the final selection of men to go to the Pole. The weary men had plenty of time to speculate about the final party as they plodded along for hours in deathly silence.

The issue came to a head on 20 December as the men climbed close to the top of the glacier. At the end of the day's march, Scott summoned Atkinson and revealed that his party – Atkinson, Wright, Cherry-Garrard and Keohane – would be sent back the following day. They were bitterly disappointed and Scott, who disliked confrontation, said he 'dreaded this necessity of choosing'.

Wright was furious at the rejection. He considered himself among the fittest of the twelve men, despite the extra weeks of man-hauling and the earlier observations of Atkinson. He wrote an indignant short note in his diary which summed up his disappointment:

'Scott a fool. Too wild to write more tonight.'[29]

Oates was pivotal to the entire selection process. He had impressed Scott with his management of the ponies in the most trying circumstances and was evidently capable of the heavy pulling necessary to ascend the Beardmore. Scott did not recognise Oates' hostility towards him and still harboured thoughts of having the army represented at the Pole.

It was not necessarily the most scientific method of selection but it ensured that Oates had been assigned a place in history.

20

Wrong man, wrong place

What Scott plainly did not appreciate was that Oates was already in decline. The heavy labour up the Beardmore had begun to drain him and his limp added to the difficulties.

The limp gave Oates a slight tilt to his pelvis, which forced his spine into an awkward curve and inevitably made the simple task of walking a more taxing exercise than was common. Nor was he accustomed to such long treks. Cavalry officers were trained to ride, not march. His ungainly posture was not designed for the back-breaking struggle of pulling the equivalent of 190 lb (85 kg) uphill over the snow and ice in sub-zero temperatures for eight to ten hours a day.

The first clear indication of Oates' decline emerged in his own diary on 19 December, the day before Scott ordered Atkinson's team to return. Crouched in his tent at the end of the day's march near the top of the Beardmore, Oates recorded:

> 'My feet are giving me a bit of trouble, they have been continually wet since leaving Hut Point and now walking along this hard ice in frozen crampons has made rather hay of them. Still they are not the worst in the outfit by a long chalk.'[1]

Oates had by now marched around 500 miles with wet feet, mostly in temperatures well below zero. His finnesko – reindeer hide boots, lined with sennegras (fine hay) for insulation against the cold – had proved inadequate against the biting cold. It is likely that his feet had been repeatedly soaked while selflessly tending the ponies on the Barrier and his condition was not helped by an unfortunate problem with personal hygiene.

Oates suffered what Atkinson politely described as 'undue perspiration of the feet' which meant that, even in dry conditions, his feet were damp with sweat. The hard work of a ten-hour march made his feet sweat profusely and in the freezing temperatures, the moisture literally froze on his feet. What had been a mess-hall joke in a temperate climate, suddenly assumed deadly importance in sub-zero temperatures on the Beardmore Glacier.

Another problem for Oates was poor circulation, which in warmer environments like India and Egypt had barely been noticed. He told Atkinson, the only person in whom he now confided, that his hands were always cold, which was also consistent with someone feeling the effects of under-nourishment and inferior circulation.

Oates evidently had his own private doubts about his ability to continue. Years later, Cherry-Garrard recalled a significant conversation between Oates and Atkinson as they climbed the Beardmore, which was the clearest indication that Oates did not want to continue the march. Cherry-Garrard remembered:

'. . . (Atkinson) did not think Titus wanted to go on, though he did not actually say so. He thinks Titus knew he was done – his face showed him to be so and the way he went along.'[2].

Oates told Atkinson that he 'did not feel fit to go on'.[3] Meares, when questioned years afterwards, added his own postscript:

'I always think what a pity it was that Titus, handicapped with his wounded leg, was taken on that ill-fated Polar party; his services would have been so valuable to his country in the Great War.'[4]

But, crucially, the valuable information that Oates was tiring was not passed onto Scott, probably because like so many in the expedition, Atkinson found Scott remote and unapproachable. Wright also spotted weaknesses among the party. But, he too, refrained from telling Scott. More than 60 years after the tragedy, he explained:

'I felt that I was the better man to go along than certainly one and maybe two of those who did. Thinking in terms of Scott's objective that he would have been wiser if he'd taken me and left A or B perhaps.'[5]

Wright never elaborated on the identities of A or B, but it is assumed that Teddy Evans was one. Evans, who had man-hauled for almost 500 miles and was near exhaustion, was an obvious choice to return. The other candidate was probably Oates.

Scott's ignorance of Oates' fitness is also illustrated by a conversation between Wilson and Cherry-Garrard shortly before the first party was sent back to Cape

Evans. Wilson spoke to Scott about the make-up of the teams and Cherry-Garrard remembered a conversation:

'It was a toss-up whether Titus or I (Cherry-Garrard) should go on . . .'[6]

It must be assumed that Oates would have gone back to Cape Evans with Atkinson's first returning party if Scott had been informed about his mood and condition. However, Oates did not feel inclined to tell Scott how he was feeling, mainly because of the breakdown in communication and also he did not wish to be seen letting the side down. It was a costly breakdown.

Oates' dislike of Scott also contributed to his silence. He was now driven more by contempt than ambition for the Pole and was determined not to show signs of weakness to a man he despised. Oates was equally consumed with his overriding sense of duty and natural stoicism, which made it difficult for him to admit a weakness. Suffering in silence was a particular characteristic of Oates.

Scott at least had made up his own mind about the composition of the final party, even if he did not share the facts with his colleagues. Atkinson's team turned northwards on 22 December and on the same day, Scott began a new diary with a revealing entry on the flyleaf. It was a death warrant, which read:

'Ages: Self 43, Wilson 39, Evans (PO) 37, Oates 32, Bowers 28. Average 36.'[7]

The remarkable feature of his selection is that Scott chose to pick his men when less than 300 miles from the Pole. It was a choice he should have made in the hut at Cape Evans during the long Antarctic winter, when he could have assessed the physical and mental strengths and weakness of the men after suitable consultation with the doctors, Atkinson and Wilson. Instead, he made the choice when his options were narrowest.

The baffling fact is that Scott liked to study human nature and generally recorded his views – often unflattering – in his private journals. Many of the comments about individuals were later deemed too insensitive and were excised or toned down in the published version of his diary.

The options before Scott were strictly limited even before he sent back Atkinson's party, leaving just eight men to choose from. Teddy Evans had been ruled out for personal reasons and because he was exhausted, taking Lashly was too risky after his strenuous exertions and even the once powerful Taff Evans was showing signs of struggling.

Wilson, it is assumed, was always likely to be included because he was a doctor and close to Scott. He was also fit and proved to be an outstanding sledger.

Bowers, with his navigational skills and immense appetite for work, had forced his way into the reckoning. Crean, a formidably strong character who had only begun man-hauling at the foot of the Beardmore, was probably the fittest of all eight men at the top of the Beardmore. He should have made the final team.

In the circumstances at the top of the Beardmore, the final party should have been Scott, Wilson, Bowers and Crean. The biggest mistake was that neither Scott nor Wilson appears to have inspected the men closely. Oates, the professional soldier, would have testified to the wisdom of inspecting troops before a battle.

But there appears to have been no open discussion about the suitability of Oates, least of all with the man who mattered above all in the circumstances – Scott. Scott, according to a conversation between Wilson and Atkinson, remained irrationally committed to the army being represented at the Pole and wanted Oates to continue. At a key moment when the coolest and most clear-headed judgements were needed, Scott let sentiment override everything.

George Bernard Shaw, an outspoken critic of Scott – despite his long friendship with Kathleen Scott – was among those who later delivered a damning judgement of Scott's choice of men for the Polar party. In a letter to Mrs Scott, written a decade after the tragedy, he observed:

> '. . . (Scott) was a man of sentiment: when his feelings were touched his judgement ceased to exist. He was therefore dependent on his luck.'[8]

Cherry-Garrard, one of the last men to see the party alive, rightly concluded that Scott had made an error of judgement in choosing Oates. Debenham recalled a conversation with Cherry-Garrard:

> 'Cherry-Garrard told me that the selection of Oates for the Polar party was a mistake.'[9]

There appears to have been little or no group discussion about the make-up of the party, aside from a brief word with Wilson who, in any event, was not the type to challenge leadership's decisions. Scott simply presented his team selection as a *fait accompli*. A life in the navy meant that Scott was accustomed to a regime of unquestioning loyalty and blind obedience to orders.

Wilson's role at this stage was hugely significant. He was Scott's mental prop and the bridge between the introverted leader and the others. Yet he appears to have failed to inform Scott about the condition of the men toiling up the Beardmore. Nor did he question his judgement over the choice of Oates, or anyone else.

Nor could Wilson have failed to notice the steady decline of Oates with whom he shared a tent for over four weeks as they laboured together up the Beardmore. Teddy Evans, writing years afterwards, pointed an accusing finger at Wilson's odd failure to speak up:

'. . . a close observer, a man trained to watch over men's health, over athletes training, perhaps, would have seen something amiss.'[10]

Wilson clearly had his own opinions and it is known that he discussed the fitness of the three remaining seamen – Crean, Evans and Lashly – with Atkinson. Atkinson said Lashly was the fittest, which was an odd choice considering that he clocked up more man-hauling miles than any of the trio. Wilson, surprisingly, agreed.

Next, said Atkinson, was Crean, though Wilson did not agree with this choice. Neither Atkinson nor Wilson chose Taff Evans, who was Scott's favourite. Either Wilson did not speak to Scott about the fitness of Evans or was ignored. Cherry-Garrard, too, felt the choice of Evans was another mistake in the final party's make-up, which meant that he, at least, had spotted the Welshman's decline.

Wilson himself was not expecting to make the final march and told Cherry-Garrard that he fully anticipated being among the next group to be sent back, the last supporting party.

The irony is that Oates began a noticeable decline at precisely the moment Scott was reaching his fateful decision. Luck had run out for Oates.

He was still suffering badly with his cold wet feet and on 26 December, a new worry emerged. He recorded in his diary:

'The back tendon of my right leg feels as if it had been stretched about four inches. I hope to goodness it is not going to give trouble.'[11]

The strain of marching and dragging a sledge with a limp was clearly taking its toll and there was little time to rest any of the inevitable aches and strains which had been picked up on the strenuous marches. There was no choice but to slog on. In a more communicative environment, Oates would have discussed his injured tendon and wet feet with Wilson. In the event he simply soldiered on uncomplaining.

The pulling was very hard, with the weaker team – Teddy Evans, Bowers, Crean and Lashly – falling steadily behind. They slogged for more than eleven hours to cover only twelve miles on 30 December and after a welcome meal were too tired even to write up their diaries. Oates, in Scott's stronger team, observed:

'They (Evans' team) had a dreadfully heavy day arriving in camp ¾ hour after us. Poor devils they are having a cruel time of it. They have a lighter load than us but their sledge must have something the matter with it.'[12]

On the same day, about 100 miles over the horizon to the east, Amundsen and his four colleagues flew unseen past the British party in the other direction, rushing to catch the *Fram* with their historic news. Almost close enough to wave, but not quite.

Scott made another startling decision the next day. He ordered Evans, Bowers, Crean and Lashly to leave their skis behind to save weight, which consigned the weakest group to an energy-sapping torment of foot-slogging over the soft, broken ground. Scott's motive appeared to be that he wanted to break Evans' team and justify his subsequent decision not to take his deputy to the Pole. In a telling entry to his diary, he wrote that the march without skis was '. . . a plod for the foot people and pretty easy going for us . . .'[13]

A welcome half-day's rest was taken on New Year's Eve, as the men camped at 87° and established Three Degree Depot, about 200 statute miles from the Pole. A group of five men – Scott, Teddy Evans, Bowers, Wilson and Oates – squeezed into Scott's tent and spent a relaxed afternoon chatting, drinking tea and doing odd mending jobs. It was an agreeable break and for a moment, the stress and heavy work were forgotten as they sipped their warming drinks and unwound.

Evans remembered that the normally reticent Oates suddenly came out of his shell and for the first time that anyone could recall, he cheerfully took the lead in the conversation. In the little green tent, at over 9,000 ft (2,700 m) on the Polar plateau Oates blossomed, charming and amusing his colleagues with engaging stories about his home and army life.

Oates brought chortles of laugher as he recounted tales about boyish escapades at Eton and pig-sticking in India. Evans remembered that Oates talked on and on, his large brown eyes sparkling as he entertained the slightly surprised group who were more accustomed to his long brooding silences. He recalled:

'Oates talked for some hours. At length, Captain Scott reached out and affectionately seized him in the way that was itself so characteristic of our leader and said: "You funny old thing, you have quite come out of your shell, Soldier. Do you know we have all sat here talking for nearly four hours? It's New Year's Day and 1 am."

This was the only occasion when we ever took a holiday on that memorable journey . . . we warmed to one another in a way that we had never thought of, quite oblivious to cold, hardship, scant rations, or the great monotony of sledge-hauling.'[14]

Oates had relaxed, probably because he felt that he was nearing his journey's end and would shortly be sent back with the last returning party. Getting the pitiful ponies to the bottom of the Beardmore was a marvellous achievement in itself and climbing the imposing glacier was a huge bonus. He had exceeded his expectations and the burden of duty and responsibility had been lifted. Quite reasonably, Oates probably assumed that his deterioration had been spotted by either Scott or Wilson and that he was probably going home.

Outside in temperatures down to −10°F (−23°C), Crean, Taff Evans and Lashly were engaged in the unpleasant task of converting the sledges from 12 ft (3.6 m) to 10 ft (3 m) with spare runners. It was hard work in the freezing temperatures and in the process Taff Evans sustained a severe cut to his hand. Evans, like Oates with his saturated feet, concealed the wound. Evans had been alongside Scott since the *Discovery* expedition a decade earlier and badly wanted to be among the select band to stand at the South Pole. He was only 200 miles from the Pole and fame, and Evans did not want a trifling cut to extinguish his burning ambition. What he did not appreciate was that in the frigid cold of the Polar regions, cuts take far longer to heal.

Scott waited until the eight men were barely 150 geographic miles from the Pole before dropping his final bombshell. On 3 January, he announced that instead of leading a four-man party to the Pole, he would take an extra person. The final five were Scott, Wilson, Bowers, Taff Evans and Oates, the names he had scribbled in his diary a few days earlier.

The Last Supporting Party of Teddy Evans, Crean and Lashly would return short-handed. It was another mistake.

Scott, ably assisted by Bowers' organisational skills, had built the entire expedition's supplies and equipment round teams of four. All the food and oil depots along the path of the return journey had been broken down into pre-packed units of four and the extra man would undoubtedly disrupt the carefully-planned organisation. Teddy Evans, Crean and Lashly, would have to extract three-quarters of the food and fuel from each depot and leave a quarter behind for the returning Polar team. It also meant losing more precious time sorting out rations and cooking for an extra person.

Observers have since calculated that Scott may have panicked as he surveyed his immediate prospects less than two weeks of decent marches from the Pole. He still faced around 1,000 miles (1,600 km) of man-hauling to the Pole and back to Cape Evans and a fifth man was a guarantee against failure. A better guarantee would have been to scrutinise his men.

Scott was torn with anguish over the decision to take an extra man. Although he had plainly decided against including Teddy Evans, he waited until the very last minute before announcing his decision and even then found it difficult to speak directly to the bitterly disappointed men he was sending back.

Scott went across to Evans' party to deliver the bad news. As he entered the smoke-filled tent Crean, a life-long pipe-smoker, was clearing his throat. Crean had served Scott with unswerving loyalty since their *Discovery* days a decade earlier but Scott did not have the courage to speak plainly. The cough was the perfect excuse and Scott declared:

'You've got a bad cold, Crean.'

The canny Crean immediately saw through Scott and refused to go quietly, responding:

'I understand a half-sung song, sir.'[15]

Scott ordered Bowers, Crean and Lashly out of the tent and told Teddy Evans that he was not going to the Pole. Scott asked if he could 'spare' Bowers. It was a devastating blow to Evans, who had spent well over two years preparing for the mission and naturally assumed as second-in-command that he would be in the final party.

The decision was also potentially threatening to Evans, Crean and Lashly, who faced a daunting 750 mile (1,200 km) return to base camp with only three men. It was a highly risky prospect when only Evans was capable of navigation and the risk of accident in the crevasses of the Beardmore was readily apparent. In addition, their sledgemeter had broken and the men would have to guess the daily distances travelled, relying heavily on the outward tracks to pick their pathway home.

Teddy Evans was deeply disappointed but had little choice. He may have disagreed with Scott but Evans was a disciplined naval officer. He stifled his disappointment.

It was different for Oates. Although he had long since dismissed Scott as a poor leader, his strong code of honour and unshakeable devotion to duty meant that Oates could not reveal his true condition. Oates suffered in silence when the occasion screamed out for frankness. Oates had spurned two golden opportunities to return, first with Atkinson and now with Evans. No one would have thought worse of the man, particularly as he had accomplished his main task.

Scott was unable to judge things coolly and unemotionally, Teddy Evans had been marginalised and Wilson and Bowers loyally kept their own counsel. Crean, Taff Evans and Lashly as ordinary seamen carried no weight with Scott and were never consulted or involved in decision-making. Nor did Scott bother to ask if Oates wanted to march on. Oates was at the mercy of events.

Oates scribbled a final letter to his mother and brother Bryan for Evans to carry back in time for *Terra Nova's* departure. The note to his mother was a slightly disjointed missive, sprinkled with optimism about reaching the Pole and offering odd hints that, in spite of the potential glory ahead, he was longing to be back home at Gestingthorpe. He also took the opportunity to reassure his mother about his health and conveniently to gloss over his own decline. He wrote:

'I have been selected to go to the Pole with Scott as you have seen by the papers. I am of course delighted but I am sorry I shall not be home for another year as we shall miss the ship. We shall get to the Pole alright. We are now within 50 miles of Shackleton's Farthest South.

It is pretty cold up here (9,500 ft) and the work has been very heavy but it is easier now as we can ski. I am very fit indeed and have lost condition less than anyone else almost.

I hope the alterations at Gestingthorpe have been carried out . . . it will be nice in there as I can have a fire at night . . .

Can you please also send me ½ doz books so that I can start working on my major's exam on the way home, these things should be addressed to *Terra Nova* at Lyttelton.

What a lot we shall have to talk about when I get back – God bless and keep you well until I come home.

L.E.G. Oates.

4th: We get plenty of food and as soon as we start back we have plenty in the depots. Please give my love to Violet, Lillian and Eric. I am afraid the letter I wrote from the hut was full of grumbles but I was very anxious about starting off with those ponies.'[16]

Oates' last letter to his mother was the only recorded occasion he mentioned God in his notes home. He invariably signed off with a formal, 'Yours affectionately' and some may feel there was something deeper at work in that final poignant letter. Except that Oates was not spiritual.

Oates handed over his final letters to Evans and asked him to write and let his family know how fit and happy he was. It was an emotional parting and Evans recorded his last conversation with Oates:

'He asked me to send him out tobacco and sweets by the dog teams, and his last words to any man now living were words of consolation at our not going forward and thanks for our undertaking the return journey short-handed, which meant as we then thought, so much to the Polar party.'[17]

Evans also carried another message for either Meares or Atkinson to bring the dogs out to 82° or 83° in mid-February to help the returning party catch the *Terra Nova* before she escaped the clutches of the ice. Scott happily assumed that Evans, Crean and Lashly would have an easy 750-mile ride home. It was a dangerous assumption.

In the event, Evans was struck down with scurvy on the return march and Crean and Lashly had to drag him over 100 miles on the sledge in a memorable act of self-sacrifice and heroism. Crean finally saved Evans' life by walking the final 35 miles to Hut Point in eighteen hours without adequate food or shelter. Crean had already marched for 1,500 miles when he set out and his solo journey to Hut Point ranks as the greatest single-handed act of heroism and fortitude in the entire Heroic Age of Polar exploration.

Evans, Crean and Lashly accompanied the five men southwards for a few miles to make sure that they were able to get along in the new enlarged formation. At around 10am on 4 January, the two parties came to a standstill at 87°34', about 170 statute miles (270 km) or a little under 150 geographic miles from the South Pole.

The parting was painful and emotion-charged, with hard-man Crean openly in tears at being denied so close to the Pole. Teddy Evans said the normally composed Oates was the most affected of the Polar party as the eight men exchanged warm well-wishes and firm handshakes. Oates was characteristically considerate. His parting words were to console the three men facing the long journey home and to offer the encouragement of fresh meat on the Barrier. Oates comforted Evans with the parting thought:

'I am afraid, Teddy, you won't have much of a slope going back, but old Christopher is waiting to be eaten on the Barrier when you get there.'[18]

With the wind howling and temperatures down to a numbing −17°F (−27°C), the five set off southwards. As they stepped out, Evans, Crean and Lashly broke the chilly silence of the Plateau with a resounding 'three huge cheers'. Oates, who was pulling in the rear, turned and cheerfully waved his hand several times.

Evans, Crean and Lashly stood silently for as long as the lacerating wind would allow, watching the party moving slowly towards the endless white horizon. The last sight was a cluster of indistinguishable black specks, silhouetted against a bleached ocean of whiteness. Both groups frequently turned round to see each other receding slowly into the distance. The black dots soon grew smaller and finally disappeared.

Scott, Wilson, Bowers, Evans and Oates were perhaps twelve to fourteen days' march from their goal. There were no traces of Norwegian dog tracks and the excitement was intense. The South Pole was within grasp.

21

The abyss of defeat

The final lap to the South Pole began optimistically. The five managed little over 11¼ miles (18 km) on 5 January, despite some very heavy dragging. Scott observed that 'everything is going with extraordinary smoothness' and Wilson wrote a businesslike entry in his diary entry predicting arrival at the Pole on 15 January.

Oates shared the optimism. He had scrawled a brief, single-page letter to his brother, Bryan, which Teddy Evans carried back to the *Terra Nova*. It began with the confident declaration:

'We shall get to the Pole alright. . .'[1]

The tragedy began to evolve on the same day that Wilson wrote his cheerful forecast. The travelling surfaces started to deteriorate and Scott noticed another unexpected problem. The extra person in a four-man tent added considerably to the discomfort and he gloomily observed:

'Cooking for five takes a seriously longer time than cooking for four; perhaps half an hour on the whole day. It is an item I had not considered when reorganising.'[2]

The loss of valuable time was critical as the men fought their way slowly over the Plateau, covering barely one mile an hour and gasping for breath in the thin air nearly two miles (3 km) above sea level. They would need every available hour in the harness to make the trek to the Pole and back to the safety of Cape Evans.

Bowers, who was travelling without skis, also struggled in the heavy surface, his short stumpy legs often sinking deep into the snow. Equally critical was the poor diet, which unknown to the men, was not providing them with enough to sustain them for the very heavy work of man-hauling. Hunger was emerging as a vital factor and Bowers conceded that the men would '. . . all eat far more needless to say. . .'

The basic daily ration was twelve ounces of pemmican, biscuits, butter, sugar, cocoa and tea, which provided around 4,500 calories per man. Modern research has indicated that a minimum of 6,000 calories per day is needed for the sort of heavy labour which the five men were experiencing for up to ten hours per day. The three men who retraced the footsteps of Scott's expedition in 1985–86 – Roger Mear, Robert Swan and Gareth Wood – were advised by nutritionists that a massive 8,000 calories a day was a more realistic figure.

The diet also lacked the necessary intake of vitamins, particularly vitamin C, which is found in fresh meat and vegetables and is now known to be necessary to combat scurvy. Fit men begin to suffer the effects of scurvy after about three months without vitamin C. Scott, Shackleton and Wilson had been struck by scurvy on the 'Furthest South' journey in 1902–3, which lasted three months. In 1909, Shackleton and his three companions barely survived a terrible four-and-a-half-month journey which took them to within 97 miles of the Pole. Teddy Evans was only narrowly saved from death by the bravery of Crean and Lashly on the last supporting party's hazardous return. Evans was on the march for almost four months.

By now Scott's Polar party had been foot-slogging for almost two and a half months with only the odd intake of horseflesh to slow the inevitable onset of scurvy. Ahead lay at least another two and a half months and close to 1,000 miles of physically draining man-hauling without fresh meat or vegetables.

Taff Evans, meantime, found that his badly cut hand stubbornly refused to heal and did not appreciate that it was another sign of vitamin C deficiency.

In addition, the men were always thirsty. All drinking water or water for a hot mug of tea or cocoa had to be melted in the Primus stove and it was not practical to stop every time the men needed a drink. Despite the biting cold of –20°F below (–29°C) on the Plateau, the men sweated heavily under the protective clothing and badly needed to maintain a steady intake of fluid. In the daily struggle, the sweat froze on their body, increasing their discomfort.

The starving, dehydrated and vitamin-deficient men marched on in a silent, monotonous struggle against the elements. An eight-hour slog in the harness was standard and Scott added to the woes on 7 January when he abruptly ordered the party to abandon their skis. It was a bizarre decision sparked by frustration with the difficult travelling surfaces. He soon came to his senses and returned to pick up the skis. But it cost them one and a half hours of lost time. At camp that night, Scott for the first time noticed that Evans had cut his hand.

A blizzard confined the men to their tent on 8 January and a day later they passed Shackleton's 'Furthest South', Scott reaching the point on exactly the same day as Shackleton. In their triumph, no one had remembered that only three years earlier, an exhausted and emaciated party of Shackleton, Wild, Adams and Marshall had escaped death by the slimmest margin on the desperately close race back to McMurdo Sound.

On 11 January Scott admitted that the hauling 'takes it out of us like anything'. The following day, just 72 miles from the Pole, he further conceded they were struggling. The men were now drawing on their reserves, even though they had yet to reach the halfway point in the long journey and Scott added:

> 'At camping tonight everyone was chilled and we guessed a cold snap, but to our surprise the actual temperature was higher than last night. . . It is most unaccountable why we should suddenly feel the cold in this manner.'[3]

Scott's mood swung between pessimism and optimism, though he was at his most positive in discussing his companions. He recognised that Oates had proved invaluable with the ponies and added:

> '. . . now he is a foot slogger and goes hard the whole time, does his share of camp work and stands the hardships as well as any of us. I would not like to be without him. . .'[4]

But Scott had not looked closely enough and did not spot that Oates was clearly feeling the strain. It was not until 14 January – about 40 miles from the Pole – that Scott finally recognised Oates might be in trouble. He entered a brief comment in his diary, which read:

> 'Oates seems to be feeling the cold and fatigue more than the rest of us, but we are all very fit. It is a critical time, but we ought to pull through.'[5]

The exhausting work and dietary deficiencies were also having an effect on Oates' morale. Although the triumph of reaching the Pole might be expected to lift his spirits, Oates was despondent and there was little sense of satisfaction or impending achievement. Nearing the goal of their ambition on 15 January, he wrote:

> 'My pemmican must have disagreed with me at breakfast for coming along I felt very depressed and homesick.'[6]

Scott lightened the sledges the following day by caching some supplies and pushed on for the remaining 30 miles (48 km) to the Pole, concerned only at the 'appalling possibility' that the Norwegians had beaten them to the prize. During the afternoon, their world caved in.

At around 5 pm on 16 January, the keen-eyed Bowers suddenly spotted a black speck in the far distance. As they stumbled forward, the dark contour began to take on the ominous shape of a ragged black flag, which fluttered menacingly in the bone-chilling wind. Within a short time ski tracks, paw-prints and dog excrement confirmed the worst. 'All the day-dreams must go,' Scott wrote.

The makeshift Norwegian banner was a devastating blow. Hopes and dreams lay in ruins. The disappointment was acute, although Oates observed the black mood with a typically laconic observation:

'We are not a very happy party tonight.'[7]

Bowers took this photograph of his dejected colleagues inspecting Amundsen's tent, flying the Norwegian flag at the South Pole. Left to right: Scott, Oates, Wilson and Evans. (SPRI)

Oates appeared to take the crushing defeat better than most, perhaps because he had not realistically expected to ever stand at the Pole. His judgement was more measured and rational than the others who, in their different ways, had slaved for the honour of being first at the Pole.

Oates had detached himself emotionally from the enterprise and alone among the group was capable of recognising the outstanding achievement of Amundsen. The best man had won and he knew it. Even at the very moment of ultimate defeat, he was able to write a generous tribute to the victorious Norwegian:

'Thirteen miles from the Pole and we have picked up the Norskies tracks pointing straight here. Scott is taking his defeat better than I expected.

The Polar party took a series of photographs during their brief stay at the South Pole. 'Great God! This is an awful place,' Scott wrote. The tortured looks on the faces of the five men show the enormous physical strain and emotional impact of their ordeal. (Left to right) Bowers, Oates, Evans, Scott and Wilson. (SPRI)

I must say that man (Amundsen) must have had his head screwed on right. The gear they left was in excellent order and they seem to have had a comfortable trip with their dog teams. Very different to our wretched man-hauling.'[8]

Wilson would only concede that Amundsen had beaten them '. . . in so far as he had made a race of it'. Bowers tapped heavily into his jingoistic vein and wrote:

'It is sad that we have been forestalled by the Norwegians, but I am glad that we have done it by good British manhaulage.'[9]

Sleep came hard to the men in the tent, huddled together for warmth as temperatures near the Pole dropped to –23°F (–30°C). To add to the discomfort, the chilling winds had inflicted irritating frostbites to the cheeks and noses of Oates, Bowers and Evans.

In the morning they marched closer to the Pole itself in vile weather. Temperatures were about –22°F (–30°C) and the cutting 30 mph winds blew directly into their frostbitten faces. Wilson, who had endured the horrors of the winter trip to Cape Crozier, said it was the coldest march he could remember. Scott wrote:

'Great God! This is an awful place and terrible enough for us to have laboured to it without the reward of priority.'[10]

The following day, 18 January, they came across a Norwegian tent with a note showing that the five explorers had captured the geographical prize a month earlier and had spent some days in the area fixing the precise location of the Pole. Inside the neat, tidy tent Amundsen had left various pieces of gear, including a sextant, half a reindeer sleeping bag and socks.

Amundsen also left a letter addressed to King Haakon of Norway and a brief covering note asking Scott to forward it. Amundsen correctly assumed that Scott's party would be the next to reach the Pole and the covering note was valuable insurance that news of his conquest would reach the outside world in the event of an accident on the return leg to the *Fram*. Nothing was left to chance.

Another interpretation, made some years later by Raymond Priestley, a member of Campbell's Northern party, was that Amundsen's apparently innocent request had effectively down-graded Scott from 'explorer to postman'.

All that remained was the anti-climatic and sorry ritual of recording their own achievement. It was, by any standards, a tremendous feat to reach the Pole, particularly as the journey had been completed largely in the man-hauling harness. But there was no sense of accomplishment.

A short note was left in the Norwegian tent announcing their visit to the Pole and Scott said they put up their own 'poor slighted Union jack' before taking some photographs of the scene.

It was perhaps the most remarkable photographic session ever taken, with Bowers pulling a length of string to take each picture of the five men clustered together at the bottom of the world. Each weatherbeaten, tortured face told its own bleak story as the five dejected men tried to compose themselves against the biting winds in temperatures down to −21°F (−29°C). They were posing for posterity and wished they were somewhere else.

Defeat. The disconsolate party photographed after the shattering discovery that Amundsen had won the race to the South Pole. Oates (left) stands aside from his colleagues, leaning uneasily on his shorter left leg and with his shoulders rounded by exhaustion. Oates is unrecognisable from the stiff-backed cavalry officer who readily volunteered to join the expedition. Scott stands (back centre) alongside Evans. Bowers (left) and Wilson are sitting. (SPRI)

Oates strikes the most disconsolate and unhappy figure of the quartet, his body language being that of a man longing to escape from his plight. In the most famous picture of the five gathered in front of the limp Union Jack, he stands slightly aside from his colleagues, his shoulders rounded by exhaustion and his head propped uneasily at an angle. Oates is a semi-detached figure, leaning heavily on his shorter left leg. The slouching, abject character is barely recognisable from the stiff-backed cavalry captain who had strutted the parade grounds in India, Egypt and Ireland.

The full cost of the exertion, cold, hunger and utter disappointment is plainly etched in the gaunt, haunted features of a man who is staring into the abyss. It is the face of a man without hope.

22

'God help us. . .'

The return journey, from the very start, was a fight for survival. The 900-mile (1,440-km) march to the Pole had drained them physically and their spirits had evaporated at the sight of the Norwegian flag.

Shortly before turning northwards, Scott had posed the ultimate question in his diary which suggests serious doubt in his mind about his own chances of survival:

> 'Now for the run home and a desperate struggle. I wonder if we can do it.'[1]

Oates found the going especially hard, the biting cold gnawing at his increasingly emaciated frame and his cold, wet feet continuing to give trouble. He was probably the first whose decline was plainly apparent to his colleagues. On 20 January, only two days after leaving the Pole, Scott observed:

> 'I think Oates is feeling the cold and fatigue more than most of us.'[2]

Oates had noticed another worrying sign of his being run-down. In a brief diary entry, he gave the first indication that his circulation had been impaired by frostbite. He wrote:

> 'One of my big toes has turned black. I hope it is not going to lame me for marching.'[3]

In fact, amputation was probably the best Oates could now expect.

He was not the only one with problems. Evans, who had taken the defeat harder than anyone, was suffering badly from frostbitten hands picked up while camped at the Pole and according to Scott, was already a 'good deal run down'.

The indefatigable Bowers was finding the labour of plodding through soft snow without skis a dreadfully tiring business and Wilson was hit by a painful attack of snowblindness. He also suffered a strained leg muscle, probably arising from a local haemorrhage which may have been related to the first signs of scurvy.

As expected, the weather was a major worry. They had recognised from the beginning that the Plateau stage posed a serious hurdle to tiring men on the return leg and the safety margin would be further eroded if a blizzard confined them to the tent for any length of time.

The men could ill afford to lose any time since Scott had cut things fine, spreading his line of supply depots of food and fuel too far apart. Nor were the depots easy to spot on the ocean of whiteness.

Amundsen had been galvanised by the fear of missing vital supply depots and constructed an elaborate system of traverse marking which reduced the risk of marching past a cache in the rush to get home. On each side of the depot, he placed ten flags at intervals of one mile, each one numbered to point the way to the precious horde. The risk of missing a depot was slim.

Scott, by contrast, built a single snow cairn over his food depots, topped off with a flag. It meant he was forced to rely heavily on the outward tracks of the party to pick up his caches on the way home and there was no fall-back if the snow covered his old steps.

The alarm bells began to sound little more than a week after turning homeward. On 24 January, a blizzard struck and a concerned Scott made an anxious entry into his diary:

> 'Is the weather breaking up? If so, God help us, with the tremendous summit journey and scant food. I don't like the easy way in which Oates and Evans get frostbitten.'[4]

On 25 January, Bowers warned they would be 'in queer street' if they missed the next depot. On the same day, about 800 miles to the north, the triumphant Norwegians sped into their Framheim base at the Bay of Whales with two sledges, eleven dogs and five men – 'all hale and hearty'. The historic 1,860-mile round-trip had taken 99 days – an average of almost nineteen miles a day. Amundsen discovered that he had gained weight during the journey.

By contrast, hunger was now preoccupying the thoughts of Scott's team as they marched silently for hour after endless hour, longing for the warming satisfaction of a full stomach. Wilson said they could eat 'twice what we have' and Scott commented 'we are slowly getting more hungry'. The once muscular Evans, he observed, was especially thin.

Oates was cheered on 28 January when they camped near the spot where the team had parted company with Evans, Crean and Lashly three and a half weeks earlier. Sticking out of the snow was his pipe, which he had inadvertently dropped. It was a welcome but brief slice of luck and comfort for the cold, tired and hungry Oates.

Sitting opposite in the tent, Wilson observed that Oates' big toe was 'turning blue black'. His nose and face, Wilson recorded, were 'dead yellow'.

Bowers perked up on 31 January when he retrieved his skis and was at last able to travel a little easier. He had trudged more than 400 miles (640 km) on foot and was inevitably drained by the extra effort. But the immediate problems lay elsewhere.

Evans began to go rapidly downhill as January faded into February and the marches began to get slower without his bull-like strength. The five underfed, overworked men had been on the Polar Plateau for seven weeks in temperatures averaging –20°F (–29°C). On 3 February, the usually optimistic Bowers made the last entry in his private journal and was now only keeping the party's meteorological log.

Frostbite, which attacked Evans at the Pole, had stubbornly refused to let go and his cut hand was a festering mess. His hands were raw and the finger nails began to drop off, leaving ghastly suppurating sores. Wilson administered as best he could, dressing the raw wounds with vaseline and offering quiet words of comfort. More worrying was the noticeable deterioration in his mental state.

Evans slipped and fell into a crevasse on 4 February and Scott remarked that the big Welsh seaman was becoming 'dull and incapable'. In the space of a few traumatic weeks, he had gone from self-confident extrovert to mumbling incoherent wreck. The man who had been chosen for his physical strength was now impeding the progress of the party.

Evans was mentally the least equipped to cope with the bitter disappointment of losing the race to the Pole and as the largest of the party, was feeling the effects of the malnourishment more than the others. After twenty years in the Royal Navy, Evans had set his heart on the fame and fortune which would attach itself to any man who had stood first at the South Pole. He had even made plans to retire from the Navy and open a pub in South Wales with his wife, Lois, the daughter of a Welsh publican. Defeat left him consigned to a bleak future in the navy and retirement on a meagre Admiralty pension.

He was also a bluejacket alone in the company of officers and lacked the friendly support and encouragement which a mess-mate would have provided at this crucial moment. Crean, his best friend, had been sent back to Cape Evans with the last supporting party and the other men jammed into the tent seemed coldly indifferent to the plight of the broken man sitting opposite.

His companions were shocked by Evans' decline and even began to lose patience when they discovered he could not help around the camp because of his cut hand and worsening frostbite. No one had expected Evans to break down and his incapacity only served to isolate him further.

Even the normally charitable Wilson was off-hand about his decline, claiming his collapse was because he had 'never been sick in his life'. Scott said he was disappointed in the way that Evans had become so demoralised. Oates took an even more uncompromising stance and said:

> 'It is an extraordinary thing about Evans, he has lost his guts and behaves like an old woman or worse. He is quite worn out with the work and how he is going to do the odd 400 miles we have still to do I don't know.'[5]

The decline in Evans' condition began to accelerate as the party started the slow and difficult descent of the Beardmore, where hidden crevasses and the jumble of broken icefalls were a major hazard. Snowdrifts also covered their outward tracks and on one occasion they became lost in the maze of icy pathways.

Locating the Mid-Glacier depot became a matter of life and death and illustrated the risks of poor signposting in the white wilderness. Inexplicably, Scott halted the march on 8 and 9 February to indulge in a spot of geology. Although the weather was relatively fine and travel conditions more favourable, he allowed Bowers and Wilson to wander off to collect some rock specimens from the feet of Mount Darwin and Mount Buckley. They spent a 'most interesting afternoon' pottering around and placed about 35 lb of rocks on the sledge when the situation demanded rapid and lightly-laden travel.

Two days later food supplies became alarmingly short and Oates recorded the men were 'absolutely done' after struggling through bad crevasses and pressure until 9 o'clock at night. On 12 February they became lost and Scott reported 'a very critical situation' as they strained to locate the depot. It was eventually spotted by Wilson and Scott said: 'The relief to all is inexpressible.'

It was only temporary relief. The haphazard nature of locating critical depots was demonstrated on 15 February when Scott admitted: 'We don't know our distance from the depot. . .' Food was cut back, sleep reduced and Scott observed the party was 'feeling rather done'.

The deterioration in Evans added to the concerns. Evans, according to Oates, suffered a 'partial collapse'. He reported Evans being 'sick and giddy' and unable to walk alongside the sledge. Oates reasoned that Evans was at the end of his tether and alone among the others, he raised the question of how the party would cope with an incapacitated colleague. He confided to his diary:

> 'If he does not get by tomorrow God knows how we are going to get him home. We could not possibly take him on the sledge.'[6]

On 16 February Scott dolefully recorded that Evans was 'nearly broken down in brain' and Wilson said he was 'now helpless'. Petty Officer Edgar Evans died the following day, 17 February, only three weeks short of his thirty-sixth birthday.

Evans began the day in the harness plodding along in the soft snow, but soon stopped to adjust his ski shoes. Scott decided they could not afford to lose time and he was allowed to fall behind as the others pushed on towards the Barrier, urging him to come on as quickly as possible. After lunch, Evans had not caught up with his companions and Oates recorded the unhappy scene:

> 'Twice Evans had to get out of his harness – the second time for good. After lunch as Evans was not up we went back on ski for him, Scott and I leading. We found him on his hands and knees in the snow in a most pitiable condition. He was unable to walk and the other three went back on ski for the empty sledge and we brought him into the tent where he died at 12.30 am.'[7]

Oates sat with Evans while Scott, Wilson and Bowers trudged back to get the sledge, probably because Oates was also in some distress. His feet were now in an appalling state, gangrene was setting in, he was very tired and hungry and as he perched alongside the dying man, he must have contemplated his own predicament and seen the grim parallels in Evans' condition. Watching Evans slip over the edge was a terrible premonition of his own fate.

The precise cause of Evans' death remains a mystery, although several explanations have been put forward. Scott and Wilson believed he had suffered concussion from the fall down a crevasse on 4 February but there was no evidence that he had hit his head. It is known that blood vessels are weakened by the effects of scurvy and he may have suffered a brain haemorrhage. At the time of Evans' death, the Polar party had been on the march for 109 days, with only a marginal intake of fresh meat and no fresh vegetables to provide necessary Vitamin C to fight off scurvy.

Another more radical suggestion was that Evans was a victim of anthrax, picked up from spores carried by Oates' ponies.[8] The pony, Bones, suffered anthrax-like symptoms of severe colic in the winter at Cape Evans and the belief is that Evans carried the typically resilient spores to the Pole in his clothing, leading to slow terminal poisoning and contributing to his mental breakdown. However, none of the other men on the expedition seems to have been troubled by the same symptoms and the judgement is inconclusive.

The loss of Evans had removed the appalling dilemma of how to handle a sickening companion hundreds of miles from safety and with food and fuel in short supply. Scott admitted that the safety of the others demanded that they abandon the sick colleague but 'Providence mercifully removed him at the critical moment'.

23

The ultimate sacrifice

Evans was left at the foot of the Beardmore Glacier in the shadows of the great mountain range. But with hundreds of miles still to go and the season advancing rapidly, there was no time to mourn. Indeed, none of the party gave any details of Evans' burial.

After a dignified interval of about two hours, the four survivors packed their gear and pressed on in search of the next depot. Luckily the flag was easily spotted and they eagerly dug up a pony carcass. Their first proper food for a week instantly revitalised the weary, undernourished men.

The following day they reached Shambles Camp. Another filling meal of horseflesh installed new life in their overworked bodies, but there was no disguising the fact that the loss of Evans presented them with another substantial problem. While his death provided a little more badly needed food to go around, his considerable muscle-power in the harness was now missing for the vital 400-mile crossing of the Barrier. Scott soon recognised the loss and conceded that they 'might have got along faster' with the Welshman.

On the same day, 400 miles away, Crean staggered into Hut Point after his epic solo march of 35 miles in eighteen hours to bring news that Teddy Evans was close to death out on the Barrier. Evans had been struck down by scurvy as he descended the Beardmore on the return journey from the Polar plateau and Crean and Lashly, despite their own exhaustion, dragged the comatose figure on the sledge for over 100 miles. Atkinson, the only doctor within hundreds of miles, was at Hut Point and he was able to save Evans.[1]

The alarming state of Crean, Lashly and particularly Teddy Evans was the first indication that the returning Polar party might also be in trouble out on the

Barrier. Gran quickly realised the severity of the situation and after a brief chat with the stricken Evans wrote:

> '. . . from what I heard it became clear to me that the prospects of our five-man polar party were not so bright as most members of the expedition imagined. Evans' frightful return journey was a pointer to what Scott and his men would be bound to undergo.'[2]

Gran also assumed Amundsen had reached the Pole before Scott but wisely chose not to disclose his private suspicion, claiming '. . . my pessimism could only cause damage'. But over a week would pass before anyone at Hut Point or Cape Evans fully appreciated the plight of the Polar Party struggling back across the Barrier.

On the Barrier, the situation went from bad to worse. Temperatures fell alarmingly as the season began to close in and travelling surfaces were very difficult, with soft snow still slowing progress. Pulling a sledge was like dragging a dead weight over loose sand.

The miles ticked by ever more slowly, draining their strength and increasing their own doubts about pulling through. The deterioration was becoming ever more clear and after finishing a punishing ordeal on 21 February, Scott said:

> 'We have never won a march of 8½ miles with greater difficulty, but we can't go on like this.'[3]

Three days later, on 24 February, the men shuffled into the Southern Barrier Depot, where they found a worrying shortage of oil for the primus stove. They also dug up the remains of Christopher, the monstrous pony who had caused Oates so much trouble on the outward leg. They looked forward to the stimulation of horseflesh, but even in death Christopher had the last word. Oates' diary dryly recorded:

> 'Picked up the depot and dug up Christopher for food but it was rotten.'[4]

It was the last scrap of Oates' fragmented diary to survive.

The drive for the Middle Barrier Depot, where the next cache of precious food and fuel awaited, was another hard-won struggle. On some days they managed to cover nearly twelve miles, despite the awful surfaces and their growing fatigue. It was an astonishing achievement in the circumstances, but the strain on their already depleted bodies was enormous and the rapidly approaching Antarctic autumn was closing in on the ragged explorers like a menacing predator.

More modern research suggests that temperatures on the Barrier were unusually low in the Antarctic autumn of 1912 and between 10° and 20°F below the average levels monitored by today's scientists. To that extent, the returning party was desperately unlucky as it struggled homewards.

It now took one and a half hours to get their footgear on in the morning, especially for Oates who was still concealing the true state of his swollen, blackened feet. Gangrene had now set in and it was only a matter of time before he would have to come clean.

Wilson, who had kept a diary for most of his life, made his final entry on 27 February, bleakly recording that the temperature had sunk to −37°F (−38°C). Alongside him Scott wrote that there was 'a horrid element of doubt' about reaching the safety of the next supply depot.

Scott glumly reported 'many cold feet' as the four men began the march on the morning of 28 February in temperatures of −32°F (−36°C). The drained, bitterly cold group stumbled into the Middle Barrier depot on 2 March. That night temperatures plunged below −40°F (−40°C).

Oates had managed to keep up the pretence of fitness, pulling his weight and maintaining a stoic silence over his waning health. But the pain from his gangrenous feet must have been intense. They had been wet for over four months and in temperatures of −40°F they were now like blocks of ice.

A few years later, thousands of soldiers on the Western Front were struck by crippling chilblains, often leading to gangrene, which was caused by standing in wet, freezing trenches. In some cases men with inflamed, swollen feet had to crawl or be carried from the trenches to field hospitals. They called it 'trench foot'. In Polar terminology, Oates' feet had 'gone'.

Only scraps of information about Oates' condition were recorded in Scott's diary but it is clear that by early March he was in a terrible state. Apart from the gangrenous feet, his old war wound was giving him severe trouble. The growing fatigue and the malnutrition exacerbated the effects of the bitter cold and his mental resolve was under immense pressure. It is at around this point that Oates probably realised he was not going to pull through.

The gangrene was the most immediate problem because there was the awful prospect that it would spread. Gangrene, which is literally the death of tissue, takes two different forms. Oates was probably suffering largely from the dry form, which is acutely painful and caused by severe frostbite destroying the blood vessels. The pain was akin to red-hot pokers inserted into his feet and somewhere on his lower legs a red demarcation line would be clearly visible, distinguishing between the living and dead tissue.

It is probable that Oates was also attacked by moist gangrene, the other form which normally arises from an infection. Oates' feet were blistered by the frostbite and his toenails had almost certainly fallen off, leaving raw weeping wounds. Because he concealed his condition from Wilson and the others, it is highly unlikely that the infection received any treatment in the crucial early stages when it would have been possible to clean the wounds and prevent the infection spreading.

The inadequate sledging diet was playing a further cruel part in Oates' fate. One debilitating side effect of being malnourished is that the body does not generate sufficient heat and the extremities – the hands and feet – suffer most from the lack of bodily warmth. The bitter penetrating cold of the Barrier's freezing temperatures was felt with increasing effect as the hunger took a firm hold.

The effects of developing scurvy will have added to his misery, since the disease also attacks the circulation system, causing anaemia and local haemorrhaging.

Finally his old leg wound from the Boer War was causing intense pain, which was not unlike the moment when he had been shot a decade earlier. A side effect of scurvy is that old scar tissue becomes weak, degenerates and often reopens. Oates, like the others, was now entering his fifth month without an adequate intake of fresh meat or vegetables and the pain of his rotting wound had become acute.

Oates was now a depleted, defeated figure. Concealment was largely irrelevant. As the party sat exhausted in the tent at Middle Barrier Depot on Friday 2 March, he finally dropped the pretence. Why he chose that moment to reveal his agony is not clear, although he would be aware that his worsening condition would ultimately slow the progress of the entire party. Scott, the only person now recording events, wrote:

> 'Titus Oates disclosed his feet, the toes showing very bad indeed, evidently bitten by the late temperatures.'[5]

His condition was so bad that to get his badly swollen feet into the finnesko one of his considerate companions – probably Wilson – had to slit the hide snowshoes from top to bottom. The state of Oates shocked the other three and it may well have been the moment when their own survival seemed most in jeopardy.

The breakdown of Oates was alarming for all. Losing a quarter of their pulling power was a terrible blow and the folly of placing the depots too far apart with no reserves of food was beginning to dawn on them. It was still about 65 miles

(105 km) to the next depot at Mount Hooper and 130 miles (210 km) to the safer haven of One Ton Depot. Hut Point, the final destination, was almost 250 miles (450 km) away.

Oates' condition once again raised the dreadful dilemma about how to cope with an incapacitated colleague. Scott, Wilson and Bowers were in no fit state to drag Oates, the heaviest of the four, on the sledge and they could not leave him behind while they went for help. The brutal alternative was to leave him behind to a certain death or invite their stricken comrade to solve the problem by committing suicide.

The death of Evans a few weeks earlier had conveniently removed the need for such an awful decision. But Oates' condition was different from Evans' and suggested that he faced a slower, more painful demise. Wilson remained the moral leader of the group and his belief that the entire party should be sacrificed to save one injured member was now put to the ultimate test.

It is not difficult to understand Oates' feelings as he huddled in the freezing tent opposite Scott, a man he detested and whose blundering leadership now threatened his life. He must have recalled over and over again the heated conversation on the Barrier only twelve months earlier, when Scott refused to locate One Ton Depot a further 30 miles (48 km) to the south because he did not want the hapless ponies to suffer. Those 30 miles now assumed critical proportions and Oates, more than anyone, knew who to blame for the costly shortfall. Oates had told Scott he would regret his decision and he was right. But there was not a shred of satisfaction in being right.

Equally, Oates must have felt intense pressure from knowing that his incapacity was slowing the others. The knowledge must have been an awesome burden and it is likely that he reflected on his conversations at Cape Evans during the winter when he advocated taking a gun on the expedition as a means of honourable exit for a mortally wounded traveller.

The rapidly worsening situation was also apparent from Oates' morale. Scott observed that 'his spirits only come in spurts now' and that he 'grows more silent in the tent' at night.

Wilson, a man who identified strongly with St Francis of Assisi, tended Oates as best he could in the grim circumstances, often at the expense of his own rest in the tent at night. Each man had enough to do looking after his own needs, but Scott acknowledged Wilson's 'self-sacrificing devotion' towards Oates.

However, the most immediate problem at Middle Barrier Depot was the discovery that fuel was in short supply. No one on the expedition had fully appreciated that paraffin evaporates in extreme cold unless the cans are properly

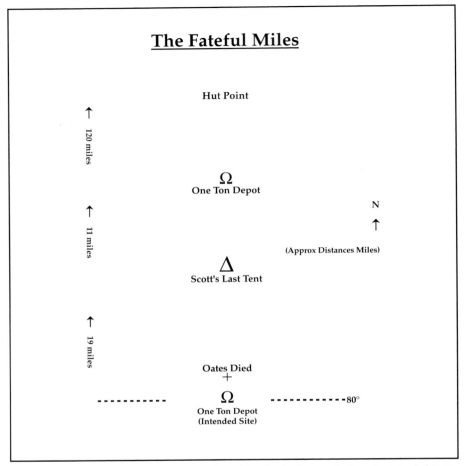

The Fateful Miles

Hut Point

↑ 120 miles

Ω
One Ton Depot

N

↑

(Approx Distances Miles)

↑ 11 miles

Δ
Scott's Last Tent

↑ 19 miles

Oates Died
+

- - - - - - - - - - -   Ω   - - - - - - - - - -•80°
One Ton Depot
(Intended Site)

*Scott's decision to locate One Ton Depot about 30 miles further north than the intended 80°S
proved decisive on the death march from the Pole.*

sealed. Scott had experienced the same problem on the *Discovery* but somehow
had overlooked taking remedial action.

Amundsen had hermetically sealed his cans to prevent the 'creep' of precious
fuel, but Scott stuck with inadequate, screwed bungs. Amundsen's oil cans were
subsequently found intact on the ice 50 years after his all-conquering expedition,
whereas Scott's had failed after less than four months.

The men, moving ever more slowly, made only five and a half miles in horrible
conditions on the first leg of the haul to Mount Hooper and their hopes were now
evaporating like the paraffin. That night, Scott wrote in his diary:

'We are in a very queer street since there is no doubt that we cannot
do the extra marches and feel the cold horribly.'[6]

At best, they were crawling along at one mile an hour but there was no question
of cutting back any further on food to extend the marching time. Without food
they could not pull and they had to pull to reach the next supply depot.

Oates was now in free-fall as the gnawing cold, tiredness and hunger took
increasing toll. His blackened feet had blown up to double the normal size and
each step was a painful, jolting reminder of his awful condition. After another
weary day's march on 4 March, the four men climbed into their sleeping bags for
an unappealing meal consisting of a single cup of warm cocoa and a hunk of solid
pemmican with just the chill taken off. The next day Scott wrote:

> 'The result is telling on all, but mainly on Oates, whose feet are in a
> wretched condition. One swelled up tremendously last night and he is
> very lame this morning. Our fuel is dreadfully low and the poor
> Solider is nearly done. It is pathetic enough because we can do nothing
> for him.'[7]

Wilson continued to administer some bandages and comfort to Oates.
Humiliation was piled on the misery when he was unable to take his place in the
harness on 6 March. Once the march stopped, Oates had to sit on the sledge, a
limp forlorn figure contemplating his own fate as the others pitched camp. The
expedition had ravaged him and it now stripped him of his dignity.

Outwardly, Oates maintained his stoicism and Scott recorded that he never
once complained about the pain or his chances of survival. Instead, he grew more
and more silent, saying less and sinking ever deeper into himself.

The crisis of how to cope with a sickening companion was coming to a head
for Scott, Wilson and Bowers. It has been suggested that Scott somehow exerted
moral pressure on Oates to 'do the decent thing' and sacrifice himself to save his
colleagues. Since only Scott's words of the time have survived, there is no
unequivocal evidence to support the claim, although his critics have conveniently
interpreted his diary to support their own conclusions.

It was no longer possible to avoid the sickening dilemma. On 6 March Scott
recorded the all-round deterioration of the party and reluctantly conceded that
Oates was now slowing up the men. He wrote:

> 'If we were all fit I should have hopes of getting through, but the poor
> Soldier has become a terrible hindrance, though he does his utmost
> and suffers much I fear.'[8]

Scott's diary of the time is far from conclusive, which is hardly surprising in view of the daily struggle. But what is abundantly clear is that as the crisis over Oates deepened, Scott became increasingly pessimistic and doubted his own ability to survive. On 7 March he ended his diary entry with the remark: 'I should like to keep the track to the end.'

Scott was already writing for posterity. His diary entries became increasingly gloomy and the language assumed the proportions of a Greek tragedy which was fast approaching the final scenes of the drama. If the Englishmen had been unable to capture the prize of the South Pole, at least Scott's diary would reveal that they died heroically. There was little doubt he wanted the journal to be found for history.

On 7 March, Scott also said the only hope of getting through was if the dogs had been brought to the Mount Hooper depot. They had not. On the same day, Amundsen's ship, *Fram*, sailed into Hobart, Tasmania, with the momentous news that the Norwegians had won the race to the South Pole. Although the dogs were now his salvation, no one at base camp realised it. Scott's orders for the animals had been changed several times and those at Cape Evans were given little clear idea of the urgency or the need to rescue the stricken Polar party. Atkinson, now effectively in charge because of Teddy Evans' severe illness, was supposed to take dog teams out to the Barrier to help the returning Polar party catch the *Terra Nova* before the ship became frozen into McMurdo Sound. 'Come as far as you can,' Scott vaguely told Meares as they parted company at the bottom of the Beardmore. But the final supporting party of Evans, Lashly and Crean had carried an entirely different message, which ordered Meares or Atkinson to drive as far south as 82° or 83° – somewhere between the Mid-Barrier and Upper-Barrier depots and a lot farther south than originally envisaged.

Unfortunately no one at base – particularly Atkinson – seemed fully to appreciate the warning signs for the Polar party which were evident in the stricken Teddy Evans. Atkinson, who was not accustomed to being in charge, opted to obey orders instead of using his initiative and launching a full-scale rescue mission.

Atkinson decided that nursing Evans was a greater priority than assisting the Polar party and it was not until 23 February – four days after Crean had staggered into Hut Point with news that Evans was close to death – that action was taken. Atkinson ordered Cherry-Garrard to take Dimitri and the dogs out to One Ton Depot and wait for Scott to come in.

It was another mistake which once again exposed the expedition's underlying conflict between science and exploration. Among the men available at base camp,

Wright was the ideal choice to make the dash to One Ton. He was an accomplished navigator and had gained invaluable experience of the ice in the first supporting party up the Beardmore. But since his return Wright had been put in charge of important scientific work at Cape Evans and Atkinson decided this took precedence over the journey to locate the Polar party. The responsibility thus fell to Cherry-Garrard.

Cherry-Garrard was the wrong man for the job. He was handicapped by severe short-sight, his spectacles fogged up behind his snow goggles, he could not navigate and had never before driven a dog team. 'Give me anything to do but navigation,' he said. Dimitri was a good dog-driver, but could not navigate.

Atkinson asked Cherry-Garrard to use his discretion if Scott had not reached One Ton, which meant he would have to decide whether to press on southwards towards Mount Hooper Depot or head back to base. But Cherry-Garrard did not have the experience of leadership or the natural confidence to take such life and death decisions and in any event he sincerely believed that the party had adequate supplies of food and fuel to reach One Ton. Cherry-Garrard saw the trip as little more than a means of hastening the conquering heroes back home and saw little danger for his friends.

Cherry-Garrard and Dimitri reached One Ton Depot late on 3 March, the same day that Scott, about 90 miles to the south, was writing: 'God help us . . .' He waited for six days, pinned down by a blizzard and his own indecision about whether to drive south.

Dimitri and the dogs were also suffering in the acute cold, with temperatures down to −37°. In the white-out conditions, Cherry was particularly worried that he might lose his way and miss his colleagues in the swirling drift if he pressed on south towards Mount Hooper depot. A shortage of dog food was the final straw. He did not have enough to feed the dogs for more than a few days and Cherry had no intention of slaughtering the weaker animals to feed the stronger ones.

An experienced dog driver – such as the men in Amundsen's party – would have raced south, killing the weaker dogs to feed the rest as the Norwegians had done on the successful trek to the Pole itself. The journey to Mount Hooper was little more than three or four days hard travelling for an expert dog handler in good conditions.

However, Cherry-Garrard felt no great anxiety about his friends and at the back of his mind were the unequivocal instructions from above. Atkinson had insisted that the 'dogs were not to be risked' and that Scott was 'not in any way dependent' on the dogs for his return.[9] Fearful of Scott's orders and unsure about handling the dogs, Cherry-Garrard packed up and headed back to Cape Evans on 10 March.

The struggling Polar party was now pinning everything on the arrival of dogs and on 9 March – the day before Cherry-Garrard turned northwards – they staggered into Mount Hooper, a little over 60 miles (100 km) from One Ton Depot. Another shortage of fuel was found.

It was a debilitating blow to Oates who was fast approaching the end. Scott surveyed the looming disaster and wrote:

> 'Things steadily downhill. Oates' foot worse. He has rare pluck and must know that he can never get through.'[10]

Oates had by now abandoned all his customary reserve and in the tent that night pointedly asked Wilson if he had any chance. Wilson avoided the truth, replying that he did not know. In reality it was apparent his colleague was as good as dead. Scott overhead the exchange and wrote a postscript in his diary:

> 'In point of fact he has none. Poor chap! It is too pathetic to watch him; one cannot but try to cheer him up.'[11]

Oates was an increasing handicap to the others, taking longer to get ready in the morning and limping uselessly alongside the sledge while his weakening colleagues pulled for their lives. Three exhausted men were now doing the work of four fit men and it showed in the distances achieved. They were now travelling at barely half the speed clocked up on the outward march in significantly lower temperatures, suffering the crippling effects of increasing scurvy and fighting permanent hunger and thirst.

Without the liability of Oates, it is possible that Scott, Wilson and Bowers had some slight prospect of pulling through to One Ton, where ample supplies of food and fuel awaited them. But their chances were virtually non-existent with a crippled passenger. On 11 March, Scott wrote:

> 'Titus Oates is very near the end, one feels. What we or he will do, God only knows. We discussed the matter after breakfast; he is a brave fine fellow and understands the situation, but he practically asked for advice. Nothing could be said but to urge him to march as long as he could.'[12]

One outcome of the grim discussion was that Scott ordered Wilson to hand out the means of committing suicide. It was a critical decision, indicating that Scott at least had surrendered all hope of pulling through – with or without Oates.

Wilson protested, but Scott insisted and Wilson handed each man a lethal dose of 30 opium tablets and kept a tube of morphine for himself. It was not the revolver which suited the military instincts of a gentleman and cavalry officer but it was enough for the grisly task.

Scott did his sums in the tent that night. At best he calculated that the drained, bitterly cold men were only capable of six miles a day and it was 55 geographic miles (63 statute miles) to One Ton Depot. They had enough food for only seven days, which was translated into the brutally simple equation of $7 \times 6 = 42$. It left them 13 miles (15 statute miles) short of the well-stocked depot at One Ton.

The following day's march fell short of the necessary average and with the autumnal season taking grip, temperatures plummeted to −37°F (−38°C). Scott noted that both Oates' hands and feet were now 'pretty well useless'. Bowers made the last entry into his meticulous meteorological log. Only Scott was now recording the closing lines of the tragedy.

Oates suffered another humiliating, possibly final, blow to his resolve when his hands became badly frostbitten in the numbing cold. He could not help around the camp and probably had to be fed by the thoughtful Wilson. The following day temperatures sank to −43°F (−42°C) and Wilson was so icily cold at the end of the march that he could not bend down to remove his skis.

The bone-chilling cold once again struck at Oates, a last wounding blow to the broken figure. At lunch on 15 March, he offered to make the ultimate sacrifice, saying he could move no further and asking Scott to leave him behind in his sleeping bag. 'We induced him to come on. . .' Scott wrote, implying that all three were united in urging him to soldier on.

The final moments of the Oates tragedy were recorded by Scott and briefly by Wilson. Scott's diary entry is the fullest account and reads:

> 'Friday, March 16 or Saturday 17. Lost track of dates, but think the last correct. Tragedy all along the line.
>
> At lunch the day before yesterday, poor Titus Oates said he couldn't go on; he proposed we should leave him to come on, on the afternoon march. In spite of the awful nature for him he struggled on and we made a few miles. At night he was worse and I knew the end had come.
>
> Should this be found I want these facts recorded. Oates' last thoughts were of his mother, but immediately before he took pride in thinking that his regiment would be pleased with the bold way in which he met his death. We can testify to his bravery. He has borne his

suffering for weeks without complaint and to the very last he was willing to discuss outside subjects. He did not – would not – give up hope till the very end. He was a brave soul. This was the end. He slept through the night before last, hoping not to wake; but he woke up in the morning – yesterday. It was blowing a blizzard. He said, "I am just going outside and may be some time". He went out into the blizzard and we have not seen him since.

We knew that Oates was walking to his death, but though we tried to dissuade him, we knew it was the act of a brave man and an English gentleman. We all hope to meet the end with a similar spirit and assuredly the end is not far.'[13]

Oates' suffering at the point of leaving the tent must have been extreme and helps explain why, as he contemplated taking his own life, he did not leave a final farewell letter to his mother. It is likely that his frostbite was so severe that he could not hold a pencil.

He was also in great pain from his gangrene and the severe cold and hunger left him sluggish and apathetic. It was probably all he could do to scramble over the out-stretched legs of his companions and crawl to the door of the tent. He did not bother to pull on his ripped boots and went slowly to his death wearing only his socks. Outside the tent a blizzard was raging and the temperature had dropped to a paralysing $-40°F$ $(-40°C)$.

Oates' last thoughts were reserved for the single most important figure in his life, his mother. Shortly before leaving the tent, Oates told Wilson how much he loved her and asked him to make sure she received his personal diary. Despite his own poor condition and knowing that he, too, was doomed, the selfless Wilson scribbled a poignant letter to Mrs Oates. He wrote:

'This is a sad ending to our undertaking. Your son died a very noble death, God knows. I have never seen or heard of such courage as he showed from first to last with his feet both badly frostbitten – never a word of complaint or of the pain. He was a great example. Dear Mrs Oates, he asked me at the end, to see you and give you this diary of his – You, he told me, are the only woman he has ever loved.

Now I am in the same case and I can no longer hope to see either you or my beloved wife or my Mother or Father – the end is upon us, but these diaries will be found and this note will reach you some day. Please be so good as to send pages 54 and 55 of this book to my beloved wife addressed, Mrs Ted Wilson, Westal, Cheltenham.

Please do this for me dear Mrs Oates – my wife has a real faith in God and so your son tells me have you – and so have I – and if ever a man died like a noble soul and in a Christ-like spirit your son did – Our whole journey's record is clean and though disastrous – has no shadow over it. He died like a man and a soldier without a word of regret or complaint except that he hadn't written to you at the last, but the cold has been intense and I fear we have all of us left writing alone until it is almost too late to attempt anything but the most scrappy notes.

God comfort you in your loss.'[14]

The testimonies of Scott and Wilson imply that Oates rejected the obvious way out by taking an overdose of opium, not in the tent at least. In the last letter to his wife, Wilson had said 'Our whole journey record is clean', a similar remark to that made in his letter to Caroline Oates. The implication is that none of the men took a fatal dose of opium.

Some observers have since argued that Scott effectively forced Oates out of the tent because he was holding up the marches and that perhaps Scott, Wilson and Bowers might have reached comparative safety of One Ton Depot without their lame companion. However, the next 120 miles from One Ton to Hut Point was almost certainly beyond their capacity.

It is impossible to make an accurate calculation of how much Oates' condition had slowed the progress of the other three. What is known is that from 2 March – when Oates first disclosed the appalling state of his feet – to his death on 17 March, Scott, Wilson and Bowers needed only to have travelled an extra one mile a day to have reached One Ton Depot. Bowers, in his last letter to his mother, wrote:

'. . . our sick companions have delayed us till too late in the season which has made us very short of fuel and we are now out of food as well.'[15]

Roland Huntford, his harshest biographer, claimed that Scott sat staring at Oates '. . . with the unspoken expectation of the supreme sacrifice'.[16] Huntford was self-evidently not there and, like many biographers who did not have the full facts at his disposal, he let his intuition run away with him.

George Bernard Shaw, another not present in the tent, lent his idiosyncratic thought processes to the argument, assisted by a close friendship with Apsley Cherry-Garrard. Shaw took a contrary view to the conventional judgement of the expedition's heroic failure. During the 1920s, he told Kathleen Scott:

Lawrence Oates, soldier and explorer. Ponting's fine portrait captures the essence of Oates – tight-lipped, resolute and slightly scruffy. (SPRI)

'There were things that Con (as Scott was known to close friends) was
not told; and perhaps one of them was that Oates was not fit to go and
did not want to go.

'This would not have made any difference with Peary, who wouldn't
have taken him anyhow, nor with Amundsen, who was an explorer
first and last and asked nothing for "the services" or for any of the
standards that were in Con's blood; but it made the final and fatal
difference to Con.'[17]

Shaw always believed that Scott was an inept explorer. He once told Kathleen's
second husband, Lord Kennet, that Scott was 'unsuited to the job' and that the
expedition ended in the '. . . most incompetent failure in the history of
exploration'.[18]

Shaw, by now in his nineties, also stoked up the argument over Scott's apparent
attitude towards the incapacitated Oates. He told Kennet:

'He (Scott) had finally to abandon Evans in the snow (he crawled to
the tent to die) and to give Oates silent hints that he should go out to
perish for a day or two before he did so, too late.'[19]

On the bottom of the neatly typed letter, Shaw scrawled in his own hand: 'Poor
Oates!'

The piercing remarks wounded the Scott family and some years later Kennet
told Scott's son, Peter:

'It is a very great pity that Shaw should have kept a copy of his letter
and that anyone should think of publishing it. I am quite sure that you
should do all you can to prevent it.'[20]

Huntford also suggested that Oates' famous last words were a work of fiction,
invented to paint a heroic gloss over the disastrous venture and remove any blame
attached to Scott for the death of Oates. Certainly Scott's diary shows that he was
writing for a public audience in the final weeks of the expedition and some have
described his famous final outpourings as his 'alibi'. Shaw's judgement was that
Scott's 'ace of trumps' was his literary talent.

But his diary also indicates that, almost two weeks before Oates crawled from
the tent, Scott had virtually given up the battle to survive and had accepted his
fate. On 4 March, he reported '. . . things look very black indeed' and on 7 March
he wrote: 'I should like to keep the track to the end.'

Scott's first letter of 'farewell' to family and friends was dated 16 March – the day before Oates left the tent. The note, written to the expedition's treasurer Sir Edgar Speyer, opens with the comment that '. . . we have been to the Pole and we shall die like gentlemen'.[21]

The only other contemporary observation on Oates came from Bowers, although his words are brief and inconclusive. In his last letter to his mother, Bowers simply noted that '. . . Oates left us the other day'.

Critics have also drawn great significance from the fact that Wilson's letter to Caroline Oates contains no mention of her son's famous parting remark. However, Wilson was contemplating his own miserable death as he scribbled the brief letter and in any event may have felt that her son's casual, matter-of-fact comment on the brink of death would offend the Victorian sensibilities of Mrs Oates. He probably felt that in the dire circumstances Caroline Oates expected something grander and more solemn. He cannot be criticised for not bothering to repeat an apparently inconsequential remark.

The pithy, off-hand comment attributed to Oates is hardly the language of Scott, a gifted writer but a conventional character. It is difficult to see the orthodox Scott delivering such an unorthodox parting shot. However, the expression is pure Oates. It is typical of the laconic, understated language he used regularly. Not for Oates the grandly eloquent valedictory speech of Sidney Carton – 'It is a far, far better thing that I do. . .' – as he climbed the steps of the guillotine in Dickens' *A Tale of Two Cities.*

For Oates, the short, nonchalant and low-key comment was a trademark. Even in death he managed to make the extraordinary act of suicide seem plain ordinary and routine. Oates hated fuss all his life and even chose to die without fuss. It would be entirely consistent for him to remark as he crawled to his death: 'I am just going outside and may be some time.' The truth of the matter is that no one really knows. The only witnesses lie deep beneath the Barrier ice.

What can be said is that Oates was an unsentimental realist and a man of great courage. Oates' calm bravery and willingness to face death had been firmly established a decade earlier on the South African veldt and his mettle was never in doubt. Both Wilson and Scott attested to his extraordinary courage in the final weeks of his terrible suffering.

But the Oates freezing in the small tent on the Barrier was a defeated man, physically wrecked and mentally crushed. His life was over. Suicide was a blessed relief when he could bear no more. The notion of self-sacrifice to save Scott, Wilson and Bowers is simply not credible. His companions were already beyond redemption when Oates crawled from the tent for the last time. His sacrifice was undeniably noble, but it was futile. Oates must have recognised that they were all facing the same death. But only Oates decided *when* he was going to die.

If Oates considered sacrificing himself to save the others, he would not have lingered until the entire party was also at death's door. If there was a 'correct' moment for sacrifice, surely it would have been somewhat earlier, perhaps on 2 March when he first disclosed the appalling state of his feet, or by 11 March when Scott was writing that '. . . Oates is near the end'.

It fell to Amundsen, the victor, to the sum up the fate of the vanquished. He said Oates' death was a great sacrifice, 'but it did no good'.

The irony is that Scott, whose bungling was partly responsible for the death of Oates, was the man who created the Oates legend. It was Scott who provided the only clue to the story of supreme gallantry, the legend that Oates had left the tent to save his colleagues. Oates would have smiled at the quirk of fate.

The death of Oates was distinguished by two other bitter ironies. 17 March, if Scott recorded the dates accurately, was his thirty-second birthday. Second, Oates died at about 80° South, precisely the point where it was planned to establish the safe haven of One Ton Depot a year earlier.

Oates' body has never been found and it is a matter of speculation what happened in the final moments of his life. Barely able to walk and his ruined feet covered only by his socks, he must have crawled away from the tent on all fours, unable to see more than a few feet ahead in the howling blizzard.

It is unlikely that Oates managed to crawl very far from the tent, perhaps less than 50 yards, before lying down and curling up in the snow like a mortally wounded animal. In vicious temperatures of −40°F (−40°C) and unimaginable wind chill levels, his body would soon have become numb. It would have brought welcome relief if he had opened his clothing, accelerating the freezing process. He may have swallowed his opium pills, blotting out the last tormented, lonely moments of his life. But that was not Oates' style. He probably just waited.

Freezing, penetrating cold invariably brings drowsiness and lethargy and it is unlikely he remained fully conscious very long in the horrifying surroundings. As he drifted off into semi-consciousness, the swirling wind whipped up a blanket of snow, which slowly covered his body like a white shroud.

Spenser's immortal lines seem singularly appropriate and could have been written with Oates in mind:

Sleep after toil, port after stormie seas,
Ease after war, death after life does greatly please.[22]

24

A very gallant gentleman

Oates' suicide was all to no avail. Scott, Wilson and Bowers trudged off northwards, leaving behind Oates' sleeping bag, spare socks, a theodolite and a camera to reduce the weight of their sledge. But they continued to drag the 35 lb (16 kg) of rock specimens, which had been gathered as they clambered down the Beardmore.

The rocks, which contained traces of fossils and vegetation, proved to be of lasting scientific value, showing that Antarctica had once formed part of a warmer environment. But the price of the knowledge could hardly have been higher.

Temperatures hovered menacingly at around −40°F (−40°C) as the autumn weather took grip and the cold in the tent was so excruciating that Scott could only write up his diary at lunch. The desolate trio struggled on a few more days, covering a very hard-won few miles and on 21 March camped just eleven miles from One Ton Depot.

The weather closed in for the kill. A raging blizzard struck, confining the three men to their last resting place. Fuel and food were almost gone and their strength had finally deserted them. Travel was impossible. Scott's right foot was struck by crippling frostbite and gangrene had set in. Amputation was inevitable. He was now in the same predicament as Oates, a 'terrible hindrance' slowing the progress of others.

The blizzard roared unbroken for another eight days, penning the men in their tent and preventing the marginally stronger Bowers or Wilson making a dash for the depot, less than a day's march for fit, well-fed men in good conditions. But Scott could not travel and a return journey of 22 miles to One Ton Depot was a marathon in those conditions. It is also possible Wilson and Bowers would not abandon their stricken leader.

Starving, freezing and facing a slow death, the three men wrote their touching farewells. Scott poured out a stream of correspondence, writing to his wife, the expedition's backers, his friends, Bowers' mother, Wilson's wife, his publisher and most memorably, his message to the public. For some unknown reason he did not write to either Taff Evans's wife, Lois, or Caroline Oates.

Scott's diary indicates they probably died on 29 March and the established line, which helped perpetuate the legend, is that Scott was the last to die. However, even this macabre detail has been challenged.

Inside the tent one of Scott's letters was found lying loosely on the floor and a short message had been scrawled on the envelope, informing the finder that Wilson's diary and sketchbook were in the instrument box. The writing is in the hand of Bowers, which prompted some to suggest that he outlived Scott and was the last to die.

Two days before, on 27 March, Atkinson and Petty Officer Keohane embarked on a hopeless mission to search the Barrier for the long overdue men. The pair, man-hauling their sledge in a howling gale and barely able to see any distance ahead, laboured about 40 miles from Cape Evans. They gave up the vain quest on 30 March when, about 100 miles (160 km) further south, Scott, Wilson and Bowers were already dead.

Atkinson was 'morally certain' the five-man party, including his friend Oates, had perished and did not launch any further attempts that season to rescue the men. Atkinson, as the senior officer left at Cape Evans, was now in charge of the depleted expedition. Teddy Evans, who had come so close to death in the last supporting party, had returned to New Zealand on *Terra Nova* along with Meares, Griffith Taylor, Ponting and several others.

Atkinson still faced a terrible dilemma, despite his assumption that the Polar party was dead. The fate of Campbell's six-man party to the North was still unknown. They had not been seen for twelve months and their return to Cape Evans was long overdue. No one knew whether they were dead or alive. As winter descended, Atkinson agonised over the difficult choice in the spring of either looking for the bodies of his dead colleagues or trying to find Campbell's lost party. Or, as Cherry-Garrard put it, 'leave live men to search for those who were dead'.[1] A free and open discussion was held and twelve of the thirteen men at Cape Evans voted to search for the dead. The other abstained.[2]

In his own quiet, unassuming manner, Atkinson proved an effective commander. The mood of the hut, inevitably, was sombre. But conditions were more comfortable, with only thirteen men occupying space where 25 had spent the previous winter and Atkinson's leadership style more relaxed and informal than Scott's.

Atkinson organised proceedings with a light touch, asking for things to be done rather than issuing orders and abolishing some of the old barriers which had needlessly separated the other ranks from the officers under Scott. Crean and Lashly, the two most formidable man-haulers who had survived the ordeal with Teddy Evans, were now brought into the fold and consulted about the search journey.

Oates' absence at Cape Evans was felt in that last winter, most obviously because of the seven new pack horses from India which had arrived on *Terra Nova* to take the place of the dead Manchurian ponies. The mules were far superior to the original batch and Cherry-Garrard noted that they were 'beautiful animals'. The irony was that the mules would now be searching for the very person who had selected them for the job.

Another bitter irony occurred on the other side of the world, which had not yet learned of the expedition's fate. In London on 6 May 1912, Oates was elected a Fellow of the Royal Geographical Society, a distinction which had earlier been given to both his father and uncle. Caroline Oates, who was delighted at the honour, generously paid £45 for her son's life membership of the Society. Oates had been dead for seven weeks.

The search for the bodies of the Polar party began on 29 October under the leadership of Atkinson. The mules were led by respected travellers like Wright, Crean and Lashly, while Atkinson, Cherry-Garrard and Dimitri took two dog teams.

The party was provisioned to travel well over 500 miles (800 km) across the Barrier, up the Beardmore and onto the Polar Plateau in the hunt for the corpses and any news of the Polar journey. Atkinson decided to stick closely to the tracks of the previous year's outward march. The hope was that the Polar party had done the same.

Opinions about the fate of the Polar party were divided. Many felt the search would be fruitless because the men had, conceivably, plunged to their deaths down a crevasse while descending the Beardmore. Lashly, who had nursed the scurvy victim Evans, was convinced they, too, had succumbed to scurvy.

The search party marched up to One Ton Depot on 11 November, with some still nurturing a faint hope that they would find their colleagues. Gran remembered that 'our hearts beat a little faster' but they soon found that the depot was undisturbed. However, one of the fuel cans had leaked and spoilt some of the food.

On 12 November 1912 the group pressed on further south, scanning the horizon for any signs of the men. Wright, who was navigating, suddenly came to a halt and then veered off to investigate an unusual black feature which had caught his eye about half a mile off to the west. It was the tip of the little tent, virtually submerged under a pyramid of snow. Inside were the bodies of Scott, Wilson and Bowers. It was neat and tidy but there was no sign of Oates or Evans.

A camp was hastily made and Atkinson sat down to read Scott's diaries recounting how Amundsen had beaten them to the Pole by a month and how Evans and Oates had died on the appalling return journey. Many of the men were in tears as Atkinson read out Scott's famous 'Message to the Public', his moving defence against the disastrous outcome of the expedition. Scott wrote:

> 'Had we lived, I should have had a tale to tell of the hardihood, endurance and courage of my companions which would have stirred the heart of every Englishman. These rough notes and our dead bodies must tell the tale . . .'[3]

Crean graciously strode across the ice and shook the hand of Gran to congratulate the Norwegians on being first to reach the Pole. Both were in tears.

It was decided to bury the three where they lay. The tent bamboo was collapsed over the men and an imposing 12-foot cairn of snow was built over the bodies. A cross made from Gran's skis was placed on top. It was bitterly cold, the sun was dipping low in the southern sky and the Barrier was almost in shadow. The eleven men stood bare-headed in the sub-zero temperatures, the burial service from Corinthians was read aloud and they sang 'Onward Christian Soldiers' as the chilling wind nipped their exposed faces.

Gran slipped on Scott's skis for the return to Cape Evans, thus ensuring that they, at least, made the round trip to the Pole and back.

A note was left, signed by all eleven men, which said the deaths were due to 'inclement weather and lack of fuel'. The note also recorded that Oates had 'walked out to his death in a blizzard to save his comrades'. Wright added his own comment, writing in his diary:

> 'A damn fine finish.'[4]

Atkinson stashed most of their supplies and pressed on, lightly-laden, in an effort to find the body of Oates, estimated to be about nineteen miles (30 km) further south. It was a cold, miserable march in temperatures near to −15°F (−26°C) and in the teeth of penetrating head winds. Most suffered painful frostbites.

After a while, they spotted one of the snow walls built on the outward march to protect the ponies. On the wall was an old piece of sacking and Oates' sleeping bag. Inside the bag they found a spare pair of socks and his finnesko, one of which was slit down the front. Evidently, Scott had carried the bag and footwear in the faint hope that Oates might somehow recover and catch them up.

Atkinson pushed on a little further south and arrived at the area where it was thought Oates had finally left the tent. There was no sign of the body, only an interminable white crust of snow as far as the eye could see in any direction. Keohane said finding a body would be like looking for 'a needle in a hayfield'. Atkinson remembered:

'The kindly snow had covered his body, giving him a fitting burial.'[5]

A cairn of snow was built and a short note was stuck to an improvised cross. The note, signed by Atkinson and Cherry-Garrard, read:

'Hereabouts died a very gallant gentleman, Captain L.E.G. Oates of the Inniskilling Dragoons. In March 1912, returning from the Pole, he walked willingly to his death in a blizzard to try and save his comrades, beset by hardship. This note is left by the Relief Expedition of 1912.'[6]

Atkinson copied the note and vowed to send it to Caroline Oates, along with her son's diaries, his portrait of Napoleon and other personal effects accumulated at Cape Evans. Atkinson was in no doubt about Oates' heroism and he told Mrs Oates that her son's bravery gave his companions 'the only chance they had'. He added:

'He sacrificed himself to try and save the others. It was a very noble act and quite fitted his ordinary character.'[7]

25

Bitter memories

The floodgates of mourning opened very slowly. While the men at Cape Evans had spent months in distant isolation coming to terms with the tragedy, the news did not penetrate the outside world until *Terra Nova* sailed back into McMurdo Sound on 18 January 1913. It was a year to the day that the five-man Polar party had put up their 'poor slighted Union Jack' and photographed themselves at the South Pole.

Teddy Evans, happily recovered from scurvy, was on board and he grabbed a megaphone to yell an enthusiastic inquiry about the health of the shore party. He was surprised at the silence that followed.

Campbell, whose northern party had survived a terrible winter ordeal, had superseded Atkinson as the most senior officer at Cape Evans. After a lengthy pause, Campbell stepped forward and broke the silence with a brisk, business-like statement:

'The Southern Party reached the South Pole on 17 of January last year
but were all lost on the return journey – we have their records.'[1]

Evans remembered a moment of 'hush and overwhelming sorrow' and immediately ordered that the flags and bunting on *Terra Nova*, which had been put up to celebrate the ship's return, should be taken down. Wright recalled that the *Terra Nova's* crew were 'greatly distressed' by the news.

The men at Cape Evans had already decided to leave behind a suitable memorial to their dead colleagues and two days later Atkinson led a party of eight men up to Observation Hill, a 750 ft (230 m) volcanic cone overlooking Hut Point Peninsula and the old *Discovery* hut. It is a spectacular lookout point for in-coming explorers from the Barrier. Cherry-Garrard said there was 'no more fitting pedestal'.

Terra Nova's carpenter, Frank Davies, spent more than two days making a giant cross from jarrah, an especially hard wood grown from a member of the eucalyptus family in Western Australia. Davies made the near 12 ft (3.6 m) cross in two halves, but it took them eight hours in a Christ-like procession to drag it on sledges across the soft, slushy ice. The cross, weighing over 20 stone (130 kg), was pulled slowly up the steep hill before Davies bolted it together.

In a brief, solemn ceremony the cross was erected, with its face pointing towards the Barrier where the five men lay under the snow. The names of Scott, Wilson, Bowers, Evans and Oates were inscribed on the horizontal limb and below on the vertical Cherry-Garrard requested that they carve a line from Tennyson's Victorian epic poem, *Ulysses*: 'To strive, to seek, to find, and not to yield.' The party gave three rousing cheers, took a few photographs and hurried down from the exposed summit to escape the biting winds that chilled them to the bone.[2]

Terra Nova slipped away from Cape Evans soon after and headed back to civilisation. The coast of New Zealand came into sight on 9 February and under cover of darkness, shortly before 3 am on the morning of 10 February 1913, the ship crept almost unnoticed into the small east-coast port of Oamaru.

Scott had an exclusive agreement with the Central News Agency in London and Atkinson rowed ashore with the reliable Crean and Lieutenant Pennell from *Terra Nova* to cable the news to the other side of the world. However, the ship had returned to New Zealand earlier than expected and word of the expedition's arrival soon spread, sparking considerable speculation among the locals. Crean reported being chased by inquisitive New Zealanders eager to learn more news, but the men escaped without divulging anything and hurried off to sea again.

The tight-lipped explorers on *Terra Nova* steamed up the coast for the port of Lyttelton, where they arrived to learn that the news had now broken. The ship, with the white ensign flapping at half-mast, sailed very slowly into the harbour as though weighed down by the sorrow of the occasion. They found a silent guard of honour formed by the people of Lyttelton who had gathered on the quayside in disbelief and sadness.

The men on board *Terra Nova* had been out of contact with civilisation for two years and could barely comprehend the scale of public mourning. The first person they met was the harbourmaster at Lyttelton, who broke down and wept. Cherry-Garrard summed up the sense of shock and wrote:

> '. . . we had been too long away and the whole thing was so personal to us and our perceptions had been blunted: we never realised. We landed to find the Empire – almost the civilised world – in mourning.'[3]

The news of Oates' death came via a personal cable from Teddy Evans to the War Office in London. In turn, the War Office sent a telegram to Gestingthorpe on 11 February, notifying Mrs Oates that her son had died almost a year earlier on 17 March 1912.[4] But Caroline Oates was blissfully unaware of events. She had gone down to her London flat at Evelyn Mansions, Carlisle Place near Victoria Station and missed the fateful cable.

The sad duty of breaking the news to Caroline Oates fell to Lillian, her eldest, who had been walking along a London street when she glimpsed a newspaper poster revealing the news that Scott's Polar party had perished a year earlier. With heavy heart Lillian hurried off to Evelyn Mansions.

Caroline Oates was distraught. One newspaper, conjuring up a suitably Victorian sense of melodrama, reported: 'Of patrician mien and Spartan mould, Mrs Oates sat in tearless grief that uttered no word of lamentation over the death of her soldier son.'

She never fully recovered from the blow, despite the long passage of time. The mourning she had practised after the death of her husband, William, was merely a rehearsal for the prolonged anguish of bereavement for her cherished son, which would continue unbroken until her own death many years later. Caroline Oates was a product of her Victorian upbringing, an age which, above all, knew how to grieve.

Each night she slept in Laurie's bedroom at Gestingthorpe, which appropriately enough, points to the south. She always carried one of his regimental epaulettes in her handbag. On one wall, she hung his snowshoes and every room in the sprawling house was muffled with black crepe. The library was transformed into a memorial chapel, which she filled with more Antarctic memorabilia lest anyone forget and each year on the anniversary of her son's death, Caroline Oates would fly a flag from the roof of Gestingthorpe.

She planted an apple tree in the garden of every cottage in the village of Gestingthorpe in memory of her son and continued for the rest of her life, like Queen Victoria, to dress only in funereal black.

The disaster also released a deluge of national mourning which absorbed Kings and commoners alike. King George V called it a 'shocking tragedy' and letters and telegrams of condolence poured in from around the world. The Royal Geographical Society in London became a focal point for the messages of sympathy, particularly from renowned fellow explorers such as Borchgrevink, Charcot and Nansen, while King Haakon of Norway offered his heartfelt sympathy for the 'dreadful loss' of the Polar party.

Newspapers produced special editions containing Ponting's remarkable photographs and long articles examining every aspect of the failed expedition.

There was also wild speculation about the causes of the catastrophe. Some of the reports were particularly macabre as conjecture replaced substance. In the absence of clear-cut facts, journalists fell back on speculation and rumour.

In one account, it was faithfully reported from New Zealand that Oates' feet had dropped off before he died because of the severe frostbite. The unlikely source of this unpleasant tale was Captain Watson, the agent of the Imperial Merchant Service Guild in New Zealand who had spoken to a shipmaster who, in turn, had discussed the disaster with Teddy Evans.

However, the reporter had conveniently overlooked the fact that Oates' body had never been found and at the time of his death, Evans was hundreds of miles away recuperating from scurvy on board *Terra Nova*, ploughing northwards through the Southern Ocean towards New Zealand.

There were other unfortunate episodes. Shortly after learning of her son's death, Caroline Oates received a bill for £4.15s (£4.07½) from the military outfitters, Humphreys & Cook, for a new dress uniform, which had been ordered while he was away.

Caroline Oates was swamped with tributes for her son, particularly as the details of his gallantry began to emerge over the wires and into the voluminous newspaper reports. Letters of condolence came from friends and strangers, all of whom were moved by the tragedy. An army friend, Colonel Ansell, said Oates' death was 'an example never to be forgotten' and another, Fergus Nixon, told Caroline: 'I have lost my greatest friend.'

Robert Henry, one of the troopers who stood alongside Oates in the skirmish at Aberdeen in 1901, wrote: 'He was known amongst us as one of the bravest of the brave.' George Maughan, a Crimean War veteran of Balaclava almost 60 years earlier, wrote that 'my heart beat with pride to read of such heroism and self-sacrifice'.

The country, too, was in deep mourning. Like all disasters involving public figures, people felt they had lost someone close. Many years later people would recall the precise moment and what they were doing when news of the tragedy first reached them.

Britain had barely recovered from the sinking of the *Titanic* ten months earlier and the Government, sensing the public mood, announced that the men would be regarded as having been 'killed in action'. In an unprecedented act, Kathleen Scott became Lady Scott when the King awarded her the status accorded to the wife of a Knight Commander of the Order of the Bath.

On 14 February, just days after the news had first broken, a large crowd gathered at St Paul's Cathedral for a memorial service to the dead men. King

George V led the mourners while outside thousands stood silently in the drizzle beneath the slate-grey London sky.

Caroline Oates, an inconsolable figure, sat with Lillian and numerous relatives, quietly longing for a more private place to grieve. At St Mary's, Gestingthorpe, a service was held simultaneously where a cousin, Mary Oates, represented the family.

Several funds were set up to provide for the dependants and pay off the expedition's outstanding debts. The public response was massive. Some £30,000 (today £1,350,000) was donated in three days, including £100 apiece from the King and Queen. By the time the various funds were consolidated into a single Lord Mayor's Mansion House Fund, the total stood at £75,000 (today £3,400,000) or almost double the £40,000 Scott had raised to launch the expedition barely three years earlier.

The Treasury insisted that the aim was to ensure that the financial health of the surviving families would be 'in as good a pecuniary position as they would have been in, had the disaster not taken place'.[5]

But, even in death, the English class system prevailed. Kathleen Scott was awarded £8,500 (today £390,000), plus a further £3,500 (£160,000) for her son Peter and £6,000 (£274,000) was granted to Scott's mother, Hannah, who also received a grace-and-favour apartment at Hampton Court. There were also modest pensions for life.

Oriana Wilson received £8,500 and £4,500 (£205,000) was given to Bowers' mother, Emily. By contrast, Lois Evans, mother of three small children and widow of the Petty Officer Taff Evans, received only £1,250 (£57,000) and a pension of £48 (£2,200) a year.[6]

Oates was different. As a wealthy member of the landed gentry, there was less obvious need for public grants. By today's standards, he was a millionaire. In his will, Oates left some £29,000, the equivalent of around £1,300,000 today.

His inheritance, which was due to pass into Bryan's hands, was also considerable. He stood to receive a share of his parent's fortune, a stake in the house and land at Gestingthorpe, plus a 50 per cent share in the Meanwood estate in Yorkshire, which he had inherited jointly with Bryan.

Nor was the family in desperate need of money. The portfolio of property and other investments which she inherited from William Oates was sufficient to give Caroline an income of nearly £10,000 a year, or about £400,000 in today's terms.

In the circumstances, the Mansion House Fund trustees did not consider the Oates family needed support, 'as he was a man of private means and left no dependant relatives'.

Money aside, the Inniskilling Dragoons were anxious to commemorate the death of their popular colleague. Lt-Colonel Neil Haig, Oates' old friend, suggested that a special fund should be raised in his name and only two weeks after news of his death, the Oates Memorial Fund was set up.

The initial aim was to provide a cottage or modest sums of money to members of the regiment who had fallen on hard times. One plan was to build cottages for needy old soldiers, but this idea was quickly abandoned and the Fund opted instead to make direct payments to regimental veterans.

The Fund attracted widespread attention from serving and retired soldiers and a total of £4,000 4s 1d (or £182,000 in today's terms) poured in from around the world in donations of all shapes and sizes. The Duke of Connaught, Colonel-in-Chief of the Inniskillings, gave £25 5s (or £1,100 today) and 10s.6d (or £24 today) came anonymously from 'Two Sappers' in Winnipeg, Canada.

Captain Moncrief, the man who had replaced Oates at Mhow in 1910, gave £5 and Lt Col Fryer, who had fought to prevent Oates joining the expedition, also donated £5 (£228).

The issue of money was an irrelevant sideshow for Caroline Oates, who wanted answers, not charity. Right from the start, she was among the very few who raised uncomfortable questions about the catastrophic outcome of the expedition. While the nation wallowed in months of drawn-out mourning and lionising of the dead, Caroline Oates simply wanted to know why her beloved son had died. She suspected incompetence and pointed her finger at Scott.

Getting to the bottom of things was no easy task, particularly as the dead men were rapidly elevated to the status of national martyrs. The causes of the disaster – such as Scott's management, the failure to deploy dogs and the poor preparation – were overlooked in the headlong rush to create legends.

Scott's poignant and powerful diary, in which he sought to justify the calamity, was published to a public eager to perpetuate the myths. But what the public did not read were the bits carefully excised from the original, including personal criticisms of colleagues such as Oates.

Caroline Oates began by accepting the official version of events. There was little option, with the survivors of the expedition still at sea en route from the Antarctic.

Teddy Evans, Scott's official deputy, was the person who sowed the early seeds of doubt. In public, Evans maintained a dignified loyalty to Scott and did as much as anyone to carry on the legend of heroic failure, delivering powerful public lectures on the expedition and carefully avoiding any hint of criticism. But he knew far more than he was divulging.

The first hint of anything out of the ordinary came when Evans wrote an

elliptical letter to Mrs Oates on his long journey from McMurdo Sound back to
Britain in the opening months of 1913. The letter, posted at Port Said as he passed
through the Suez Canal, said:

> 'I have much to talk about.
> 'One cannot state facts plainly when they reflect on the organisation,
> but I often feel inclined to.'[7]

Evans had his own misgivings about events on the expedition. He had
reservations about the overall management and suffered worse than most from
Scott's erratic behaviour and intemperate outbursts. He was particularly scathing
about Scott's decision to carry the 35 lb of rock specimens and other surplus items
on the sledge when the men were literally dying in their tracks on the Barrier.
Evans said he 'deplored' Scott's decision to put his party in jeopardy by carrying
unnecessary 'trash' instead of adequate quantities of food.

The significance of his comments are that they were contained in a letter,
written to his secretary, Silvia Gifford, and her husband Ralph, while Evans was
on board *Terra Nova* sailing away from McMurdo Sound to New Zealand. This
was weeks before the outside world was alerted to the disaster and before the
torrent of mourning swept aside all rational considerations.

Shorn of the diplomatic niceties, Evans went straight to the point and wrote:

> 'It seems to me extraordinary that they stuck to all their records and
> specimens, we (the Last Supporting Party) dumped ours at the first big
> check. I must say I considered the safety of my party before the value
> of the records and extra stores – not eatable. Apparently Scott did not.
> His sledge contained 150 lb of trash.'[8]

He added a grim footnote, declaring that '. . . thank God I was not included in
the advance party . . .'

After *Terra Nova* docked at Lyttelton, Evans hurried to catch a P&O liner back
to Britain. One of his first duties was to visit Caroline Oates at Gestingthorpe,
where he handed over Oates' personal effects. Evans gave her two sealed packages
containing his precious journal, the poignant last letter written by the dying
Wilson, his watch and £2 6s 8d in (£2.33) cash. He also gave her the portrait of
Napoleon which had hung over her son's bed in The Tenements at Cape Evans.

Evans had meticulously sealed the diary at Cape Evans and promised Caroline
Oates that the journal had not been read by anyone. In a covering letter written
while *Terra Nova* was steaming away from Antarctica, he underlined the word
'anyone' to emphasise the sanctity of her son's words.

Oates' diaries and the critical letters he had written while at Cape Evans told a different version of events from those being served up to the general public. The biting criticism of Scott's management and shortcomings were laid out before her and Caroline Oates trusted no one more than her son. For the first time she realised there was more to the disaster.

She also came to trust Evans, who made frequent visits to Gestingthorpe and her flat in Victoria. Teddy Evans and Caroline Oates had something in common. They were both grieving. Evans had suffered a severe loss on the return journey from the ice. His wife Hilda had developed fatal peritonitis while they were sailing from New Zealand to Britain and died on the return journey.

Caroline Oates had been drawn to Teddy Evans, perhaps because she understood his personal loss and perhaps because she saw Evans as the person who might provide vital details about the circumstances surrounding her son's death. She later demonstrated her feelings by making a rare public appearance in January 1916 when Teddy Evans took a new bride, marrying Elsa Andvord, the daughter of a Norwegian businessman.

Ahead of that, Evans had other problems, which he gladly shared with Caroline Oates. In wrapping up the expedition's business affairs he found a chaotic jumble of contracts and commitments. 'I cannot find in one (contract) anything that is not contradicted in another,' he told her. 'I personally would never have embarked on the expedition had I known how we were being misled in the original expedition agreement.'9

The information supplied by Evans and her son's own words reinforced her determination to get to the bottom of the story. In her eagerness to discover the truth, Caroline Oates also began sounding out other survivors of the expedition.

Atkinson and Meares, Oates' closest friends on the expedition, made several visits for tea at Gestingthorpe or dinner at her flat, where she began to uncover more uncomfortable details about the expedition. Meares revealed that it was not the happy harmonious venture portrayed to the public. Scott's rows with the expedition members, particularly Teddy Evans, were 'shocking', Meares reported. He said that Wilson 'tried to pour oil on troubled waters' and was known as 'Peace-making Bill'.

Atkinson admitted that Oates was 'so disgusted with the way the whole thing was done'. It was little consolation to Caroline Oates that her son had been 'the most popular officer' on the expedition. But she did derive a little satisfaction from the fact Scott and his companions were never forced to carry the stricken Oates. 'Laurie was never dragged on the sledge,' she wrote.

She also pressed Atkinson to reveal whether Oates regretted joining the expedition. Atkinson, who was feeling the strain of the disaster, hesitated for a

long time before finally confessing that there were times when Oates did indeed
regret going south.

Nelson and the ship's biologist Lillie were also consulted and Caroline Oates took soundings from the ranks by entertaining Lashly, Forde and an experienced *Terra Nova* seaman, Alf Cheetham.

Tom Crean, whom she described as a 'magnificent character', went to visit and pointed out that Oates felt the cold because of his bad circulation but was otherwise happy. Crean, who marched alongside Oates for hundreds of miles, said he 'walked quietly along on the march just as though he were walking around this room'.

She also approached Ponting, who was among those to recognise the tragic failure to make better use of dogs on the expedition. Within days of hearing about the tragedy, Ponting was quoted in newspapers as saying:

> 'It is my genuine personal opinion that had Scott had dogs with him on the last journey, this disaster would not have happened. But Scott did not like the idea of employing dogs and then having to kill them.
> 'It is an interesting point whether such an act is justifiable where human lives are being affected.'[10]

She also widened her circle, establishing contact with other experts on Antarctic exploration, such as Sir Ernest Shackleton and Hugh Mill, the highly respected Polar authority and former librarian of the Royal Geographical Society. She also became friends with Shackleton's wife, Emily, and generously helped meet the cost of her children's school fees.

Mrs Oates also met the expedition's three widows, Kathleen Scott, Oriana Wilson and Lois Evans. Lois Evans warmly reciprocated by crocheting a fine altar cloth for St Mary's Church at Gestingthorpe.

In contrast, Kathleen Scott was very uncomfortable in the company of Caroline Oates. It is likely Lady Scott sensed Mrs Oates' growing – but unspoken – belief that Scott had indirectly killed her son. Tense and ill at ease, Kathleen Scott gabbled anxiously during their meeting. 'She was very nervous,' Caroline noted.

Kathleen Scott had another reason for feeling uncomfortable. She felt privately that the two sick men – Oates and Evans – had contributed to her husband's death because they had slowed up the return march.

The two women were not ideally suited. They had very little in common, apart from the loss of loved ones. There was little warmth between the two and Mrs Oates airily described the 35-year-old Kathleen Scott as a 'pretty woman with very good eyes'. The buttoned-up Caroline Oates was the epitome of the stern, conventional Victorian matriarch who was a natural to the role of long-suffering dowager. Kathleen Scott, by contrast, was a new woman of the liberated Edwardian age, a gifted sculptress with a Bohemian free spirit who moved effortlessly among Royalty and Prime Ministers and artists and writers. One observer described her as 'extravagantly histrionic'. While the imperious Caroline Oates reigned in the drawing room at Gestingthorpe, Kathleen Scott flourished on the dance floor or at dinner parties.

The pair saw each other regularly in the period immediately following news of the disaster. They had at least three meetings in the six weeks between mid April and the end of May 1913 and Caroline Oates became increasingly suspicious. As her concerns mounted, Caroline went to the extraordinary length of keeping a handwritten record of the conversations over tea with Kathleen Scott. Her notes from one meeting at Scott's home in Buckingham Palace Road on 22 April extended to two and a half carefully written pages. The notes, which illustrated the tension between the pair, revealed:

> 'She (Lady Scott) was not at her ease and evidently embarrassed throughout the visit, perhaps quite natural.
>
> 'I asked Lady Scott whether she realised the risks and dangers, which indeed I had not and she said she knew they were considerable.
>
> 'I contrived to ask her what she considered was the cause of the whole disaster and she said everything had gone against the expedition from first to last and there were difficulties on every hand and a condition of weather which it was absolutely impossible to battle against.'[11]

Caroline Oates was far from satisfied by what she heard but protocol dictated that she did not press too hard. She had wanted to ask Kathleen why Scott had not postponed the Pole venture for a year after losing so many ponies on the miserable depot laying journey in 1911. It was a good question, particularly as Oates had personally arranged for a new batch of replacement ponies to be sent from India. But she elected to keep her own counsel.

Kathleen Scott was preserving the more acceptable line that Scott was an unlucky explorer and that the five dead men were merely victims of misfortune. There was barely a mention of the word scurvy, although experienced Polar explorers had their own unequivocally strong views about the reasons for the ultimate failure of the expedition.

Nansen, the man whose exploits had paved the way for Amundsen, Scott, Shackleton and other explorers of the age, believed that the men had succumbed to scurvy. In one newspaper interview he explained:

'. . . Captain Oates' illness must surely have been scurvy also. Frostbitten hands and feet are just what scurvy patients are liable to, because their circulation is impaired.'[12]

Nansen also explained that scurvy 'gives no pain' and warned that it had a seriously debilitating effect on human resolve, commenting that '. . . in the first stages (scurvy) only lowers the vitality and depresses the spirits'. He said that if Oates had been attacked by scurvy, '. . . his action is quite explainable'.

Shackleton, who had been brought to the brink of death by exhaustion and scurvy on the Barrier only four years earlier, held the same view. On being told of the disaster he remarked:

'There is something behind it and in my opinion that something is scurvy.'[13]

Amundsen, whose feat of reaching the South Pole first had now been eclipsed by the tragedy, found the deaths 'horrible, horrible'. But he was among those who saw there was more to the story. He also had his own views on the death of Oates. Interviewed while visiting America, he said:

'Oates went bravely, you know, out into the blizzard that his sickly condition might not hinder the others. He knew the others wouldn't desert him so he deserted them. That was an epic deed – wonderful, wonderful! A great sacrifice – but it did no good.'[14]

Caroline Oates' belief that her son was a victim of bungling began to harden the more she canvassed opinion and, the more she learned, the more penetrating her questioning became. As she delved further into the details of the expedition, the more Scott's mismanagement became apparent and the less Caroline accepted the official version of events She was among the first to question the critical loss of paraffin on the return journey. Henry Oates, a cousin, told her that recent scientific studies showed that fuel cans became porous under certain conditions. 'If this can be established it may solve one of the mysteries of the South Pole business,' she responded.

The finger of blame was directed at Scott, even though Bowers was in charge of supplies. Years later she concluded:

'I am absolutely convinced, knowing what I know of Bowers, that he would never have made so grave an error of judgement and calculation to allow a shortage (of fuel). I am most conscious to do away with any impression which my notes might give to the effect that Bowers was in anyway to blame.'[15]

Caroline Oates also questioned the underlying conflict of mixing exploration with the heavy scientific workload on the expedition. She saw the inevitable tension between the two as a primary cause of the disaster, doubtless encouraged by Evans' criticism.

She also demanded to know why there had been no co-ordinated rescue from Cape Evans as the men struggled back across the Barrier. Her bitterness and misgivings were summed up in a long letter written some years after Oates' death, in which she even raised the suggestion that her son had been deliberately sacrificed to save the others. She wrote:

> 'I was never satisfied with the accounts of Scott's book. I have persevered trying to obtain all the information possible from reliable sources re the causes of the failure.
>
> I will say the members of the expedition who knew me best have been very helpful and told me all they could. Distressing as it very much is, I feel, *I would rather know*.
>
> I have a dear and intimate friend who was a childhood playmate of my boy. He and I have had many talks about the Expedition. He told me there were many circumstances of commanding officers sacrificing numbers of valuable lives from sheer obstinacy and self.
>
> It is pretty ghastly when you think of the fourteen fresh dogs and seven well-trained Indian mules over which my boy took so much trouble – ready there at the base – and no transport officer to make use of them – whilst the southern party were deserted and dying. Horrible.
>
> My opinion may be worthless, but I always feel Scott allowed too many "side shows" if I may use the expression. If the objective was the South Pole, he should have focussed everything on that.
>
> His base was denuded and when relief should have been sent, there was seemingly, no one to take the initiative. Scott overwhelmed his men from the very outset . . . that man hauling was so terrible . . .'[16]

But the public wanted heroes, not villains, and despite her deep suspicions, Caroline Oates kept her views private. It is possible that someone as determined and articulate as Mrs Oates might have forced the authorities to open an inquiry into the causes of the disaster if she had pursued the matter with more vigour. In the event, no investigation was ever launched.

A little over a year after the expedition emerged from the ice, Britain was at war with Germany and heroic defeat was more acceptable than debunking its public heroes. Indeed, the dead explorers were seen as role models for others. Ponting's celebrated film of the expedition, *90° South*, was shown to rally troops and set an example to the men in the trenches. Over 100,000 soldiers, who faced slaughter on a daily basis, were taken from the trenches to watch the film about noble death.

The Reverend F.I. Anderson, Senior Chaplain to the Forces, wrote to Ponting:

> 'I cannot tell you what a tremendous delight your films are to thousands of our troops. The splendid story of Captain Scott is just the thing to cheer and encourage us out here . . .
>
> 'The thrilling story of Captain Oates' self-sacrifice, to try and give his friends a chance of "getting through", is one that appeals so at the present time. The intensity of its appeal is realised by the subdued hush and quiet that pervades the massed audience of troops while it is being told. We feel that we have inherited from Oates and his comrades a legacy and heritage of inestimable value in seeing through our present work.'[17]

The rush to adulation had other curious side-effects, which occasionally involved bending the truth. Amundsen, in his autobiography, coldly recounted how English schoolchildren of the time were taught that Scott was the discoverer of the South Pole. The British, he added, are 'a race of very bad losers'.

Caroline Oates took very little part in the many public ceremonies of dedication or commemoration for the dead men, preferring to mourn in the privacy of Gestingthorpe. In private she could give full vent to her sadness. Although she travelled to Cardiff in June 1913 to welcome the *Terra Nova* back to Britain, she avoided most other occasions when the nation gathered to mourn the loss of the Polar party.

Most notably Caroline Oates declined to visit Buckingham Palace in July 1913 when the King decorated members of the expedition with their Antarctic Medals. Alone among the five grieving women, she pointedly boycotted the ceremony. While Kathleen Scott, Oriana Wilson, Emily Bowers and Lois Evans collected the medals for which their menfolk had died, Caroline Oates was noticeable by her absence. It was a calculated snub to the official version of events.

Bryan Oates had been asked to stand in for his mother but unaccountably no one at Gestingthorpe ever replied to the formal invitation from the Palace. Teddy Evans, who had helped Royal officials with the arrangements for the ceremony, hurriedly volunteered to receive the medal on behalf of the Oates family.

Nor did Caroline Oates attend the formal ceremony in November 1913 when the Royal Geographical Society gave its medals to the expedition's survivors and relatives. On this occasion she asked Francis Drake, secretary to the expedition, to receive her son's medal on her behalf.

Caroline Oates only came out of seclusion when the Inniskillings came to Gestingthorpe to pay their respects. She led Lillian, Violet and Bryan across the road from Gestingthorpe Hall on 8 November where the regiment placed a brass memorial plaque on the north wall of St Mary's. The 2 ft × 3 ft brass was dedicated to a 'very gallant gentleman' and placed in 'in affectionate remembrance' by brother officers.

It was a memorable day for the village as the Oates family, soldiers, explorers and the local community packed into the church. The sombre black attire of the family and villagers clashed with the brilliant dash of colour provided by the scarlet and gold-braided uniforms of the dragoons and the gold-embroidered blue of naval officers.

Major-General Edmund Allenby, who had distinguished himself with the Inniskillings in the Boer War and would later gain national recognition in the Turkish campaign of 1917–18, performed the unveiling ceremony. Regimental friends, Lt-Colonel Ansell and Captain Nixon, attended and standing alongside was Captain Moncrief from Mhow. Atkinson and Meares were there along with Teddy Evans, Pennell, Levick and Lillie from the expedition. In the porch six regimental trumpeters played the 'Last Post'.

The plaque erected by the Inniskillings became an important focus of attention for Caroline Oates, the public place where the memory of her son could be kept alive. The local legend is that she went across to the church and dutifully polished the brass every week up to the end of her life.

The story of Oates' gallantry touched a chord throughout the world and encouraged a flurry of other memorials to be put up in his memory. Fellow officers placed a memorial tablet at the Cavalry Club in London and in October 1913, Teddy Evans unveiled a memorial brass at St Anne's Church, Eastbourne, near to South Lynn school. A few days later Bryan Oates performed a similar ceremony at the Parish Church, Leeds.

One of the most unexpected memorials was a small bronze plaque placed in the school library at Eton on 23 May 1914. The inscription noted that Oates was 'A very gallant gentleman' who willingly went to his death 'trying to save his comrades'. The plaque was fashioned by Kathleen Scott, who put aside the friction between the two families to honour Oates at his old school.

In 1916, at the height of the carnage in Europe, Prime Minister Herbert Asquith unveiled a memorial tablet at St Paul's Cathedral and observed that Oates had become 'the most striking personality' because of the circumstances of his death.

Others followed in places as far apart as South Africa and Argentina. The **Bitter memories** Inniskillings also decided to hold a memorial service every year on the Sunday closest to 17 March, a ceremony which continues to this day.

There was also one lasting memorial to Oates which would have been established even without his unfortunate death. It was Oates Land, a rugged mountainous area about 400 miles to the north of McMurdo Sound on the Antarctic Continent and one of the last sights of the ice which explorers see as they sail northwards to New Zealand on the homeward journey.

Lt Harry Pennell, commander of the *Terra Nova*, discovered Oates Land in February 1911 as the ship was returning to New Zealand for the first time and while Oates was struggling with the ponies on the depot-laying journey. It was the only important new geographical discovery of the ill-fated *Terra Nova* expedition.

Less surprising is that the Oates story has endured the passage of time and continues to appeal to later generations. By the mid-1950s, over four decades after the tragedy, interest in Oates remained so strong that a permanent museum was opened in his name.

The opportunity arose when a relative, Robert Washington Oates, was approached to help finance the purchase of 'The Wakes', the home of the famous eighteenth-century naturalist, Gilbert White at Selborne, Hampshire. He agreed to provide £30,000 in return for a commitment that part of the house would be dedicated to Laurie Oates.

There is some symmetry in Oates being remembered alongside White, whose *Natural History of Selborne* is widely regarded as one of the most influential books ever written about the subtle and intricate relationship between nature and English village life. Charles Darwin said White's classic book had stimulated his own interest in biology and the nineteenth-century American writer, James R. Lowell, generously applauded it as the 'journal of Adam in Paradise'.

Oates would have felt comfortable at Selborne, whose soft pastoral landscape has changed little over the centuries and harks back to a bygone age for which he seemed more suited. The village, like Gestingthorpe, features a centuries-old church called St Mary's and opposite 'The Wakes' a commanding yew tree stood for an estimated 1,400 years as a seemingly indestructible symbol of Englishness.

The White-Oates Museum was formally opened in September 1955, displaying important relics of the *Terra Nova* expedition and other memorabilia of his life. It is a measure of the lasting interest in the story of Oates that the museum continues to attract a steady procession of visitors from around the world.

A final living link with the expedition was provided by Tryggve Gran, who as a distinguished 83-year-old, came to London in 1972 to attend a commemorative dinner on the sixtieth anniversary of Oates' death. Gran, the oldest surviving member of the expedition, had overcome Oates' dislike of foreigners to become 'my great, great friend'.

He stunned the audience with a remarkable story in which he claimed to have had an eerie premonition about his death.

A local newspaper recorded the event:

> 'But the most dramatic point came when, to a silent audience, Major Gran spoke of the night of March 17th, 1912 (in fact it was the night of March 16th), when he was with a support party trying to sleep in a fragile tent in a howling blizzard and he had a vivid dream which he can still recall.
>
> He woke his companions to tell them he had heard the voice of his friend, Oates, speaking to him and that he had the premonition that, somewhere in the frozen void, Oates had died.'[18]

Gran told the audience he heard Oates cry out in his dream and then had the premonition that Oates had died. 'It is very strange, but it is true,' he added.

He also wondered what Oates was thinking as he prepared to leave the tent to face certain death. 'Today no one is giving me any birthday presents,' Gran speculated 'but I am going to give one – I am going to give my life.'[19]

Gran's dreams were the subject of some debate on the expedition. On 15 December 1911 when the Polar party was over 400 miles away struggling up the Beardmore Glacier, Gran woke one morning to tell his colleagues he had dreamt of reading a telegram which proclaimed: 'Amundsen reached Pole, 15–20 December.'[20] The story was later confirmed by Griffith Taylor, although he recorded the date of Gran's dream as 20 December.[21] In fact, Amundsen was at the Pole from 14–17 December.

Shortly after Gran's intriguing speech, Willington School at Putney opened The Oates Library in memory of its most celebrated former pupil and in 1973, a commemorative 'Blue Plaque' was unveiled at his former home, then called Stroud House, at 309 Upper Richmond Road, Putney.

The tragedy has had a profound effect on the Oates family, largely because of the commanding influence of Caroline Oates, whose obsessive devotion to her eldest son always prevented her from fully coming to terms with his death. The cavalry officer, explorer and gallant national hero was always referred to as 'my boy'.

Caroline Oates was a tormented figure in the years after the tragedy. At the back of her mind was the awful knowledge that her money had contributed to the expedition which had extinguished the most precious thing in her life. She read

all the Polar literature she could lay her hands on, often bristling with dissent over
passages which dealt with her son. She read the newspaper reviews of Stephen
Gwynn's 1929 work, *Captain Scott*, and even before reading the book itself
decided she did not like it. Bryan later gave her a copy, whereupon she
complained about various 'mistakes'.

Her hostility probably owed much to the fact that Gwynn was a good friend of
Kathleen Scott. Ironically, Kathleen Scott also disapproved of Gwynn's book,
despite their long friendship. She was unhappy that Scott had become 'public
property', though this overlooked how the tragedy as a whole had been hijacked
as propaganda during the Great War.

Caroline Oates' obsession also caused some odd contradictions. On the one
hand she was desperate to protect and control her son's memory, ensuring that all
talk about Laurie was kept from the public gaze. On the other hand, she
complained that her son never received the recognition he deserved, particularly
for his army career. She once wrote:

> 'I always felt that my boy's military career was a little overshadowed by
> subsequent events and not sufficient was made of it.'[22]

Caroline Oates was particularly keen to ensure that she alone controlled the
memory of her son. In the 1930s she deliberately blocked the first attempt to
write an authoritative book about her son and was not ashamed to resort to lying
in an attempt to preserve her authority.

The idea of a book on Oates came from Louis Bernacchi, a man with
impeccable credentials for the task. He was a distinguished Polar explorer who
had been on Borchgrevink's historic *Southern Cross* expedition in 1898–1900 and
on *Discovery* with Scott between 1901 and 1904. Bernacchi was among the first
explorers to suggest using motor transport for travelling over the ice. Bernacchi,
the wealthy son of an Italian silk merchant, wrote several books about Polar affairs
and became a council member of the Royal Geographical Society. Scott was best
man at his wedding in 1906.

But he quickly found his path blocked by the obdurate Mrs Oates. She refused
to deal directly with him and would only correspond through intermediaries.
Bernacchi recruited Hugh Mill to act as go-between, still fondly hoping that she
would release family papers and her son's important expedition diary. Mrs Oates
got on well with Mill but refused to budge.

She also perjured herself by saying that Oates did not keep a diary. Bernacchi
knew she was lying and commented that she would find it difficult to 'hark back'
on that statement. The old lady is 'very difficult', he added.

In frustration Bernacchi turned to Bryan Oates who, unknown to his mother, discreetly provided a modest amount of information about his brother's early life. Bryan lived in fear of Caroline Oates and told Bernacchi that the 'very few details I have gladly given you will most probably be placed at my door'. Bryan also told Bernacchi that 'nothing will alter' his mother's unwelcoming attitude towards the book.[23]

Bernacchi was as thorough as circumstances would allow in compiling a reliable biography. He knew many of the expedition's veterans and also approached those outside Polar exploration circles who knew Oates, such as Algernon Rayner-Wood, the former housemaster at Eton and Dr Whyte, who tended Oates' leg wound after the fight at Aberdeen. He also persuaded Frank Debenham, Oates' former colleague and now a Professor at Cambridge University, to read the final proofs of the book for accuracy.

The book, although severely hampered by Caroline Oates' intransigence and inevitably lacking in some depth, was nevertheless generally well received when finally published in 1933. Bernacchi admitted it had been a 'curiously difficult' task, which was presumably a reference to the deception and obstruction of the Oates family.

King George, who had led the mourning for the expedition twenty years earlier, was sent a copy and responded with a highly personal and emotional review. He declared:

> 'I have read your book with a beating heart and tears in my eyes. It is splendid.'[24]

Caroline Oates continued to repel boarders for the rest of her life, a brooding figure who resented outside intrusion and ordered her children and other relatives not to speak publicly about the family. Generations were repeatedly told 'not to talk to people about your family'.[25] The similarity with Queen Victoria became more pronounced as she withdrew further into her embittered isolation and one of her descendants took the analogy a stage further by recalling her as having a 'regal appearance'.

Violet Oates, who never married, remained by her mother's side throughout the years of angst, loyally supportive and unquestioning of her behaviour. She quietly played a diplomatic role as the go-between between Caroline Oates and the outside world, humouring the old lady and avoiding any confrontations which might reopen old wounds.

While Lillian and Bryan married and brought up their own families away from the suffocating atmosphere of Gestingthorpe, Violet's life was inevitably

overshadowed by the tragedy of her eldest brother's death and her mother's
fixation.

Caroline Oates' influence was apparent in another way. It was not until after her death that any member of the large Oates family was named Lawrence. It was regarded as 'too sensitive' before then. The first person to carry their ancestor's forename was Lawrence Grace Oates, the grandson of Bryan Oates, who was born in South Africa in 1943.

Caroline Oates remained a dominating influence in the village of Gestingthorpe, where she continued to exercise a stern, matronly benevolence over the local community. She seldom left the grounds of Gestingthorpe and in later life only communicated with villagers through a series of formal hand-written notes.

She re-entered normal life each Christmas by throwing a party for the local children, tenants and members of staff at Gestingthorpe. Each was graciously given a joint of meat for the festive period. Despite her charity, however, Caroline Oates never won the real affection of the villagers. She was respected, not loved.

Caroline Oates, bitter and inquisitive to the end, finally died on 26 November 1937, at the age of 83. One newspaper reported her as saying:

'When I die, I wish to die alone and no one must know.'[26]

She almost got her wish. Only the pantry boy was in the house at Gestingthorpe when a 'sudden haemorrhage' ended her life.

Lillian, the eldest, skated over her mother's long years of bitterness and mourning by pronouncing that it was the end of a 'full and wonderful life' and added a slightly mystical postscript. She wrote:

'It is wonderful to think of her glorious awakening with her loved ones
who have crossed before.'[27]

Gestingthorpe's villagers were asked not to talk about her death and there were no cars following the hearse that carried her body through the Essex countryside for the last time to the crematorium at Ipswich for a quiet funeral on 29 November 1937. Popular newspapers speculated that her ashes would be flown to the Antarctic and scattered over the Barrier snows where her beloved son lay.

But she also carried her bitterness beyond the grave. Caroline Oates ordered Violet to destroy Oates' precious Antarctic diary immediately after her death. Caroline had controlled Laurie Oates throughout his life and insisted on exercising her authority even after her own death.

It was a premeditated act of historical barbarism, which assumed only she was capable of remembering her son. Fortunately, the usually faithful Violet disobeyed her mother, sitting up late into the night copying some important extracts from the diary. But the full diary, which would have provided a valuable alternative perspective on events leading up to the Polar disaster, was reportedly destroyed.

It is impossible to state categorically that the valuable diary was, in fact, burnt in view of events down the years. But, either way, generations of historians have lost access to an important document about the expedition and a priceless opportunity to examine the one alternate view of events provided by Oates' singular, but ultimately well-founded, view of proceedings.

Among the five doomed men on the final Polar march, Taff Evans did not keep a diary and while the records of Wilson and Bowers have survived, they are respectful and uncontroversial. Scott's leadership and judgement are barely questioned in these contemporary accounts.

Only Oates took a different view of the unfolding tragedy. While the fragments copied by Violet are precious, the wanton destruction – or removal from public examination – of the Oates diary leaves an irreplaceable gap in the story that can never be adequately filled.

It is possible that the historic reassessment of Scott's last expedition, which did not begin seriously until the 1970s and 1980s, would have occurred decades earlier if the Oates family had allowed Bernacchi and other writers to read the diary and letters. The irony is that Caroline Oates' blind devotion to her son undoubtedly helped perpetuate the legend of Scott – the man she blamed for Oates' death – as the unlucky, tragic hero.

Violet Oates, in keeping with family wishes, kept the copied pages from the diary tucked away in a box for safe keeping and out of sight of prying eyes. Few outside the family even knew of their existence.

But Reginald Pound, an experienced author who had already written a biography of Teddy Evans, learned about the diary in the 1960s and asked her to reveal their contents. Violet insisted the diary was 'brief and suitably personal' and that her mother 'did not wish it published'.[28] At this point, Caroline Oates had been dead for 28 years but her influence remained as potent as ever.

What Violet did not tell Pound was that she had already agreed to lift the veil of secrecy by revealing the contents to someone else. The beneficiary of Violet's about-turn was a young writer, Sue Limb, who was also preparing a new biography of Oates.

Limb was introduced to Violet Oates by Frank Debenham and she invited the aspiring writer to her double-fronted cottage in a peaceful lane near Long Melford, a few miles from Gestingthorpe. Violet left Gestingthorpe in 1948 and lived happily into her old age, surrounded by a mass of tall trees and wild flowers and the scores of birds which flocked to her rambling garden. On the garden gate a handwritten note reminded visitors: 'Please leave water out for the birds.'

The slight, sixteen-year-old Limb found Violet Oates, a tall large-boned woman in her eighties, an 'irresistibly sympathetic woman'. They developed a close friendship and before long Violet surprisingly ditched the family tradition and began to open up.

Debenham, who had to stand over Oates in the Antarctic to bully him into writing home, had warned Limb that Laurie was not a prolific correspondent. She was told not to expect much archive material to inspect. But Limb received an unexpected windfall. She was shown a 'trunkful of letters', written over a period of more than twelve years from his time at the South Lynn 'crammer', through his military career and up to the final scribbled notes he wrote home shortly before reaching the South Pole in January 1912. Most importantly, Violet Oates allowed Limb to see the diary entries she had copied from the original.

Violet Oates underwent considerable soul-searching before releasing the previously unseen documents. It was a tough decision which went against the family conviction. Limb, who was amazed at Violet's trust for a teenage stranger, recalled:

> 'I feel she was weighing constantly the obligation to knowledge and history with the family inclination to privacy.'[29]

It was a courageous and generous gesture by the independently-minded Violet, who shared her brother's contempt for convention. She probably enjoyed one final act of rebellious defiance against the family custom of concealment and subterfuge.

Violet Oates was attracted by Limb and only two months before her death in February 1966, she drew up a new will and left £150 to 'my friend Susan Limb' to assist her in researching the book, which was eventually published in 1982.[30] In what Limb called another 'breezy defiance of convention' Violet also made arrangements for her body to be left to science.

Violet Oates was 84 years old when she died, the last of the four children of William and Caroline Oates of Gestingthorpe. Lillian, the eldest, died in November 1965 at 87 and the youngest, Bryan, was 80 when he died in 1963. Given the longevity of the family, it is tempting to believe that Laurie Oates would have enjoyed a long life.

Lawrence Edward Grace Oates now lies in his unmarked tomb on the Barrier, almost perfectly preserved by the hostile environment which overwhelmed him in 1912. He rests undisturbed from the agonising moment when he could not

*Violet Oates. Laurie's younger sister who dutifully supported her mother in the long
years of recrimination and mourning after the death of Oates. She never married.
(White Oates Museum)*

crawl an inch further, impeccably embalmed about 75 ft (23 m) below the cold white surface. He is frozen in time.

The Barrier, now called the Ross Ice Shelf, is constantly on the move, heading inexorably towards the Ross Sea where its great icebergs break off into the waters and drift slowly out into the Southern Ocean. Oates, too, is on the move.

Modern research shows that he is inching slowly northwards, initially at a rate of around 2,000 ft a year (600 m) and accelerating to over 3,000 ft a year (1,000 m) as he nears the Ross Sea. It is estimated that Oates will reach the sea about 275 years from now, when a giant berg 'calves' away from the Barrier and carries him into the waters off the Antarctic Continent.[31]

Lawrence Edward Grace Oates, a restless man all his life, will find his last resting place only when the merciless Barrier finally releases its grip in the year 2275.

26

A second tragedy

There was a second tragedy in the life of Lawrence Oates. The first was his unfortunate presence in the South Pole party and lingering suffering on the return march. The other was fathering a child, whom he never saw. Lawrence Oates became a father in 1900, shortly before gaining his cherished commission in the Inniskilling Dragoons. But it is highly unlikely that he ever set eyes upon his child and probably died without knowing that he was a father.

The unknown and secret child emerged after a brief liaison during the summer of 1899, when Oates was flitting between Gestingthorpe and the 'crammer' at Eastbourne or his uncle's family home at Meanwood and the militia barracks at York.

His girlfriend was Henrietta Learmont McKendrick, the daughter of master builder, Walter McKendrick and his wife, Mary Grainger McLelland, a former domestic servant. Henrietta was one of four daughters born to the McKendricks in the small Scottish town of Johnstone, near Paisley during the 1880s. Walter McKendrick died of cirrhosis of the liver in 1896 at the early age of 41 and Etta, as she was called, is thought to have left Johnstone soon afterwards.

It may never be possible to provide conclusive proof that Laurie Oates fathered the child, although enough evidence exists to offer a powerful case that he did. The vital clue to the child's parentage – the birth certificate – is missing, probably because like many young girls of the Victorian age, the birth was never registered. It is also reasonable to assume that the young mother's pregnancy was so embarrassing that the birth was kept a closely guarded secret.

The circumstances of the romance are unclear but anecdotes passed down through the family suggest that Etta was shipped off to an unknown destination in Ireland to have the child in secrecy.

Immediately after the birth, the child was taken from Etta and handed over to the care of Blanche Wright and Ellen B Kingsford, two resourceful former nurses who ran a special home for the unwanted children of unmarried mothers in the south of England, far from Johnstone. The two women raised the child in the firm but benevolent atmosphere of their home and named her Kathleen Gray.

Kathleen Gray's birthday was given as 24 March 1900, a few days after Laurie Oates' twentieth birthday.

Blanche Wright, who never married, became closely attached to little Kathleen and some years later formally adopted the child. Kathleen, who was invariably called Kit, knew Wright only as 'Auntie'. By coincidence, Kit was regularly taken to Wright's holiday home at the Devon resort of Sidmouth where a young Laurie Oates had spent many happy days during his childhood.

The Wright-Kingsford refuge, which provided a sanctuary for some of the most defenceless outcasts of Victorian society, was established in 1898 in a six-roomed

Kathleen Gray, the mystery woman who was the illegitimate child of Laurie Oates. The child was brought up in a home and named Kathleen Gray by one of the spinsters who later adopted her. She was always known as Kit and died in 1981, aged 81.
(Angela Wilson)

rented cottage in the quiet Surrey backwater of Hersham. The two women financed the venture from their own pockets and assorted donations and gifts of furniture from friends, plus occasional small payments from the families of the unfortunate mothers.

Demand for places grew rapidly and by 1902 the doughty pair had taken on the considerable responsibility of a mortgage to buy a larger property at Granville Road, Finchley in North London where they established the Fallows Corner Home for Children. The home ran into severe financial difficulties when swamped with appeals for help towards the end of the First World War and by 1918 the shelter faced closure. It was rescued by the Shaftesbury Trust, the long-established patrons of the disadvantaged, who renamed it the Wright-Kingsford Home.

Blanche Wright received the OBE in 1932 and by the time she retired in 1946, had provided kindness and shelter to more than 1,700 illegitimate infants like Kit Gray.

Kit enjoyed a happy but strict upbringing at the home, where the boys and girls were kept apart and long prayer sessions were held every night. A little later she went to the nearby Henrietta Barnett School for girls in Finchley, distinguishing herself at games.

Kit was brought up to believe that her parents were both dead. The only clue to their identity came from Blanche Wright, who knew the full story but would only divulge that Kit's father was a great hero. It was a morsel of information which inevitably aroused Kit's curiosity, but over the years she found it impossible to prise any more details from 'Auntie'.

Kit Gray helped out at the home after leaving school and by her middle twenties had developed a close relationship with John 'Jack' Pearson Sayer, a talented commercial artist who lived in nearby Mill Hill. Sayer married Kit Gray in January 1926 and Blanche Wright, Kit's adopted mother, was witness to the ceremony at the Parish Church, Finchley.

Shortly after the marriage, Kit again tackled 'Auntie' about the identity of her real parents and Blanche Wright finally relented. It was at this point Kit Gray was told that her father was the national hero, Captain Oates. But what astonished her even more was that her mother was someone she knew well, Mrs Toby Cooper.

Toby Cooper, in fact, was Henrietta Learmont McKendrick, who had overcome her early motherhood and in 1918, had married Anthony Cooper, a doctor in the Royal Army Medical Corps. Although known as Etta during her childhood, she later adopted the unusual name of Toby and lived most of her adult life in London under the name, Mrs Toby Cooper. But she never had another child.

There is little doubt that Etta McKendrick and Toby Cooper were the same person. Her mother, Mary McKendrick, died of pneumonia in Scotland in 1936 at the age of 82. The person nominated as informant is Henrietta Learmont Cooper of Earls Court Road, London – Etta McKendrick/Toby Cooper.

Toby Cooper – Etta McKendrick – was one of a number of well-to-do women in the affluent North London suburbs who took an interest in the Wright-Kingsford refuge and was a regular visitor to the home, supporting the various fundraising events and helping to generate interest in the undertaking among her friends.

She had taken a particular interest in the attractive, energetic Kit Gray and had watched from a discreet distance as she matured into a confident, self-assured young woman. But the rigid social customs of the day prevented her from disclosing the real reason for her fascination and Toby Cooper was forced to endure the slow torture of watching her child develop in front of her own eyes. Even the smallest gesture like a maternal cuddle was impossible in case it betrayed her dark secret.

Toby Cooper's secret was indeed dark. It appears that she was little more than a child when she slept with Laurie Oates in 1899. Toby Cooper was born Henrietta Learmont McKendrick on 7 October 1887 at the family home in Johnstone, which suggests she was a few months short of twelve years of age when she became pregnant and only twelve and a half when she gave birth to Kit Gray.

The highly sensitive nature of the affair helps explain why successive generations have fought to keep the matter private and why barely anyone has felt able to speak about the matter. The Oates family, in particular, has remained tight-lipped about the child for precisely 100 years and both Toby Cooper and Kit Gray were reluctant to speak openly about their secret – even with close members of their families.

It is highly probable that Laurie Oates never saw his child and it is unlikely that he even knew she existed. There are no mentions of the relationship or a child in any of his surviving letters. In addition, most of his adult life was spent away from Britain serving with his regiment in South Africa, Ireland, Egypt and India or on Scott's expedition.

Oates was a very honourable man and if he had been aware of the child's existence, it is equally improbable that he would have wilfully abandoned her. We can only speculate whether his life would have been changed by the knowledge that he was a father. Quite possibly the responsibilities of a child might have given the drifting character the sense of purpose he lacked in the army and

A photograph of Kathleen 'Kit' Gray probably taken around the time of her marriage to commercial artist, Jack Sayer, in 1926. It was around this time that Kit finally discovered her father was the famous soldier and explorer, Captain Oates.
(Angela Wilson)

never found in the ice of Antarctica.

Kit Gray, having established the truth about her parents, immediately tried to establish contact with the Oates family. Shortly after her marriage in 1926, Kit went to Gestingthorpe where she confronted Caroline Oates with the news that she was her son's child and therefore her granddaughter. The details of what must have been a very tense meeting are not known, but Caroline Oates offered no encouragement to the woman on her doorstep.

A friend of Kit Gray later remembered:

> 'Not sure of the details but she got a cold reaction. Mrs O did not admit anything and did not wish to see Kitty again.'[1]

It is quite possible that the story of Oates' child is a fabrication. But it is difficult to discover a motive for such an elaborate lie when there has been no obvious attempts by anyone down the years to exploit the link – either by seeking money from the Oates family or by attaching themselves to the memory of a national figure. Indeed, the story has remained under wraps for a century.

Blanche Wright, Kit's adopted mother, was the original source of the story in the 1920s and she never sought to gain from her delicate secret. Nor was Blanche Wright the type of person who would lie to her adopted daughter about sensitive matters like her parentage. Had she wanted to maintain the secrecy of Kit Gray's parents, Blanche could easily have given a totally fictitious and untraceable name and not the name of well-known character whose relations were easy to locate. In the event, she only divulged information about Laurie Oates and Toby Cooper after being placed under intense pressure by Kit.

The secrecy was carried into the next generation by Kit Gray herself, who refused to divulge details of her parentage for the next 30 years. Kit, like Blanche Wright, never sought to exploit the association with Oates. Details only emerged in the 1950s when Kit began to speak to a small number of people about her background.

Kit Gray and Jack Sayer had two children, John and Gillian. John died in a car crash in his mid-20s without knowing his mother's secret past. Kit finally unburdened herself after her daughter Gillian's own marriage in the 1950s. The secret weighed heavily on Kit Gray and she seemed tormented by the knowledge. Gill Sayer recalled how Kit 'longed to talk' about her parents and felt a deep frustration at being unable to speak freely about her origins.

Gill Sayer, who was born in 1929, remembered that her mother had always taken a particular interest in Mrs Toby Cooper. But Gill only discovered her real identity after Toby Cooper's death and she, too, was never able to get closer to the truth.

By a strange twist, there was a touch of Caroline Oates in Toby Cooper. She was known as an intolerant, austere disciplinarian with a reputation for being fanatically house-proud. Gill Sayer remembered her as a 'stern old lady'. She was a snob who mocked the working classes as the 'great unwashed', despite her own working-class roots in Scotland. Contemporaries also recalled with some irony that she took a hard line on the slack moral values of the nation's youth.

Toby Cooper – Etta McKendrick – died in 1956 at the age of 69, taking with her the full story of her illicit relationship with Laurie Oates.

Kit Gray did not resemble Laurie Oates but her only son, John, who died in 1956, bore an uncanny likeness to him. On one occasion Kit took her children, John and Gill, to see Charles Friend's film, *Scott of the Antarctic*, at London's Odeon Leicester Square. In the foyer they were confronted by life-size cut-out figures of Scott's party and Gill recalled:

> 'I got a shock because the figure of Captain Oates could have been John standing there. The likeness was so striking. It was a weird experience.'[2]

Laurie Oates and his child, Kit Gray, shared some similar characteristics. Kit, like Oates, was a quiet person with a strong personality and a laconic sense of humour. One close friend said she had 'hidden depths', a term that could be applied equally to Oates. She was also very brave and won considerable admiration during the Second World War for driving a fire engine throughout the London Blitz.

Another friend recalled:

> 'She struck me as being like a racehorse that was straining to be released for some adventures.'[3]

Kit Gray's marriage to the artist Jack Sayer ran into difficulties after the war and they separated in the 1950s. Kit threw herself into other adventures, including running a children's dress shop in fashionable Hampstead during the mid-1950s. She also took an active role in politics and gave energetic support to the Conservative Party in the 1970 General Election.

The strain of her busy life took a heavy toll and Kit suffered a debilitating stroke in the early 1970s from which she never fully recovered. Kit Sayer – Kathleen

Lookalike. John Sayer, the only son of Kit Gray, bears a striking resemblance to Laurie Oates and particularly his brother, Bryan Oates. (Angela Wilson)

Gray – died in 1981, aged 81.

The full account of Laurie Oates' illegitimate child and the life of Kit Gray can never be written because vital records, perhaps deliberately, were not kept. The extreme sensitivity of the affair and the prevailing social attitudes towards illegitimacy also meant that the relationship could never be examined rationally.

Nor could any kind of formal acknowledgement possibly compensate for the personal losses suffered by the young mother and the child who never knew her father. Or the tragic man who died never knowing he was a father.

Chapter notes

Chapter 1

1. The last member of the Oates family to live at Meanwoodside was Charles Oates, who died in 1902. The property passed into the hands of his nephews, Lawrence and Bryan who never lived there. Between 1904 and 1917 Meanwood was rented to a prominent Leeds citizen, Lt Col Edward Kitson Clark, who purchased the home in 1917. Leeds Corporation bought the site from his widow in 1954 for £8,500 (about £130,000 in today's terms) with the intention of developing a natural history trail and a Polar room to commemorate Lawrence Oates. But the project failed and the house was demolished soon after. It now forms part of Meanwood Park, Leeds.
2. Royal Geographical Society, *Geographical Journal*, 1896 (VII), pp667–68.
3. London Borough of Wandsworth, Memo, 15 September 1967, BDL.
4. *Ibid.* The house was later renumbered to 309 Upper Richmond Road, BDL.

Chapter 2

1. Caroline Oates, household account books 1896–1921, ECA.
2. C. Oates letter to Rudmose Brown, 3 March 1924, SPRI.
3. The house was later renumbered to 313 Upper Richmond Road, BDL.
4. Klaus Marx, quoting Sir Maurice Bowra, *Willington School,* p10.
5. *Ibid*, pp5–7.
6. *Ibid*, p5.
7. Sue Limb and Patrick Cordingley, *Captain Oates: Soldier and Explorer,* p19.
8. Marx, p8.
9. *Ibid*, p7.
10. The British Dyslexia Association officially defines dyslexia as 'a complex neurological condition which is constitutional in its origin. The symptoms may affect many areas of learning and function and may be described as a specific difficulty in reading, spelling and written language. One or more of these areas may be affected. Numeracy, notational skills (music), motor function and organisation skills may also be involved. However it is particularly related to mastering written language, although oral language may be affected to some degree.' Source: *The Dyslexia Handbook.*
11. Robert Scott, diary, 22 October 1911. This entry was removed from the published version.

I am just
going outside

Chapter 3

1. Gestingthorpe Hall had only two other owners since William Oates purchased the property in 1891, remaining in the Oates family until 1947. The Cooke family bought the house in 1948 and did not sell it until 1998.
2. Philip Morant, *The History and Antiquities of the County of Essex,* 1768.
3. Sue Limb & Patrick Cordingley, *Captain Oates: Soldier & Explorer,* p21.
4. Proverbs, Chapter 27, verse 11.
5. Mark Girouard, *The Return to Camelot: Chivalry and the English Gentleman,* p176.
6. G.G. Coulton, *Fourscore Years,* p260.
7. *Ibid,* p260.
8. Louis Bernacchi, *A Very Gallant Gentleman,* p25.
9. Coulton, p261.

Chapter 4

1. Caroline Oates, diary, 17 March 1896.
2. Oates family papers, ECA.
3. Henry Pelham, President of Trinity College, Oxford letter to Lawrence Oates, 20 May 1899, SPRI.
4. Caroline Oates, household account books, 1896–1921, ECA.
5. Lawrence Oates, letter to Caroline Oates, 17 June 1899.

Chapter 5

1. Lawrence Oates, letter to Caroline Oates, 1 February 1900.
2. Oates letter to C. Oates, 5 March 1900.
3. Oates, Army service record, PRO.
4. In 1922, the 6th Inniskilling Dragoons were merged with the 5th Dragoon Guards and in 1935 became The 5th Royal Inniskilling Dragoon Guards. Later this was shortened to The Royal Dragoon Guards.
5. Oates letter to C. Oates, 30 March 1900.
6. Oates letter to C. Oates, 30 March 1900.

Chapter 6

1. Lawrence Oates, letter to Caroline Oates, 24 June 1900.
2. Oates letter to C. Oates, 26 September 1900.
3. Oates letter to C. Oates, 20 January 1901.
4. Oates letter to C. Oates, 25 January 1901.
5. Oates letter to C. Oates 24 February 1901.
6. Oates letter to C. Oates, 6 March 1900.
7. Oates letter to C. Oates, 2 July 1900.

Chapter 7
1. *Essex & Halstead Times*, 29 June 1901. Oates kept the Boer commander's note and Caroline Oates proudly displayed it in the hall at Gestingthorpe.
2. Reuters dispatch, 7 March 1901.
3. Lawrence Oates' version of the Aberdeen 'scrap' was contained in a letter written in 1908 to Major E.S. Jackson who was commissioned to write a history of the regiment's activities during the Boer War. SPRI.
4. Oates' response was widely reported by the contemporary press, later in the records of the Inniskilling Dragoons and subsequently in various books, including Louis Bernacchi, *A Very Gallant Gentleman* p42 and Sue Limb & Patrick Cordingley, *Captain Oates: Soldier and Explorer*, p41.
5. Major E.S. Jackson, *The Inniskilling Dragoons*, p217.
6. Bernacchi, p44.
7. Suffolk & Essex Free Press, 13 March 1901.
8. *Ibid.*
9. Lawrence Oates letter to Caroline Oates, 7 March 1901.
10. Limb & Cordingley, p42.
11. Limb & Cordingley: A recollection of C.A. Fleury-Teulon, 6th Inniskilling Dragoons, footnotes p48.
12. *The Inniskilliner*, February 1913.
13. Oates letter to C. Oates, 30 March 1901.
14. Oates letter to C. Oates, 1 April 1901.

Chapter 8
1. *Essex & Halstead Herald,* 29 June 1901.
2. *Ibid.*
3. The bells of St Mary-the-Virgin can still be heard.
4. Lawrence Oates, letter to Caroline Oates, 24 October 1901.
5. Louis Bernacchi, *A Very Gallant Gentleman*, p46.

Chapter 9
1. For a detailed study of the Curragh camp under British occupancy see: *A Most Delightful Station,* by Con Costello.
2. Lawrence Oates, letter to Caroline Oates, 14 October 1902.
3. *Ibid*, 5 March 1903.
4. George Seaver, notes on discussion with Frank Debenham, undated. SPRI.
5. Louis Bernacchi, *A Very Gallant Gentleman*, p48.
6. Oates letter to C. Oates, 9 October 1900.
7. Oates letter to C. Oates, 12 May 1903.

8.   Oates letter to C. Oates 5 May 1905.
9.   Oates letter to C. Oates, 20 September 1904.
10. Oates letter to C. Oates 11 April 1906.

Chapter 10
1.   Sue Limb notes from conversations with Violet Oates, (undated), RDG.
2.   Sue Limb & Patrick Cordingley, *Captain Oates: Soldier & Explorer*, p87.
3.   Headley Bennett, quoted in *The Willington Magazine*, 1984.
4.   *Daily Telegraph*, 15 February 1913, quoting Colonel Yardley of the Inniskilling Dragoons.
5.   Report of conversation between Col Johnnie Brooke and Clive Holland of SPRI, 7 April 1979, RDG.
6.   Lawrence Oates, letter to Caroline Oates, 27 January 1910.
7.   Commander Edward R.G.R. Evans (later Lord Mountevans) *The Strand Magazine*, December 1913.
8.   *Ibid.*
9.   Lt-Col. A.B. Fryer, letter to Commander-in-Chief, India, 21 March 1910, ADM 1/8595/162 WO 138/35, PRO.
10. War Office, telegram to C-in-C, India 17 March 1910, ADM 1/8595/162 WO 138/35, PRO.
11. Limb & Cordingley, reported conversation with Susan Ingall, (Captain Terrot's daughter), p90.

Chapter 11
No notes

Chapter 12
1.   Commander Evans (later Lord Mountevans), 'My Recollections of a Gallant Comrade', *The Strand Magazine*, December 1913.
2.   Sue Limb & Patrick Cordingley, *Captain Oates: Soldier & Explorer*, p95.
3.   War Office file on Bryan Oates, ADM 1/8595/162 WO 339/20752, PRO
4.   Lawrence Oates, letter to Caroline Oates, undated.

Chapter 13
1.   Lawrence Oates to William King, 14 August 1910.
2.   Lawrence Oates, letter to Caroline Oates, undated.

Chapter 14
1.   Lawrence Oates to William King, 13 November 1910.
2.   Lawrence Oates, letter to Caroline Oates, 23 November 1910.

3.   Hjalmar Johansen, who was born in Ibsen's hometown of Skien, was an experienced Polar traveller who accompanied Nansen on his epic 'Furthest North' crossing of the Arctic Ocean in 1893–96. Nansen persuaded Amundsen to take Johansen on the *Fram,* but the two clashed and Amundsen ejected him from the final South Pole party. Johansen later became depressed and committed suicide in January 1913.
4.   Oates letter to C. Oates, 23 November 1910.
5.   Kathleen Scott, diary October, 1910, KFP.
6.   Frank Debenham, *The Quiet Land*, p109.
7.   Cecil H. Meares to Major Meares, 18 March 1910, BCA.
8.   Meares to Major Meares, 22 August 1910, BCA.
9.   The nineteen ponies were given names, which were: Blossom; Blucher; Bones; Chinaman; Christopher; Davy; Guts; Hackenschmidt; Jehu; Jimmy Pigg; Jones; Michael; Nobby; Punch; Snatcher; Snippets; Uncle Bill; Victor; Weary Willy.
10. Oates diary undated.
11. Oates letter to William King, 15 November 1910.
12. Oates letter to C. Oates, 23 November 1910.
13. *Ibid.*
14. Oates letter to C. Oates, 17 November 1910.
15. Henry Bowers, letter to Emily Bowers, 28 November 1910, SPRI.
16. Oates letter to C. Oates, 23 November 1910.

Chapter 15
1.   Lawrence Oates, letter to Caroline Oates, 28 November 1910.
2.   E.R.G.R. Evans, *South With Scott*, p47.
3.   Robert Scott, diary, 5 December 1910.
4.   *Ibid,* 28 December 1910.
5.   *Ibid,* 7 January 1911.
6.   Oates, Notes on the Ponies, SPRI.
7.   Scott diary, 14 January 1911.
8.   Oates letter to C. Oates, 22 January 1911.
9.   Oates letter to C. Oates, 22 January 1911.
10. Evans, *The Strand Magazine*, December 1913.
11. George Seaver, notes of conversation with Frank Debenham, undated. Seaver wrote several books about members of the expedition and the notes were attached to his personal copy of Apsley Cherry-Garrard's *The Worst Journey in the World,* SPRI.
12. Oates letter to Colonel N. Haig, 20 January 1911.
13. Oates letter to C. Oates, 22 January 1911.

Chapter 16
1.   Apsley Cherry-Garrard, *The Worst Journey in the World*, p147.
2.   Robert Scott, diary, 28 January 1911.
3.   Lawrence Oates, letter to Caroline Oates, undated.
4.   Oates letter to C. Oates, 22 January 1911.
5.   Oates, Notes on the Ponies, SPRI.
6.   Edward Wilson, *The Diary of the* Terra Nova *Expedition, 1910–12*, p104.
7.   Scott, diary, 15 February 1911.
8.   Scott, diary, 18 February 1911.
9.   Frank Debenham, *The Quiet Land*, p95–96.
10.   Cherry-Garrard, p157.
11.   Tryggve Gran, *The Norwegian With Scott*, p59.
12.   Scott, diary, 17 February 1911.
13.   *Ibid,* p60. Tryggve Gran was born in Bergen, Norway and enlisted in Britain's Royal Flying Corps at the outbreak of the First World War in 1914. He was credited with seventeen 'kills' and won the Military Cross. Gran was the last surviving member of the *Terra Nova* expedition's shore party when he died in 1980, just twelve days from his 91st birthday.
14.   *Ibid* p59.
15.   *Ibid* p59.
16.   Cherry-Garrard, p172.
17.   Oates diary.
18.   Gran, p63.
19.   *Ibid*, p64.
20.   Cherry-Garrard, p191.
21.   Scott, diary, 1 March 1911.

Chapter 17
1.   Lawrence Oates, diary.
2.   Louis Bernacchi, *A Very Gallant Gentleman*, p106.
3.   Frank Debenham, quoting Captain Scott, *The Quiet Land,* p104.
4.   Edward Wilson, *The Diary of the Terra Nova Expedition*, p128.
5.   Caroline Oates, notes from discussions with Edward Atkinson, 27 April 1913.
6.   Cecil Henry Meares continued travelling for the rest of his life. He joined the Royal Flying Corps at the outbreak of war in 1914, rising to the rank of Lieutenant-Colonel. He was reputedly a member of British Intelligence. Meares finally settled in British Columbia, Canada with his wife, Annie, and died in May 1937, aged 61. The restless wanderer asked for his ashes to be sprinkled in 'some convenient woods or garden'.

7.   Robert Scott diary, 17 March 1911.

8.   Edward Leicester Atkinson served with distinction during the First World War, fighting in Flanders and at Gallipoli. He was severely wounded, losing an eye in 1918. Badly scarred from war wounds and the emotional strains of the *Terra Nova* expedition, he died in 1929 at the relatively early age of 46 and was buried at sea.

9.   George Seaver, notes on discussion with Frank Debenham, undated, SPRI.

10.   Herbert Ponting, *The Great White South,* p161.

11.   Debenham, *The Quiet Land,* p126.

12.   Debenham, letter to Sue Limb, undated, RDG.

13.   E.R.G.R. Evans, *The Strand Magazine,* 1913.

14.   Anton Omelchenko returned to Russia, fought in the First World War and after the Revolution in 1917 joined the Red Army. He married, and helped set up a collective farm at his birthplace of Batki in Russia. He was killed by lightning in 1932 at the age of 49.

15.   T. Griffith Taylor, *With Scott: The Silver Lining,* p225.

16.   Seaver, undated, SPRI.

17.   R.C.F. Falckh, *The Death of Petty Officer Evans, The Polar Record* 23 (145), pp397–403.

18.   Evans, *The Strand Magazine.*

19.   Lawrence Oates, letter to Caroline Oates, 24 October 1911.

Chapter 18

1.   Caroline Oates, household account book, 1911, ECA.

2.   Caroline Oates, notes from a discussion with Teddy Evans, 25 April 1913.

3.   George Seaver, notes of conversation with Frank Debenham, undated, SPRI.

4.   Lawrence Oates, letter to Caroline Oates, dated 24–31 October 1911.

5.   *Ibid.*

6.   *Ibid.*

7.   *Ibid.*

8.   Robert Scott letter to C. Oates, October 1911, SPRI.

9.   Oates letter to C. Oates, 24–31 October 1911.

10.   Edward Wilson, diary, 15 October 1911.

11.   Oates letter to C. Oates, 24–31 October 1911.

Chapter 19

1.   William Lashly, *Under Scott's Command: Lashly's Antarctic Diaries,* p121.

2.   T. Griffith Taylor, *With Scott: The Silver Lining,* p326.

3.   Robert Scott, diary, 31 October 1911.

4. Tryggve Gran, *The Norwegian With Scott*, p138.
5. Lawrence Oates diary, 7 November 1911. In today's terms, £1,000 is worth around £47,000; £5 is £235 and 30/- (£1.50) is £70.
6. *Ibid.*
7. Scott, diary, 13 November 1911.
8. Oates diary, 18 November 1911
9. *Ibid.*
10. Cecil Meares, reported conversation (source unknown), RDG.
11. Herbert Ponting, *The Great White South*, p288.
12. David Wilson & D.B. Elder, *Cheltenham in Antarctica*, p101
13. Caroline Oates, notes from discussions with Mrs Oriana Wilson, 29 April 1913.
14. Stephen Gwynn, *Captain Scott*, p227.
15. *Glasgow Herald*, 13 February 1913, reporting a conversation with Edward Wilson.
16. Oates diary, 24 November 1911.
17. *Ibid*, 29 November 1911.
18. E.R.G. Evans, *My Recollections of a Gallant Comrade*, 1913.
19. Apsley Cherry-Garrard, *The Worst Journey in the World*, p405.
20. *Ibid*, p407.
21. Edward Wilson, *The Diary of the Terra Expedition*, p213.
22. Scott diary, 19 December 1911.
23. Cherry-Garrard, p468.
24. Henry Bowers, diary, 1 December 1911, SPRI.
25. Cherry-Garrard, p409.
26. Roald Amundsen, *The South Pole*, vol 2, p122.
27. Roald Amundsen returned from the South Pole and continued Polar exploration. He completed the Northeast Passage around Siberia and became the first to fly across the North Pole. He died in 1928 when his aircraft crashed while searching for the survivors of Umberto Nobile's airship in Arctic waters. Olav Bjaaland, the ski champion, returned to his native Telemark and died in 1961 at the age of 89. Helmer Hanssen made further trips to the ice in the 1920s and died in 1956, aged 86. Sverre Hassel went back to his job in the Norwegian Customs but dropped dead at Amundsen's feet when visiting his old leader in 1928. Oscar Wisting became a captain in the navy and took part in the search for Amundsen. In 1936, the 65-year-old Wisting asked for permission to sleep on board *Fram* and was found dead next morning in his old cabin.
28. Bowers, diary, 14 December 1911.
29. Charles Wright, *Silas*, p221.

Chapter 20
1. Lawrence Oates, diary, 19 December 1911.
2. Apsley Cherry-Garrard, diary, 1911.
3. George Seaver, notes from conversation with Frank Debenham, undated, SPRI.
4. Louis Bernacchi, *A Very Gallant Gentleman*, p17.
5. Charles Neider, *Edge of the World: Ross Island Antarctica*, quoting Sir Charles Wright, p282.
6. Apsley Cherry-Garrard, *The Worst Journey in the World*, p423.
7. Robert Scott diary, 22 December 1911. Scott made two errors with this entry. Oates, born on 17 March 1880, was 31 years of age, not 32 and Edgar 'Taff' Evans, whose Naval record gives his birth date as 9 March 1876, was 35 and not 37.
8. George Bernard Shaw, letter to Kathleen Scott, 23 March 1923, KFP.
9. Seaver.
10. E.R.G.R. Evans, *South With Scott*, p228.
11. Oates, diary, 26 December 1911.
12. *Ibid,* 31 December 1911.
13. Scott diary, 2 January 1912.
14. E.R.G.R. Evans, *The Strand Magazine*.
15. The exchange is attributed to Tryggve Gran after conversations with Tom Crean. One version is contained in his book, *Kampen om Sydpolen* and a slightly different account is contained in the English translation of his diaries, *The Norwegian With Scott*.
16. Lawrence Oates, letter to Caroline Oates, 3–4 January 1912.
17. Evans, Strand Magazine, 1913.
18. *Ibid.*

Chapter 21
1. Lawrence Oates to Bryan Oates, 3 January 1912.
2. Robert Scott, diary, 5 January 1912.
3. *Ibid,* 12 January 1912.
4. *Ibid,* 8 January 1912.
5. *Ibid,* 14 January 1912
6. Lawrence Oates, diary, 15 January 1912.
7. *Ibid,* 16 January 1912.
8. *Ibid,* 16 January 1912.
9. Henry Bowers, letter to Emily Bowers 17 January 1912, SPRI.
10. Scott, diary, 17 January 1912.

I am just going outside

Chapter 22
1. Robert Scott, diary, 17 January 1912.
2. *Ibid,* 20 January 1912.
3. Lawrence Oates, diary, 25 January 1912.
4. Scott, diary, 24 January 1912.
5. Oates diary, undated.
6. Oates diary, 15 February 1912.
7. Oates diary. This entry is dated 18 February, although Evans death occurred on 17 February.
8. R.C.F. Falckh, *The Death of Petty Officer Evans,* The Polar Record, 1987.

Chapter 23
1. Tom Crean and Bill Lashly were awarded the Albert Medal for gallantry, the equivalent of today's George Cross, for saving the life of Teddy Evans.
2. Tryggve Gran, *The Norwegian With Scott,* p177.
3. Robert Scott, diary, 21 February 1912.
4. Lawrence Oates, diary, 24 February 1912.
5. Scott, diary, 2 March 1912.
6. *Ibid,* 2 March 1912.
7. *Ibid,* 5 March 1912.
8. *Ibid,* 6 March 1912.
9. Apsley Cherry-Garrard, *The Worst Journey in the World,* p473.
10. Scott, diary, 10 March 1912.
11. *Ibid,* 10 March 1912.
12. *Ibid,* 11 March 1912.
13. *Ibid,* 17 March 1912.
14. Edward Wilson letter to Caroline Oates, March 1912, SPRI.
15. Henry Bowers, letter to Mrs Emily Bowers, March 1912, SPRI.
16. Roland Huntford, *Scott & Amundsen,* p535.
17. George Bernard Shaw letter to Kathleen Scott, 6 April 1923, KFP.
18. Shaw letter to Lord Kennet, 21 February 1948, KFP.
19. Shaw letter to Kennet, 28 February 1948, KFP.
20. Kennet letter to Peter Scott, May 1957, KFP.
21. Scott, letter to Sir Edgar Speyer, 16 March 1912.
22. Edmund Spenser, *The Faerie Queene,* Book 1.

Chapter 24
1. Apsley Cherry-Garrard, *The Worst Journey in the World,* p492.
2. *Ibid,* p500.

3.   Robert Scott, diary, March 1912.
4.   Charles Wright, *Silas*, p346.
5.   Edward Atkinson, *Scott's Last Expedition*.
6.   *Ibid*.
7.   Edward Atkinson, letter to Caroline Oates, 31 January 1913, SPRI.

Chapter 25
1.   Reginald Pound, *Evans of the Broke*, p123.
2.   The cross has withstood the rigours of Antarctica and remains perched on top of Observation Hill, Ross Island.
3.   Apsley Cherry-Garrard, *The Worst Journey in the World*, p638.
4.   War Office telegram, 11 February 1913, PRO.
5.   HM Treasury correspondence on the annuities awarded to members of the British Antarctic Expedition, PRO.
6.   The residue of the Fund was given to Cambridge University which later established the Scott Polar Research Institute, now an internationally recognised centre of historical and scientific information on Polar matters. The first director was Frank Debenham.
7.   E.R.G.R. Evans, letter to Caroline Oates, 13 April 1913, SPRI.
8.   Evans to Silvia and Ralph Gifford, 6 February 1913.
9.   Evans letter to Caroline Oates, 22 January 1914.
10. Herbert Ponting, quoted in numerous newspapers, 13 February 1913.
11. Caroline Oates, note of meeting with Kathleen Scott, undated.
12. Fridtjof Nansen, quoted *Daily Chronicle*, 13 February 1913.
13. Sir Ernest Shackleton, quoted *The Morning Post*, 12 February 1913.
14. Roald Amundsen, quoted in numerous newspapers, 13 February 1913.
15. Caroline Oates, notes 16 February 1922.
16. Caroline Oates, letter to Rudmose Brown, 26 March 1928, SPRI.
17. Ponting, *The Great White South*, pp297–98.
18. Tryggve Gran, quoted *Wandsworth Borough News*, March 1972.
19. Gran speech at Dryburgh Hall, London, 17 March 1972.
20. Gran, *The Norwegian With Scott*, p153.
21. Griffith Taylor, *With Scott: The Silver Lining*, pp434–435.
22. C. Oates, letter to Rudmose Brown, 9 April 1924, SPRI.
23. Louis Bernacchi, quoting Bryan Oates, in a letter to Hugh R. Mill, 14 November 1932, SPRI.
24. Bernacchi letter to Hugh R. Mill, 26 May 1933, SPRI.
25. Lawrence Oates (grandson of Bryan Oates), letter to the author, 26 July 1999.

26. *Daily Express*, 29 November 1938.
27. Lillian (Oates) Ranalow letter to 'Bob', 3 January 1938, WOM.
28. Violet Oates, letter to Reginald Pound, 27 December 1965, SPRI.
29. Sue Limb correspondence with the author, 2001.
30. Violet Oates, last will and testament, 15 December 1965. Sue Limb produced a first draft of the book in 1965 and Patrick Cordingley, an officer in the 5th Royal Inniskilling Dragoons, joined the project in 1979. The book was finally published in 1982 and dedicated to Violet Oates and Frank Debenham.
31. Professor Charles R. Bentley, University of Wisconsin, papers and correspondence with author, 1999.

Chapter 26
1. Muriel 'Judy' Miller, letter to Angela Mack, 10 September 1984.
2. Gillian Ward, the daughter of Kathleen Gray, interviews with author, 1999.
3. Miller.

Bibliography

Books

A considerable number of books were consulted in writing this biography of Lawrence Oates, particularly in the area of Polar exploration. Those listed below were most helpful in my researches. It is, of course, a personal selection.

Aldridge, Don	*The Rescue of Captain Scott,* Tuckwell Press, 1999
Amundsen, Roald	*My Life as an Explorer,* William Heinemann, 1927
Amundsen, Roald	*The South Pole,* Hurst & Co, 1976
Bainbridge, Beryl	*The Birthday Boys,* Duckworth & Co, 1991
Baughman, T.H.	*Pilgrims on the Ice,* University of Nebraska Press, 1999
Bernacchi, Louis	*A Very Gallant Gentleman,* Thornton Butterworth, 1933
Brent, Peter	*Captain Scott and the Antarctic Tragedy,* Weidenfeld & Nicolson, 1974
British Antarctic Expedition (*Terra Nova*) 1910–13	Miscellaneous Data, compiled by Colonel H.G. Lyons, Harrison and Sons, 1924
Burke's Landed Gentry	Re: *Oates, Formerly of Gestingthorpe Hall,* 18th Edition, Vol 2, 1969
Campbell, Victor	*The Wicked Mate: The Antarctic Diary of Victor Campbell,* (Ed. H.G.R. King), Bluntisham Books/Erskine Press, 1988
Card, Tim	*Eton Reviewed,* John Murray, 1994
Cherry-Garrard, Apsley	*The Worst Journey in the World,* Penguin Books, 1970
Costello, Con	*A Most Delightful Station: The British Army on the Curragh of Kildare, Ireland, 1855–1922,* The Collins Press, 1996

I am just going outside	Coulton, G.G.	*Fourscore Years*, University Press, Cambridge, 1943
	Debenham, Frank	*In the Antarctic*, John Murray, 1952
	Debenham, Frank	*The Quiet Land: The Antarctic Diaries of Frank Debenham*, (Ed. June Debenham Back), Bluntisham Books/Erskine Press, 1992
	Evans, E.R.G.R. (Lord Mountevans)	*South With Scott*, Collins & Co, 1924
		The Antarctic Challenged, Staples Press, 1955
	Evans, Roger	*The 5th Inniskilling Dragoon Guards*, Gale & Polden, 1951
	Gentleman, A.	*A New and Complete History of Essex*, 5 vols, Lionel Hassel, 1770
	Gran, Tryggve	*The Norwegian With Scott: Tryggve Gran's Antarctic Diary, 1910–13*, (Ed. Geoffrey Hattersley-Smith), HMSO, 1984
	Gregor, Gary	*Swansea's Antarctic Explorer: Edgar Evans*, Swansea City Council, 1985
	Gwynn, Stephen	*Captain Scott,* The Bodley Head, 1929
	Hanssen, Helmer	*Voyages of a Modern Viking*, George Routledge & Sons, 1936
	Harrowfield, David	*Icy Heritage,* Antarctic Heritage Trust, 1995
	Huntford, Roland	*Nansen,* Duckworth & Co, 1997
	Huntford, Roland	*Scott & Amundsen*, Hodder & Stoughton, 1979
	Huntford, Roland	*Shackleton,* Hodder & Stoughton, 1985
	Huxley, Elspeth	*Scott of the Antarctic*, Weidenfeld & Nicolson, 1977
	Jackson, Major E.S.	*The Inniskilling Dragoons*, Arthur L. Humphreys, 1909
	James, Lawrence	*The Rise and Fall of the British Empire*, Little, Brown and Company, 1994
	Johnson, Anthony M.	*Scott of the Antarctic and Cardiff*, University College Cardiff Press, 1984
	Jones, A.G.E.	*Polar Portraits*, Caedmon of Whitby, 1992
	Kennet, Lady (K. Scott)	*Self-Portrait of an Artist*, John Murray, 1949
	King, H.G.R.	*The Antarctic*, Blandford Press, 1969
	King, Peter	*Scott's Last Journey*, Duckworth & Co, 1999
	Kruger, Rayne	*Goodbye Dolly Gray*, Cassell & Co, 1959
	Lagerbom, C.H.	*The Fifth Man: The Life of H.R. Bowers*, Caedmon of Whitby, 1999

Lashly, William	*Under Scott's Command: Lashly's Antarctic Diaries*, (Ed. Commander A.R. Ellis), Victor Gollancz, 1969
Limb, Sue & Patrick Cordingley	*Captain Oates, Soldier & Explorer*, B.T. Batsford, 1982
Mabey, Richard	*Gilbert White*, Pimlico, 1999
Markham, Sir Clements	*Antarctic Obsession*, edited by Clive Holland, Bluntisham Books/Erskine Press, 1986
Marx, Klaus	*My First and Best School,* Trustees of Willington School, 1985
Mason, Theodore	*The South Pole Ponies*, Dodd, Mead & Co, 1979
Maxtone-Graham, John	*Safe Return Doubtful*, Patrick Stephens, 1989
Meare, Roger & Robert Swan	*In the Footsteps of Scott*, Jonathan Cape, 1987
Mountfield, David	*The History of Polar Exploration*, Hamlyn Publishing, 1974
Neider, Charles	*Edge of the World: Ross Island, Antarctica,* Doubleday & Co, 1974
Pakenham, Thomas	*The Boer War,* Abacus, 2000
Ponting, Herbert	*The Great White South,* Duckworth & Co, 1921
Pound, Reginald	*Evans of the Broke*, Oxford University Press, 1963
Pound, Reginald	*Scott of the Antarctic,* Cassell & Co, 1966
Preston, Diana	*A First Rate Tragedy,* Constable and Co, 1997
Priestley, Raymond	*Antarctic Adventure*, Hurst & Co, 1974
Quartermain, Les	*Antarctica's Forgotten Men,* Millwood Press, 1981
Richards, Dr Robert	*Dr John Rae*, Caedmon of Whitby, 1985
Savours, Anne	*The Voyages of the* Discovery, Virgin Books, 1992
Scott, Robert	*Scott's Last Expedition*, arranged by Leonard Huxley, Smith Elder & Co, 1913
Scott, Robert	*The Diaries of Captain Robert Scott*, Facsimile Edition, University Microfilms, 1968
Scott, Robert	*The Voyage of the Discovery,* Smith Elder and Co. 1905
Seaver, George	*'Birdie' Bowers of the Antarctic*, John Murray, 1938
Seaver, George	*Scott of the Antarctic*, John Murray, 1940

I am just **going outside**	Seaver, George	*Edward Wilson of the Antarctic*, John Murray, 1934
	Shackleton, Sir Ernest	*The Heart of the Antarctic*, William Heinemann, 1909
	Smith, Michael	*An Unsung Hero – Tom Crean, Antarctic Survivor*, The Collins Press, 2000
	Solomon, Susan	*The Coldest March*, Yale University Press, 2001
	Spufford, Francis	*I May Be Some Time*, Faber and Faber, 1996.
	Taylor, Griffith	*With Scott: The Silver Lining*, Bluntisham Books/Erskine Press, 1997 (Originally published by Smith Elder & Co, 1916)
	Thomson, David	*Scott's Men*, Allen Lane, 1977
	Turley, Charles	*Roald Amundsen, Explorer*, Methuen & Co, 1935
	Turley, Charles	*The Voyages of Captain Scott*, John Murray, 1914
	Watkins Yardley, Lt Col J.	*With the Inniskilling Dragoons: The Record of a Cavalry Regiment During the Boer War, 1899–02*, Longmans Green and Co, 1904
	Wheeler, Sara	*Cherry*, Jonathan Cape, 2001
	Wheeler, Sara	*Terra Incognita*, Jonathan Cape, 1996
	Wilson, David & D.B. Elder	*Cheltenham in Antarctic: The Life of Edward Wilson*, Reardon Press, 2000
	Wilson, Edward	*Diary of the* Terra Nova *Expedition to the Antarctic, 1910–12*, Blandford Press, 1972
	Wright, Charles	*Silas: The Antarctic Diaries and Memoir of Charles S. Wright*, (Ed. Colin Bull and Pat F. Wright), Ohio State University Press, 1993
	Young, Louisa	*A Great Task of Happiness*, Macmillan, 1995

Archive sources and abbreviations

Bank of England, London (BoE)
Battersea District Library, London (BDL)
British Colombia Archives, Victoria, BC, Canada (BCA)
British Dyslexia Association, Reading, Berkshire (BDA)
British Library, London (BL)
Cambridge University Library, Cambridge (CUL)
Cheltenham Art Gallery & Museums, Cheltenham (CAG)
Essex County Archives, Chelmsford, Essex (ECA)
Eton College Archives, Berkshire (EC)

General Medical Council, London (GMC)
Public Record Office, London (PRO)
The Museum of the Royal Dragoon Guards, York (RDG)
Royal Geographical Society, London (RGS)
Scott Polar Research Institute, Cambridge (SPRI)
The Shaftesbury Society, London (SS)
Suffolk County Libraries & Heritage, Bury St Edmunds, Suffolk, (SCL)
University Library Cambridge (ULC)
The University of Wisconsin, Madison, Wisconsin, US (UoW)
West Yorkshire Archives, Sheepscar, Leeds, Yorkshire (WYA)
Gilbert White Museum-The Oates Memorial Museum, Selborne, Hampshire (WOM)

Newspapers, magazines, periodicals, etc.

A considerable number of publications, too many to list, were consulted in the research of this book. The sources include the large collections of newspapers, magazines and periodicals contained at the Battersea District Library (BDL), the British Library's Newspaper Library (BL), the Museum of the Royal Dragoon Guards (RDG), the Royal Geographical Society (RGS), the Scott Polar Research Institute (SPRI) and the Gilbert White Museum-The Oates Memorial Museum (WOM). The publications consulted include:

Blue Peter
Cavalry Journal
Daily Chronicle
Daily Mail
Daily Express
Daily Mirror
Daily Sketch
Daily Telegraph
East Anglian Magazine
East Anglian Times
Encounter
Essex Countryside Magazine
Essex & Halstead Times
Essex Review
Evening News

**I am just
going outside**

Evening Standard
Geographical Journal
Glasgow Herald
The Guardian
Halstead Gazette
The Inniskiller (The journal of the 6th Inniskilling Dragoons)
Manchester Dispatch
Morning Post
The Observer
Polar Record
Quarterly Bulletin (South African Library)
The Shaftesbury Magazine
The Spectator
Strand Magazine
Suffolk & Essex Free Press
Sunday Times
The Times
Wandsworth Borough News
Western Mail
Willington Magazine
Yorkshire Post

Articles

The articles which were most useful in compiling this book were:

Anon	*The Inniskilliner: The Journal of the 6th (Inniskilling) Dragoons*, February 1913
Anon	Lawrence Edward Grace Oates, *The Essex Review*, Vol XXII, April 1913
Anon	William Edward Oates, Obituary, *The Geographical Journal,* Vol VII, 1896
Anon	*South Lynn,* Eastbourne Civic Society, 1975
Bank of England	Equivalent Contemporary Values of the Pound: A Historical Series, 1270–1999
'A Brother Officer'	No Surrender Oates, *The Cavalry Journal*, 1913

Butler, A.N.	Antarctic Hero, *East Anglian Magazine* Vol 22
	The Antarctic Disaster: *The Inniskilliner,* *February, 1913*
Evans, E.R.G.R.	Captain Oates: My Recollections of a Gallant Comrade, *The Strand Magazine*, December, 1913
Falckh, R.C.F.	The Death of Petty Officer Evans, *Polar Record* 23 (145) 397–403, 1987
Jaye, R.C.	Captain Oates: The Ponting Photographs, *East Anglian Magazine,* Vol 1 1935.
Limb, Sue	Hero of Their Times, *The Observer*, 24 June 1984
	Why a Very Gallant Gentleman Went Out For A Walk, *Sunday Times*, 14 November 1982
Mack, Angela	Oates the Father, *The Observer*, 26 October 1984
Marx, Klaus	Captain Oates Relived, *Willington Magazine*, 1984
Marx, Klaus	Willington School Honours Its Most Famous Pupil, *Willington Magazine*
McLoughlin, A.A.	The Very Gallant Gentleman, *Essex Countryside*, Vol 10, April, 1962
Robin, Gordon	Memorials to Lawrence Oates, *Willington Magazine,* November, 1973
Rogers, A.F.	The Death of Chief Petty Officer Evans, *The Practioner,* April, 1974.
Shearing, Taffy	The Antarctic Tragedy: Legacy of the Boer War? *Quarterly Bulletin*, The South African Library, June 1985, 39 (9)
Young, Wayland (Lord Kennet)	On the Debunking of Captain Scott: A Critique Against Myths, Errors & Distortions, *Encounter*, Vol 54, May, 1980.
Young, Wayland	An Exchange Between Roland Huntford & Wayland Young on Scott and Amundsen, *Encounter*, vol 55, November, 1980.

I am just going outside

Unpublished diaries, documents, interviews, letters, etc.

Atkinson, Edward, L.	Account of discovering the bodies of the Southern Party, 1912 (SPRI)
	Letter to Mrs Caroline Oates, 31 March 1913, (SPRI)
Bentley, Charles R.	(Professor Emeritus of Geophysics, Geophysical and Polar Research Center, University of Wisconsin). Studies of glaciology, the movement of the Ross Ice Shelf and the current location of the bodies of Lawrence Oates and other members of the Southern Party. *Journal of Glaciology* (Vol 44, No 46). Correspondence with the Author
Bernacchi, Louis	Letters to Hugh R. Mill, 1932–33 Re: Oates biography (SPRI)
Bowers, Henry	Antarctic journal, 1910–12 (SPRI)
	Letter to mother, March, 1912 (SPRI)
Chambers, Florence	Letter to BBC (undated), re: Lawrence Oates (RDG)
Cooper, Ashley	Recollections of Oates family at Gestingthorpe, correspondence with author
Cordingley, Patrick	Interview with Colonel J.A. Brooke, re: L.E.G. Oates (RDG)
Dagnall, Tony	Interviews with author, re: the Oates family in Gestingthorpe
Debenham, Frank	Correspondence with Sue Limb (RDG)
East Essex Hunt Club	Minutes 1900–35 (ECA)
	Letter to Caroline Oates, 22 February 1913 (ECA)
Eton College	School records, 1894–96 (EC)
Evans E.R.G.R.	'Teddy' (Lord Mountevans), Telegram to War Office, 11 February 1913 (PRO)
	Letters to Mrs Caroline Oates, 3 February 1913; 13 April 1913 (SPRI)
	Copy of Address at Oates Memorial Service, Colchester, Essex, 14 March 1937 (WOM)
Gran, Tryggve	Tape recording of speech at Dryburgh Hall, London, 27 March 1972, re: Lawrence Oates (courtesy of Klaus Marx)

Holland, Clive — Interview with Colonel J.A. Brooke, 7 April 1979, re: Lawrence Oates (SPRI)

Kennet, Lord — Letter to Peter Scott, May 1957 (UCL)

Limb, Sue — Interviews with author, 2001
Letter to Frank Debenham undated (SPRI)

Lloyd, Dr Evan, MBCWB, CRCPed, FSARCS, Dip. Sports Medicine — Medical effects of frostbite, interviews with author, 1999

Mack, Angela — Interviews with author, 1999
Letters and notes, re: Kathleen Gray

McKendrick, Henrietta Learmont — Personal details: including Birth Certificate, Marriage Certificate, family tree

Meares, Cecil Henry — Letters, postcards to Major Meares, 1910–13, (BCA)
Military Service Record, 1900–1920 (PRO)
Will and Probate, 1937 (BCA)

Oates family — A large amount of correspondence, diaries, family pedigrees and other material relating to many generations of the Oates family, is deposited at the White-Oates Museum, Selborne, Hampshire (WOM)
A considerable amount of correspondence, diaries and family papers concerning the Oates family connections with Yorkshire (mainly Headingley, Meanwood and Leeds) is deposited at West Yorkshire Archives, Sheepscar, Leeds, Yorkshire (WYA)

Oates, Bryan William Grace — Last will and testament 22 November 1957

Oates, Caroline Annie — Fragments of diaries and letters, copied by Violet Oates (RDG)
Notes on meetings with Kathleen Scott, Oriana Wilson and members of the British Antarctic Expedition between 1913–1922.
Household account books 1896–1921; Bank pass books, receipted bills, 1913–1940; Accounts of Hall Farm, Gestingthorpe; Particulars of properties, investments, schedule of lands, (ECA)

	Letter to Major E.S. Jackson, re: 'Aberdeen incident,' 22 August 1908 (SPRI)
	Correspondence Re: Commemorative 'Blue Plaque', (BDL)
	Last will and testament 15 May 1906
Oates, Laurie G.	Correspondence with author, 1999
Oates (Ranalow) Lillian	Letter to 'Bob' 3 January 1938 (WOM)
	Last will and testament, 17 June 1961
Oates, Violet	Correspondence with Sue Limb (RDG)
	Letter to Reginald Pound, 27 December 1965 (SPRI)
	Last will and testament, 14 January 1966
Oates, William	List of investments, property, shares, etc, 3 April 1896 (ECA)
	Last will and testament, 3 June 1891
Pannell, Cecil	Recollections of Oates family at Gestingthorpe, correspondence with the author
Pelham, Henry	Letter (from Trinity College, Oxford) to L.E.G. Oates, 20 May 1899 (SPRI)
Priestley, Raymond	Letter to Mrs Caroline Oates, 7 March 1915 (SPRI)
Royal Dragoon Guards	The Oates Memorial Fund, papers, correspondence (RDG)
Royal Geographical Society	Correspondence, papers relating to British Antarctic Expedition, (Terra Nova) 1910–13; Correspondence, papers re: The Mansion House Fund, 1913; Correspondence, papers re: RGS Polar Medals (RGS)
Scott, Kathleen (Lady Kennet)	Kennet Family papers: Diaries, engagement books, letters, 1896–1946 (CUL)
Scott, Robert F.	Letter to Mrs Caroline Oates, October 1911 (SPRI)
Seaver, George	Notes on discussions with Frank Debenham, undated. Bound in personal copy of *The Worst Journey in the World* (SPRI)

I am just going outside	Shaw, George Bernard	Letters to Kathleen Scott (Lady Kennet), 23 March 1923; 6 April 1923; 21 February 1948; 28 February 1948 (KFP), (CUL)
	Teverson, Frances	Recollections of the Oates family at Gestingthorpe, correspondence with the author
	HM Treasury	Letters, telegrams, documents, Re: Annuities, payments to members of British Antarctic Expedition, 1910–12, T164/404 (PRO)
	Wandsworth, London Borough	Correspondence re: Commemorative 'Blue Plaque' at Oates family home Putney, London, (BDL)
	War Office	Correspondence, documents, Re: Oates application to join British Antarctic Expedition, 1909–10, ADM 1/ 8365/3 (PMG) 74/42 (PRO) LEG Oates, personal file; Correspondence re: Oates application to join British Antarctic Expedition, ADM 1/8595/162 WO 138/35 (PRO) Telegram to Caroline Oates, 11 February 1913 (PRO)
	Ward, Gillian	Interviews with author, 1998–2000 Correspondence, Re: Kathleen Grey
	Williamson, Thomas	Antarctic Diary, 1912–13 (SPRI)
	Wilson, Edward A.	Letter to Mrs Caroline Oates, March 1912 (SPRI) Letter to Reginald Smith, 21 March 1912 (CAG)
	Wright-Kingsford Home	Material relating to home is contained in the archives of The Shaftesbury Society, notably *The Shaftesbury Magazine,* 1918–1943 (SS)

Films

Last Place on Earth, written by Trevor Griffith, Central Television, 1985
90° South, by Herbert Ponting, British Film Institute, 1933
Scott of the Antarctic, Directed by Charles Friend, Ealing Studios, 1948

Index